W9-AOE-280

DATE DUE

GAYLORD

PRINTED IN U.S.A.

International Political Economy Series

General Editor: **Timothy M. Shaw**, Professor of Commonwealth Governance and Development, the Director of the Institute of Commonwealth Studies, School of Advanced Study, University of London

Titles include:

Glenn Adler and Jonny Steinberg (*editors*)
FROM COMRADES TO CITIZENS
The South African Civics Movement and the Transition to Democracy

Glenn Adler and Eddie Webster (*editors*)
TRADE UNIONS AND DEMOCRATIZATION IN SOUTH AFRICA, 1985–1997

Einar Braathen, Morten Bøås and Gutermund Sæther (*editors*)
ETHNICITY KILLS?
The Politics of War, Peace and Ethnicity in Sub-Saharan Africa

Deborah Bräutigam
CHINESE AID AND AFRICAN DEVELOPMENT
Exporting Green Revolution

Gavin Cawthra
SECURING SOUTH AFRICA'S DEMOCRACY
Defence, Development and Security in Transition

Jennifer Clapp
ADJUSTMENT AND AGRICULTURE IN AFRICA
Farmers, the State and the World Bank in Guinea

Neta C. Crawford and Audie Klotz (*editors*)
HOW SANCTIONS WORK
Lessons from South Africa

Susan Dicklitch
THE ELUSIVE PROMISE OF NGOs IN AFRICA
Lessons from Uganda

Kevin C. Dunn and Timothy M. Shaw (*editors*)
AFRICA'S CHALLENGE TO INTERNATIONAL RELATIONS THEORY

Kenneth Good
THE LIBERAL MODEL AND AFRICA
Elites against Democracy

Kees Kingma (*editor*)
DEMOBILIZATION IN SUBSAHARAN AFRICA
The Development and Security Impacts

Clever Mumbengegwi (*editor*)
MACROECONOMIC AND STRUCTURAL ADJUSTMENT POLICIES IN ZIMBABWE

Nana Poku
REGIONALIZATION AND SECURITY IN SOUTHERN AFRICA

Howard Stein, Olu Ajakaiye and Peter Lewis (*editors*)
DEREGULATION AND THE BANKING CRISIS IN NIGERIA
A Comparative Study

Peter Vale, Larry A. Swatuk and Bertil Oden (*editors*)
THEORY, CHANGE AND SOUTHERN AFRICA'S FUTURE

International Political Economy Series
Series Standing Order ISBN 0–333–71708–2
(*outside North America only*)

You can receive future titles in this series as they are published by placing a standing order.
Please contact your bookseller or, in case of difficulty, write to us at the address below with
your name and address, the title of the series and the ISBN quoted above.

Customer Services Department, Macmillan Distribution Ltd, Houndmills, Basingstoke,
Hampshire RG21 6XS, England

The Liberal Model and Africa

Elites against Democracy

Kenneth Good
Professor of Political Studies
University of Botswana

palgrave

© Kenneth Good 2002

All rights reserved. No reproduction, copy or transmission of this publication may be made without written permission.

No paragraph of this publication may be reproduced, copied or transmitted save with written permission or in accordance with the provisions of the Copyright, Designs and Patents Act 1988, or under the terms of any licence permitting limited copying issued by the Copyright Licensing Agency, 90 Tottenham Court Road, London W1T 4LP.

Any person who does any unauthorized act in relation to this publication may be liable to criminal prosecution and civil claims for damages.

The author has asserted his right to be identified as the author of this work in accordance with the Copyright, Designs and Patents Act 1988.

First published 2002 by
PALGRAVE
Houndmills, Basingstoke, Hampshire RG21 6XS and
175 Fifth Avenue, New York, N.Y. 10010
Companies and representatives throughout the world

PALGRAVE is the new global academic imprint of
St. Martin's Press LLC Scholarly and Reference Division and
Palgrave Publishers Ltd (formerly Macmillan Press Ltd).

ISBN 0-333-79042-1

This book is printed on paper suitable for recycling and made from fully managed and sustained forest sources.

A catalogue record for this book is available from the British Library.

Library of Congress Cataloging-in-Publication Data
Good, Kenneth, 1933–
    The liberal model and Africa : elites against democracy / Kenneth Good.
        p. cm.—(International political economy series)
    Includes bibliographical references and index.
    ISBN 0-333-79042-1
    1. Democracy. 2. Elite (Social sciences) 3. Botswana – Politics and government – 1966- 4. South Africa – Politics and government – 1994- 5. United States – Politics and government. I. Title. II. International political economy series (Palgrave (Firm))
    JC423.G6335 2001
    321.8—dc21   2001036490

10 9 8 7 6 5 4 3 2 1
11 10 09 08 07 06 05 04 03 02

Printed and bound in Great Britain by
Antony Rowe Ltd, Chippenham, Wiltshire

To **Clara, Rosa, Hannah** and **Ursula**,
further along their roads

'Never believe governments, not any of them, not a word they say; keep an untrusting eye on all they do.'

Martha Gellhorn

'The first task of free men is to call all things by their right names.'

Judge Irving Younger

Contents

List of Abbreviations

ADS	Africa Defence Systems
AIDS	Acquired Immune Deficiency Syndrome
AMB	African Merchant Bank
ANC	African National Congress
AZT	Azidothymidine (anti-retroviral AIDS medication)
BBC	British Broadcasting Corporation
BCP	Botswana Congress Party
BDF	Botswana Defence Force
BDP	Botswana Democratic Party
BIDPA	Botswana Institute of Development Policy Analysis
BMC	Botswana Meat Commission
BNF	Botswana National Front
CBNRM	Community Based Natural Resource Management
CEO	Chief Executive Officer
CIA	Central Intelligence Agency
CKGR	Central Kalahari Game Reserve
CMI	Christian Michelsen Institute
CODESA	Convention for a Democratic South Africa
COSATU	Congress of South African Trade Unions
DP	Democratic Party
DWNP	Department of Wildlife and National Parks
EU	European Union
FBI	Federal Bureau of Investigation
FBS	Futuristic Business Solutions
GDP	Gross Domestic Product
HATAB	Hotel and Tourism Association of Botswana
HIV	Human Immunodeficiency Virus
HRC	Human Rights Commission
IBM	International Business Machines
IDASA	Institute for Democracy in South Africa
IEC	Independent Electoral Commission
IFP	Inkatha Freedom Party
JVP	Joint Venture Partnership
KZ-N	Kwazulu-Natal
LBRP	Labour-based Relief Programme
LWD	Livestock Water Development

MDM	Mass Democratic Movement
MK	Umkhonto weSizwe
MP	Member of Parliament
NAIL	New Africa Investments Limited
NDB	National Development Bank
NEC	National Executive Committee
NGOs	Non-governmental Organizations
NP	National Party
NWC	National Working Committee
OAU	Organization of African Unity
PDIs	Previously Disadvantaged Individuals
PDL	Poverty Datum Line
PR	Proportional Representation
RAD	Remote Area Dwellers
RADP	Remote Area Development Programme
RDP	Reconstruction and Development Programme
RUF	Revolutionary United Front
SACP	South African Communist Party
SGL	Special Game Licence
SLOCA	Services to Livestock in Communal Areas
SSRC	Soweto Students Representative Council
STMT	Sankuyo Tshwaragano
SWAPO	South West African People's Organization
SWAT	Special Weapons and Tactics
TGLP	Tribal Grazing Land Policy
TRC	Truth and Reconciliation Commission
UDM	United Democratic Movement
UNISA	University of South Africa
UNITA	National Union for the Total Independence of Angola
USAID	United States Agency for International Development
WEFA	Wharton Economic Forecasting Associates
WIMSA	Working Group of Indigenous Minorities in Southern Africa

Value of the Botswana Pula

At end of*	SA Rand	$US
1976	1.00	1.15
1978	1.05	1.21
1980	1.01	1.35
1982	1.02	0.94
1984	1.27	0.64
1986	1.20	0.54
1988	1.23	0.52
1990	1.37	0.53
1992	1.36	0.44
1994	1.30	0.36
1995	1.33	0.36

*Selected years.

Source: *Barclays Botswana Economic Review*.

Preface

This is a study of the complex interrelations between development, democracy, and elitism, chiefly in contemporary Africa and the United States, but also in Athens and in seventeenth-century England, and by implication elsewhere. In an Africa characterized by human and physical destruction wrought chiefly by autocratic elites, southern Africa stands out both for its capitalist development and for its democracy. Botswana is the continent's longest established liberal democracy, with a multi-party system and regular elections in existence since the eve of independence in 1965.[1] A similar system was established in South Africa in 1994, although a popular, participatory movement, literally of world-historic importance, had developed through the previous two decades out of the student movement, and a vibrant civil society, with the growing trade unions in its van. Both these liberal democracies are notable for their dominant autocratic elites and deep inequalities. Presidents Festus Mogae and Thabo Mbeki are vividly different from the likes of Charles Taylor, Blaise Compaore, Daniel arap Moi, Robert Mugabe, and the late Joseph Mobutu, but they are empowered to act alone and they readily do so, invariably with scant resort to their people.

This is not altogether surprising. The United States is the most advanced capitalist economy and the quintessential liberal polity. America's elites are powerful, highly manipulative, and non-accountable, and voter turnout in elections is extremely low. In the world's wealthiest liberal nation, inequalities, and injustices for a burgeoning underclass, are equally high.

When the liberal democratic model is chosen, where everything revolves around the act of voting in periodic elections, elitism and inequalities readily flourish. Voting *is* necessary, but it is also *insufficient* in and of itself as a means of empowering citizens to control the opportunism and self-aggrandisement of leaders. Elections within liberal democracy essentially function to enable elites to get elected, and the brief act of voting, and of counting, are wide open to abuse, whether in the state of Florida, Nigeria, or Ivory Coast. Capitalism and liberal democracy are, furthermore, overly compatible with each other. The former creates the inequalities and injustices which the latter, with its non-interventionist state and non-participatory citizenry, is unable and unwilling to resolve. Little wonder if African people sometimes seem unenthusiastic about the electoral democratic model, which leaves the big problems of health, education, and poverty untouched, yet facilitates and legitimizes autocracy.

It could be – it has been – different. Democratic Athens existed for two centuries, with active, direct participation in politics by worker/peasant citizens, and institutionlized methods for restricting the ambitions and presumptions of elites of wealth, education, and status. Elections were viewed by the citizens with suspicion, as likely to confer unfair advantage on the rich and the well-born, as elections in the United States frequently exemplify. Athenian democracy was a manifest reality for far longer than modern French republics, Hitler's Third Reich, or the Soviet Union, and it was no accident that the elite theorists who arose during the first great wave of democratization around the turn of the twentieth century sought to obscure or ignore its significance.

Similarly, the Levellers arose in the early stages of capitalist development in a revolutionary Britain. They existed briefly, and never acquired political power. But they spoke at their height for many thousands of common people in London and the parliamentary army, and enunciated a critique of constitutional, parliamentary power which attests to the endurance of the popular democratic aspiration.

The mass movement in South Africa, beginning in the 1970s, grew out of the schools, cities, factories, and communications networks of the country's relatively advanced and growing capitalist economy, and it became far more profound in structural and socio-political terms than other contemporary People's Power formations in central Europe and the Philippines.[2] It represented at its peak some two million people in about 700 affiliated groups. It developed a theory and a practice of organizational democracy which focused upon the accountability of leadership to the mass membership, and the necessity of sustained criticism of all leaders. Majority rule was important – and it was the domestic popular movement which arguably did most to bring an end to apartheid – but it would be nothing if it was not accompanied by new participatory democratic forms which placed power in the hands of the people in their factories, schools, and households. Perhaps the greatest testament to the effectiveness of these ideas came soon after 1990, from the leaders who not long after acquired power in Pretoria. A year after the unbanning of the nationalist parties and the return of the established leaders from exile and prison, the mass democratic movement was unceremoniously disbanded. It was the empowerment, not of the people, but of the African National Congress elite that was realized in the elections of 1994, and their non-accountability soon followed.

Much has been done to erase even the memory of the mass democratic movement from popular consciousness, as Athenian democracy was removed from the scholarly record. The 'Class of 76' might be denied due recognition by the new power holders, but an advanced capitalist economy persists, with the working class and large trade union organizations embedded within it, not easily airbrushed from history. The popular democratic aspiration was powerfully redeveloped in South Africa through the 1970s–1980s, and the class, urban and educational structures which supported it then largely remain today. The racist regime has gone, replaced by an aloof and non-accountable elite, and by inequalities among the black majority even greater than before – the further concomitants of liberal democracy. Yet struggles lost and half-realized in England, and hopes dashed across Africa since the early 1960s, could still be reinvigorated and advanced in South Africa.

Liberalism first embraced democracy only a century ago, largely in order to stifle it, to remove its participatory, egalitarian practices and values from the agenda. The enforced compromise, the restricted outcomes, are with us still in the obscurantism and elitism of liberal politics. The problem with participatory democracy, Arblaster reminds us, is not chiefly of a technical and practical kind, but derives instead from the active opposition of the democratic leaders,[3] from the handsome, smiling Bill Clinton and Tony Blair, the saintly Nelson Mandela, the seemingly benign Thabo Mbeki, and Festus Mogae, who boldly prefers Botswana's elections dull and non-participatory.

This study aims to critically interrogate the realities of liberal democracy, its elitism and non-accountability, its inequalities and injustices, celebrated universally since 1990 as the democratic epitome. Participatory systems and movements, whether in Athens, or seventeenth- and nineteenth-century England, or contemporary South Africa, are more effective in satisfying the democratic aspirations of the people *and* in curtailing ambitious elites, than is what is passed off today as 'democracy'. By examining contemporary democratic regimes, in the United States, or in the vaunted African cases of Botswana and South Africa, the limitations and constraints inherent in liberal democracy are highlighted. The need for a clear re-think of what constitutes democracy, both in the West and in Africa, is emphasized.

Part I
Autocratic Elites and Enfeebled Masses: Africa, Botswana and South Africa

'When law and order start to break down, the distinction between a politician and a warlord quickly becomes blurred.'
Barnaby Phillips, BBC journalist

'I must have received 400 murderers and 2,000 drug traffickers in my office. When you deal with Africa, you cannot avoid dirtying your hands.'
Bruno Delaye, foreign policy adviser to President Mitterrand

1
Autocratic Elites and Enfeebled Masses: Africa, Botswana and South Africa

Botswana is an established liberal democracy in existence since pre-independence elections in 1965. Open, competitive, free and fairly fair elections occur regularly. The rule of law is generally upheld, though not necessarily equally available to all in every sphere. Good levels of rationality and efficiency commonly prevail in government and the private sector. Corruption occurs among the ruling elite in the nexus that exists between government and business, but it appears moderate at the lower levels of administration especially in such public instrumentalities as the police, customs and immigration.[1] Even in the late nineteenth century, Bamangwato, the Central District of modern Botswana, possessed, as is noted below, a strong state. Sustained growth is the norm, albeit on a narrow sectoral base. Throughout the 1980s the country enjoyed an annual average growth of gross domestic production (GDP) of 10.9 per cent, by far the highest in Africa.[2]

Capitalist barbarism

Most of the rest of Africa is very different. Over much of West Africa, in the two Congos, in the Great Lakes and the Horn of Africa, and elsewhere, conditions of actual or incipient 'capitalist barbarism' prevail.[3] Liberia moved early and decisively towards destruction. Conditions in the late 1990s, some seven years after Charles Taylor initiated civil war, according to Huband, were as follows: 'Acts of appalling violence and mass executions' have been 'committed by all sides' throughout the country. 'As destructive has been the fear', which 'prevailed from the first moment' the armies of youngsters began 'overturning traditional authority, annihilating the small educated class and quickly evolving into a generation of teenage psychopaths', whose 'rule of terror' made

Liberia a 'wilderness'.[4] Up to 100 000 lives may have been lost and about half the population displaced.[5] Taylor brought depravity to Liberia, while he amassed 'vast wealth' for himself.[6] He gained control over 'the royalties from the world's largest commercial shipping fleet and the rents to be earned from narco dollars' passing through the country, contributing in so doing to the criminalization of the economy and the remnants of the state.[7] With these acquisitions he promoted possibly worse depravity and destruction in neighbouring Sierra Leone. By early 1999, the Revolutionary United Front (RUF) and its Liberian ally controlled most of the diamond-mining areas of that country, providing valuable spoils through smuggling. 'More than half' of its 15 000 to 30 000 fighters were said to be children and youths. Its brutality rivalled perhaps only that of the Hutu leadership in Rwanda in 1994. Few residents survived the massacres in the towns which it seized, and those who did were 'gruesomely disfigured'.[8] Children killed their parents, cannibal gangs roamed in the countryside and, as the RUF entered Freetown in January, 'barbarism flourishe[d]'.[9]

While Liberia and Sierra Leone were 'possible sources of contagion for the whole region',[10] notably Guinea and Congo-Brazzaville,[11] war continued in Angola. By the end of the century, Jonas Savimbi was, for Jonathan Steele, Africa's 'greatest surviving war criminal'. For 25 years he had brought destruction and deaths totalling about 800 000 to his country.[12]

The Angolan government controlled the main towns and handsome, fast-growing oil revenues. They were worth in 1999 around $3.5 billion a year, and were expected to increase substantially as new off-shore fields came into production. The bulk of the money bypasses the budget and goes straight into the hands of the presidency. According to a report at the end of that year, 'the entire profits' from the country's oil 'for the next three years' had already been spent – either on armaments or to finance the super-rich lifestyles of the 'oiligarchy'.[13] Both it and the leadership of Savimbi's forces appeared to accept 'indefinite war as a natural state of affairs'. Below both the ruling and rebel elites, at the level of the conscripted foot-soldier and the person in the shattered streets, however, it was in the words of an unnamed diplomat, 'a war of poor people against miserable people'.[14] By 2000, on a recent United Nations report, some 200 Angolans were dying every day because of malnutrition, and 90 per cent of the four million inhabitants of Luanda were in poverty. The resource-rich country had become 'the worst place in the world to be a child' – almost one-third of infants died before the age of five.[15]

Charles Taylor emerged as the most ruthless and richest warlord in Liberia, and in July 1997 he was elected as President, with about 75 per cent of the vote, after disbursing a good part of the wealth he had amassed from exploiting the country's resources. His closest election rival, Ellen Johnson-Sirleaf, a former United Nations and World Bank official, got some 10 per cent of the votes. The turnout was put at 85 per cent.[16] He continued the debasement of the society. One of the slogans used in his Presidential campaign was: 'He Killed my Pa, He Killed my Ma, I'll vote for Him'.[17] Huband says that 'if [Taylor] had lost there would have been another war', and Chris McGreal reported that Liberians said they voted for him to prevent more war.[18]

Taylor's influence in Sierra Leone saw no diminishment. By July 1999, the RUF, guilty of wide-scale murder, mutilation and rape, had received an 'absolute and free pardon and reprieve', and Foday Sankoh and other rebel leaders were offered prominent and profitable government positions.[19] This was a blanket amnesty which included gross human rights violations against civilians.[20] The rebel practice of inflicting mass amputations – 'chopping' – had given Sierra Leone 'its special place in the annals of human wickedness'.[21] By December 1999 Sankoh had been helped to form a supposed political party, and rebels were being given $300 each on arrival at special camps. But his chief lieutenant, Sam Bockarie or 'Mosquito', remained armed and in the bush. *The Economist's* correspondent noted that Taylor, Sankoh's mentor, had won the presidency by threatening to resume fighting, and believed there was 'no doubt Mr Sankoh will make the same threat in the election due in 2001'.[22] General Timothy Shelpidi, commander of the West African peacekeeping force, Ecomog, accused Liberia earlier in the year of creating upheaval in the region, and later said: 'As long as Taylor is in power in Liberia, the Sierra Leone crisis will never end'.[23]

After Sankoh fell into the hands of United Nations units in Freetown in May 2000, an event precipitated by further rebel attacks, the government of President Ahmed Tejan Kabbah acted as if the amnesty (or Lomé) agreement with the RUF remained in force. The Kabbah government did not look 'remotely capable' of rebuilding the wrecked country.[24] RUF leaders continued to receive material assistance from both Charles Taylor and Blaise Compaore in Burkina Fasso. Three of them travelled with the Liberian president to a joint meeting in Ougadougou on 5 June. Five days later, one of the same rebel leaders carried diamonds to Monrovia. Taylor had arranged transport of arms, munitions, fuel, food and soldiers to the RUF, and had produced a plan to fortify the Kono diamond producing areas, which the rebels firmly controlled.[25]

President Charles Taylor's intimidation and exploitation is constant, but his means of achieving his ends have increased. In early 2000 he passed a law that gives him the right to dispose of all 'strategic commodities'. These are defined as mineral resources, forest, agricultural and fishery products, all art, and anything else the President names.[26] The economy, state and people of Liberia have effectively becomes the property of Taylor.

War radiated east and southwards from the two Congos and Angola. Zambian businessmen-politicians provided lucrative supply facilities to Savimbi, and, in apparent reprisal, bombs were detonated in Lusaka in February 1999, damaging water and electricity services. Namibia was sucked into the fighting at the end of the year – police and civilians were killed, Namibians were recruited into the Angolan army, foreign tourists were murdered, and the country's vital tourism industry was damaged. Violence was flowing out from Angola like oil and diamonds.[27]

Legitimized autocracy

Elsewhere, the contrast with capitalist barbarism was not meaningful democratization, but the legitimization of autocracy through the ballot box. Democracy understood as merely the act of voting, over 24 or 48 hours once every five or seven years, not as a sustained participatory process, is wide open to manipulation and abuse. Electoral processes have been effectively manipulated by the holders of state power in, among others, Ivory Coast, Gabon and Cameroon.[28] Blatantly oppressive techniques were sometimes utilized, but the outcomes accorded legitimacy and recognition to existing autocrats. President Gnassingbe Eyadema held power in Togo for 31 years, and got a renewed term in 1998 through fiddling the electoral lists, denying the opposition access to the state-run media, and direct intimidation of the opposition; when it seemed that Gilchrist Olympio might nonetheless win, paramilitary units stopped the count in Lome, and seized and burnt ballot boxes.[29]

In October 1987, Blaise Compaore gained power in Burkina Fasso by brutally murdering his close friend – 'brother officer' – President Thomas Sankara. He got himself elected as a civilian President four years later, and in November 1998 he was returned through the ballot box for another seven years in office. Since only 25 per cent of voters had turned out in 1991, government thugs went into people's homes and urged them to register. Opposition parties who called for a boycott of the polls were beaten-up with clubs, batons and hammers. The official turnout was put at 56 per cent, and 88 per cent of them voted for President Compaore.[30]

Democratic pressures elsewhere led only to elections which produced partially democratic systems at best, 'democratic despots' at worst.[31] In Zambia, the movement which triumphantly brought back a multi-party system in 1991 proved unable to control the autocratic tendencies of President Frederick Chiluba, as he pursued a destructive vendetta against his failed and aged predecessor, Kenneth Kaunda,[32] and harassed his critics in the media and elsewhere. Civil society exists in Kenya along with a powerful tradition of protest, but President Daniel arap Moi retained power over more than 20 years, while shifting from a single-party dictatorship to a multi-party despotism, with the same misrule throughout.[33]

The military handed over power in Nigeria to widespread relief in 1999, but its legacy was woeful,[34] and the democratic foundations of the government of President Olusegun Obasanjo seemed deeply flawed. Some 50 million people were perhaps eligible to vote in 1999. Election turnouts in Nigeria have usually been low, with 30 per cent good or the norm, and 40 per cent considered high. But this time nearly 30 million voters were said to have been counted, indicating a rate of participation of 60 per cent, and the gap between the winner and loser was supposedly seven million votes. The 'only logical conclusion' was that 'as many as half the votes counted...must have been fakes'.[35] Cunliffe-Jones reported that voting figures were wildly inflated in many areas, and the totals counted were more than double the figure for the last election in 1993. With wealthy friends in and out of the military, Obasanjo had 'benefited from a powerful political machine', which his opponents completely lacked.[36]

Toad Kings: old and new

Soyinka's Old Toad Kings not only remained firmly anti-democratic at the end of the century, but their ranks were joined by some of the supposed 'new leaders' of Africa, those younger, sober and thoughtful men, as President Bill Clinton had admiringly described them.[37] President Robert Mugabe, a Toad aged 76 in 2000, flagrantly depicted democracy as a possible 'factor for instability rather than stability', suggested that governments were being 'stampede[d] willy-nilly to adopt democracy', and insisted that African nations 'be left alone to evolve our own institutions', at the opening of a summit meeting of the Organization of African Unity in Harare on 2 June 1997.[38] Not long after,

his Namibian counterpart, President Sam Nujoma, used his governing party's parliamentary predominance to change the country's
advanced, democratic constitution and accord a third term in office to
himself.[39] But it is in the broad area of human rights, of more actual-
ized rather than mere formalized electoral democracy, that the rigidity
of the Toad Kings is most apparent, and where the new leaders have
joined them.

Robert Mugabe dismisses the whole question of gay and lesbian
rights, pronouncing firmly that such people are 'worse than pigs and
dogs'; President Moi is certain that 'homosexuality is against African
norms and traditions'; President Sam Nujoma has said that 'homosexu-
ality must be condemned and rejected in our society'; and Frederick
Chiluba affirms that 'homosexuality is the deepest level of depravity.
It is unbiblical and abnormal.' Nujoma's Home Affairs minister, Jerry
Ekandjo, went further and called on graduating police officers, in
October 2000, to 'eliminate' gays and lesbians 'from the face of
Namibia'.[40]

President Yoweri Museveni of Uganda was conspicuously placed
among the small group of Africa's new leaders, but seemed as intolerant as Mugabe. When his government re-wrote Uganda's constitution
and penal code in 1990, the maximum penalty for 'unnatural carnal-
ity' was increased from 14 years to life imprisonment. In 1994 he said
that his government would 'shoot at' anyone bringing homosexuality
into his country.[41] Efforts to promote gay rights emerged later within
civil society in Kampala, and on 27 September 1999, President
Museveni declared that he had instructed the police 'to look for homo-
sexuals, lock them up and charge them'.[42]

The treatment of felons was another area where the human rights of
the new leaders were on a par with those of the old. The Zambian
penal code imposes a mandatory death sentence for treason, murder
and aggravated robbery. In September 1999, the High Court in Lusaka
condemned 59 soldiers to death for their involvement in a failed coup
attempt in 1997; they joined another 168 murder and aggravated robbery convicts already awaiting execution. Hangings, it was believed,
tended to be carried out at intervals of ten years. The last executions in
the country, of eight people, occurred in January 1997, and all these
had been convicted between 1982 and 1990. The attempted coup was
not the country's first, and it seemed to suggest rather wide dissatisfaction with the government. A movement against the death penalty
had arisen in Zambia. Imposing the death penalty for the political
offence of treason, as Wakabi has noted, is a serious deterrent against

legitimate opposition to an existing government.[43] But President Chiluba declared that he would not deliver a judgement that contravened the decision of the court.[44]

Prisoners are treated no less harshly in Uganda, and appeals to President Museveni for clemency have fallen on the same deaf ears as those of his notorious predecessors. At the turn of the twenty-first century, Abdallah Nabulere, 68, described as a peasant from the district of Pallisa, had been on death row in Luzira maximum security prison for 22 years. He had been sentenced to death for murder in February 1978. His younger brother Hussein Mubbala, convicted with him, died of natural causes in the prison's condemned section in 1986, while his father, who had also been on death row, passed away two years earlier. 'I feel the President should pardon me', said Nabulere. 'I am an old man whose back is broken and I have suffered enough'.[45]

In 1998 there were 179 convicts awaiting execution in Uganda. Near the end of 1999 some 28 people were hanged for various offences including treason and armed robbery. The European Union, international human rights agencies, and others had appealed for clemency without avail. 'Sexual defilement' was reclassified as a capital offence shortly after. In late November 1999 about 500 treason suspects were awaiting trial; they had been on remand for more than three years, accused of waging war against the government. Ugandan prisons were holding five times their intended capacity. As district commissioner, Ngoma Ngime, reported: 'The prisoners are sleeping like sacks of beans packed on top of each other'.[46]

Barbarism intensified

Hopes of change faded further at the end of the 1990s when the leading new modernizers fell out among themselves utilizing heavy military force in the process. The resort to arms was initiated by President Museveni in association with the Rwandan leader, Paul Kagame, crossing into Congo-Kinshasa, on the comprehensible grounds that the government of Laurent Kabila had not put a stop to the Hutu extremist forces still operating destructively along the Rwandan–Ugandan borders. But their armed intervention against Kabila was quickly followed by that of Zimbabwe, Namibia and Angola in support of the Congo government, and in the protracted stalemate that ensued, Rwandan and Ugandan units clashed with each other in the eastern half of the country.

In early June 2000, their forces rained shells and mortar fire on each other in Kisangani. Some 250 civilians were reported killed, and over

1000 wounded. Much of the centre of the city, including the cathedral on the river's edge, was destroyed. This was the third and the most brutal time that the two armies had battled for control of Kisangani since they first began fighting each other there a year earlier.[47] Museveni's and Kagame's military initiatives had led to a large and wasteful escalation of militarization in the region, and brought no new light to the Congo.

Robert Mugabe's military engagement was especiallly heavy – some 6000 troops in 1998, and 11 000, with helicopters and fighter aircraft, shortly after. It involved access to the Congo's diamond wealth for Zimbabwean generals and their backers, and great hardship for the people.[48] Inflation, unemployment and interest rates all moved above 50 per cent, and some 70 per cent of the population were impoverished. GDP was expected to shrink by 5 per cent in 2000, the annual budget deficit moved into double figures, and an estimated 150 000 jobs were threatened as businesses faced bankruptcy.[49] After Mugabe suffered his first electoral loss in an important constitutional referendum in February 2000, state-organized anarchy and thuggery quickly engulfed much of the once well-developed country. 'Leaders like Mugabe', said Soyinka, 'would rather see their countries on fire than give up power'.[50]

Worse occurred in the north. Prime Minister Meles Zenawi of Ethiopia and President Issaias Afwerki of Eritrea were a prominent duo among the new leaders of Africa. Their seriousness had been displayed on more than one occasion. They had joined together to overthrow the corrupt and dictatorial Mengistu regime in 1991, and had cooperated in the uniquely smooth secession of Eritrea two years later, though this left Ethiopia landlocked. They had a reputation for 'usually settl[ing] any problems with a quick telephone call'.[51] The core leadership in both countries came from the same basic group of Tigrayan Christian highlanders, described as proud, self-reliant, and also as uncompromising. Issaias Afwerki, only in his mid-fifties, was unlike many of his African presidential peers in being austere and unpretentious. But he also embodied, it was noted, the Eritrean slogan 'never kneel down'.[52] They had fought a 30-year struggle for independence, their army was huge for such a small, poor state, and they had acquired, Clapham notes, 'a contempt for the diplomatic conventions'.[53] Qualities of openness, egalitarianism and independence were intermixed with rigidity and militarism.

Relations between the two brotherly nations plummeted through a series of provocative and irrational actions beginning in early 1998.

Eritrea introduced its own currency, which soon fell sharply in value against the Ethiopian birr; Ethiopia insisted that bilateral trade must be based on hard currency; and Eritrea abrogated their 1991 agreement on Ethiopia's free access to the ports of Assab and Massarwa. Ethiopia is stronger economically,[54] it possessed better weaponry, and its population is some 18-times larger than its neighbour. Nevertheless, 'there is no question', states Clapham, that the resort to war 'came from the Eritrean side'.[55] Issaias, adds *The Economist*, 'made a huge mistake'. He wanted to show the Ethiopians that he would not be pushed around. 'Within a few days' the two countries were at war in the vicinity of a disputed village, Badme.[56]

As the new leaders fell out, bad moved quickly to worse and soon the very worst imaginable. In one battle between 14 and 16 March 1999 the Ethiopians advanced in waves of tanks and infantry on a four-kilometre front, towards Eritrean trenches, in the face of a barrage of artillery, mortar and machine-gun fire. They were repulsed after 60 hours of intense hand-to-hand fighting. The Eritreans claimed to have killed 10 000. A month later, hundreds of Ethiopian corpses still lay unburied among burnt-out tanks, under a stench of decomposition.[57] Carnage and waste were the fruits of the determination of the two leaders. Eritrea, around this time, had some 180 000 soldiers at the front – out of its total population of 3.5 million – and it was spending 20 per cent of its national income on war. Six sophisticated MIG-29 aircraft, for instance, had been purchased from Russia at around $20 million each, and two were already lost.[58] If the weaponry was heavy and sometimes advanced, the tactics were those of 1914–18, and the medical treatment was of an even earlier period.[59] By the end of the year, in the words of Steele:

> 500 000 Ethiopian and Eritrean conscripts face[d] each other in squalid trenches which display the senseless tragedy of World War 1. Up to 50 000 have already gone 'over the top' and been mown down in the 18 months since their leaders started the conflict.[60]

Mediation efforts by the United States and the Organization of African Unity had both proved fruitless. But the ostensible reason for the war was just a few hectares of barren mountain and desert.[61]

Welcoming Canadian ambassador Robert Fowler to Botswana in May 1999, the country's Foreign Minister, Lieutenant-General Mompati Merafhe, said that the conflicts raging in Africa were a cause of shame to the continent. War was draining Africa of its much needed material and human resources, he said.[62] If deaths alone are counted, the numbers are indeed daunting. In the wars considered above: some 100 000 people dead in Liberia on the instigation chiefly of Charles Taylor over nine years; uncounted 'tens of thousands',[63] mostly civilians, in rebellion in Sierra Leone, over much the same period, in which Foday Sankoh's RUF acquired ascendancy; up to 800 000 dead in Angola over 25 years, where indefinite warfare is accepted as normal by both the governing and the rebel elites; some 50 000 soldiers killed in battle between the forces of Prime Minister Meles and President Issaias in an 18-month period. Eritrea killed another 25 000 Ethiopians, it claimed, in the first three days of renewed fighting in May 2000. Ethiopia had quadrupled its military spending before it asserted its dominance on the battlefield soon after.[64]

And in the greatest enormity of all, some 800 000 people – Tutsis and moderate, pro-democratic Hutus – slaughtered in one hundred days in Rwanda in mid-1994. This was no spontaneous, primordial outburst. It was a planned extermination organized by an elite of Hutu extremists – the Akazu circle – who utilized their high levels of administrative and social control, who anticipated that the world would react neither effectively nor in time, and who ultimately misjudged only the rapid advance of the Rwandan Patriotic Front into Kigali, as they themselves retreated under French military protection into Mobutu's Zaire. The rate and scale of their killing rivalled that of Pol Pot and even Hitler's industrialized exterminations.[65]

Barbarism, depravity, destruction and wastage of what material resources exist,[66] with new modernizing elites inflicting carnage on their own young men and women, and others like Museveni displaying a contempt for human rights rivalling that of the oldest and worst regimes. Democracy as a living, participatory system cannot exist in such conditions. As Zainab Bangura, head of the Campaign for Good Governance in Sierra Leone, said of her country's rulers: the 'political class has not just become inherently corrupt, it has lost the remotest understanding of popular government'.[67] Chinua Achebe wrote in 1983 that the trouble with Nigeria is 'simply and squarely a failure of leadership ... the unwillingness or inability of its leaders to rise to the responsibility ... of personal example ...'[68] Francis Nyamnjoh generalized firmly near the end of the 1990s: 'Africa's greatest enemy is its leaders, with barely a few exceptions.'[69]

Movements or tendencies for popular change face crippling difficulties.[70] Leys quotes Bayart as earlier observing that the role of the African masses has been reduced to that of mute accompaniments – 'paid extras' at best – in the crowd scenes organized by the kleptocrats.[71] Their induced muteness has made it very difficult, almost impossible, for any concept of citizenship to develop.[72] Leys posed the fundamental problem as 'the weakness of the social formations' on which the state rests.[73] But this is profoundly a two-way affair, an interrelationship in which the rulers play the determining role. Corrupt and autocratic elites have a deeply debilitating affect on the mass of the people; after years of crude despotism, 'Nigeria has no tradition of democracy, nor of effective governance.'[74] Autocratic elites foster popular passivity, and perpetuate themselves more comfortably upon it. Mobutu ruled for over 30 years, not only on the assistance he skilfully obtained from the United States, France, Belgium and the Bretton Woods institutions, but even more because the 'population was kept in a state of infantilism'. No other kleptocrat exceeded his depredations, but economic collapse and wide-ranging brutality were tolerated by a people 'steeped in passivity' for over a century.[75]

Silence is the hand-maid of elitism and ultimately the cloak for tyranny, even where an electoral politics exists. Democracy had not developed roots in most African countries, said Mamphela Ramphele, because people had failed to see that new ruling elites had the potential to be just as autocratic as their colonial predecessors. Only five years after majority rule in South Africa, a 'culture of silence', she said, threatened the country's infant democracy.[76] Out of a prevailing lack of vision and leadership, in a related formulation, a situation had come about where 'Africa's population appear[ed] to be more tolerant of inadequate standards of governance than the peoples of almost all other parts of the world…'[77]

What characterised most of Africa in the twenty-first century was therefore a largely static interrelationship between autocratic elites and enfeebled masses, the former literally uninterested in democracy and governance, and the latter without the moral, material and organizational means to do anything about it. Decades of decay and despotism had effaced citizenship, and an empty electoral democracy had done little or nothing to engender it.

The insufficiency of elite democracy

Southern Africa is in many ways totally different from the barbarism and despotism, and yet in some essentials much the same. It is obviously the most advanced region both economically and democratically, but the political feature that characterises the region, with the exception of

Mauritius with its functioning liberal democracy, is the existence of predominant party systems and the elitism accompanying them.

The continental background has underlined the attractiveness of Botswana's democracy, and the rosy perceptions of world leaders have magnified the enhancement further. Arriving in Gaborone on the fifth leg of his six-nation tour in March 1998, President Clinton said that he had travelled from 'Africa's youngest democracy, South Africa, to its oldest, Botswana'. He had seen 'the promise of a new Africa ... its roots are here deep in your soil for you have been an inspiration to all who cherish freedom'. He praised the economic leadership of President Ketumile Masire, and the peaceful transfer of power, due in two days time, to his deputy, Festus Mogae. 'Botswana's success was built by its people' and, he declared, 'by the dedicated leaders they choose'.[78]

Nelson Mandela added his great prestige to praise no less extravagant: 'The manner in which the people of Botswana have combined the modern forms of democracy with the long-held traditions of indigenous democracy', he announced on 14 October 1999, 'is an example that can be looked to' in what he called 'the current rebirth of our continent.' An honorary degree was being conferred on Mandela by President Festus Mogae, chancellor of the University of Botswana, and the people were due to vote in national elections in just two days time. Botswana's democracy 'served as a guiding star' to all South Africans, he said, as they 'falteringly took [their] first steps towards [their] new democracy'. Botswana, Mandela added, 'was an example of African democracy that had sustained itself over time'.[79]

When Botswana's democracy is examined more closely, it is the strong elitism of the model, and the dominance of form over participatory substance, which stand out.[80]

Empowered elites, passive masses

Botswana holds regular free and partly fair, open competitive elections, but no change of government resulted over the period 1965–99. Elections in democratic Mauritius, by contrast, have led to a change of government on more than one occasion, with a sitting Prime Minister actually conceding defeat, in December 1995, even before the final results were officially announced. Other predominant party systems have existed in other democracies coterminously – notably in Italy, Japan and Sweden.[81] But the continuing predominance of the Botswana Democratic Party (BDP) becomes rather more problematic beyond a span of 35 years. Before the national elections of October 1999, the then official opposition, the Botswana Congress Party (BCP), held 11 seats in the National Assembly of 44 members, the highest opposition representation ever. It was acquiring credibility as an alternative government. After the vote, its parliamentary representation fell to one seat, while the strength of the BDP rose further. As 2000 was entered no credible alternative to the ruling party was in existence.[82] For Darnolf and Holm, Botswana was a democracy without an opposition[83] – a near contradiction even in liberal terms.

No limitation on the Presidents's term in office existed before 1998 – death or retirement were the effective limiting factors on the power and longevity of the BDP-bolstered state President. Nor is the President, contrary to Clinton's assertion, chosen by the people. He is instead indirectly elected by the members of the National Assembly, an electorate which has ranged in size over the years from 30 to 44 mostly male people. Sir Seretse Khama was succeeded smoothly by his Vice-President Masire in 1980, and Masire by his Vice-President Mogae in 1998, without reference to the popular will. He is not required to hold an elected parliamentary seat, but has the right to speak and vote in parliament nonetheless.

Great centralization of power in the presidency exists. Under the constitution the President decides alone; he appoints and removes the Vice-President and all cabinet members, and determines on the sitting and dissolution of parliament. He nominates four specially elected MPs, who enjoy the same voting rights as those who are actually elected, and may – often do – acquire senior ministerial position. He commands the Botswana Defence Force, appoints and promotes its officers, and may control its operational deployment. The President has influence over the appointment of the Chief Justice of the High Court. He can appoint and constitute a commission of inquiry, determine whether it sits in public or private, and whether its report is published or not. The Office of the President exercises direct control over the police, the public service, the Directorate on Corruption and Economic Crime, and Information and Broadcasting (embracing the only daily newspaper – distributed nationally, free of charge – Radio Botswana, Botswana Television and the government news agency), as well as the military;[84] the panoply of state power in the President's hands.

The presidency's control over opinion and information is extensive. The Immigration Act confers wide powers on the President alone – declaring, say, that a resident foreigner is a prohibited immigrant – which are not subject to review in a court of law. The Penal Code encompasses such broad and political matters as sedition, defamation and contempt, and can encourage self-censorship among publishers, editors and journalists. The provisions of the National Security Act of 1986 are both vague and totalizing, and involve a penalty of up to 25 years' imprisonment regardless of public interest. Civil servants are not allowed to speak to the press, but following a series of corruption scandals in 1991–94, punitive confidence laws were introduced in a number of parastatals further restricting the availability of information to the public; those in the Botswana Housing Corporation, for instance, carried a possible fine of P5000 and imprisonment for up to five years for an ethically-conscious employee.

The rise of senior bureaucrats into high office is a characteristic of Botswana's democracy, and it may be rapid and direct. Festus Mogae was only 59 on his accession in 1998, and his experience of elective office was slight. His career was chiefly that of an official in national and international finance before President Masire made him a nominated MP and also Minister for Finance and Development Planning in 1989, and then Vice-President in 1992. He only obtained an elected parliamentary seat in the national elections in October 1994.[85] When he became President and thus resigned his constituency seat in 1998, his acquaintance with elective office covered just four years.

Mogae entered the presidency with some suggested capacity for new and critical thinking; it was time for Africans to stop blaming colonialism for their failings, he told a banquet of political and business leaders in Johannesburg in December 1997. The blame had to be shifted, he said, to the post-independence policies and strategies adopted by black leaders.[86] As President he told a meeting of the OAU, in no more relevant a place than Blaise Compaore's Ouagadougou, that autocrats should not lead Africa: those who used unconstitutional means to oppress their own people should not have access to high office in the OAU.[87] He also had some reputation for domestic fiscal probity;[88] he opposed the subsidies to cattle-owners and the handouts to businessmen with which the BDP government was firmly associated.[89] His self-perception was significant: 'I am one of a new breed of African leaders', he declared, just hours after his inauguration, 'who [a]re aware of the importance of economic management'. He referred specifically to 'people like President Museveni, President Mandela, and Thabo Mbeki', and while 'differences in our style and temperaments' exist, 'strategically and technically we believe in the same sort of things'. He affirmed, 'governance nowadays is about economic management'.[90]

Despite his tendencies towards critical thinking on important Africa-wide issues, Mogae has accommodated himself since 1998 within

Botswana's constitutionally autocratic system. In three of his most important decisions he decided alone or well-nigh alone. On 1 April that year President Mogae appointed Lieutenant-General Ian Khama as Minister for Presidential Affairs, and the next day nominated him as Vice-President; he had retired as army commander only on 31 March. Aged 45, General Khama's experience of elective politics was non-existent. Mogae had kept both his front and back-benchers in parliament, and the BDP itself, in the dark about his decision. Leading, long-serving ministers like Daniel Kwelagobe, Ponatshego Kedikilwe and Mompati Merafhe were bypassed in the process.[91] The people were not consulted. When Kgosi Ian Khama Seretse Khama later won a constituency seat within his chieftaincy in Central District, he appeared before the voters explicitly as their Chief.[92] He was more apolitical than the President, and his interests and values seemed firmly authoritarian.[93] He opposed alcohol consumption, and as Minister for Presidential Affairs he sent police and paramilitary units to close bars and restaurants throughout the country one hour before midnight on 31 December 1998.[94] Both the country's President and Vice-President had entered politics by way of nomination directly to high office. The people's choice played no role in either case.

When Botswana committed military forces along with those of South Africa purportedly to quell political unrest in Lesotho on 22 September 1998, the decision to deploy the BDF was taken by President Mogae, and perhaps Vice-President Khama, alone. Cabinet was not consulted, and parliamentarians were not informed. General Khama correctly pointed out later that there was no law which required the President to consult, and the BDF Act also authorized him to act alone. A news-blackout was imposed on Radio Botswana and the government-owned *Daily News*, even though the intervention was being extensively covered in the South African and international media. The President's Office allegedly endeavoured to mislead the independent press about the train of events. Mogae informed the Leader of the Opposition as the Botswana force approached the Lesotho border, but he did not inform the nation over Radio Botswana of this unprecedented intervention into a friendly neighbouring country.[95]

The Vice-President retained not only his chiefly status but also continued to enjoy his military prerogatives as before. He regularly trained at the BDF gym in Gaborone, and he piloted an army helicopter to BDP election campaign meetings in Nkange and Molepolole on two occasions in September 1999.[96] Those who criticized his actions as conferring unfair advantages on himself and his party were, he said, merely 'jealous' people, who did not know how to fly.[97]

Khama's disdain for responsible, democratic politics seemed vast. Right at the outset of his Vice-Presidency, he had informed his interviewer, Rebaone Odirile, that 'If I do not feel happy, I will soon leave.'[98] He did not assume one of the established roles of the Vice-President, that of Leader of the House in parliament, and towards the end of 1999 he was absent from parliamentary sittings when questions pertaining to his Ministry were being asked.[99] At the beginning of December, President Mogae announced that he had granted General Khama 'up to one year's sabbatical leave of absence from his duties as Vice-President and Minister of Presidential Affairs' effective from 1 January 2000.

Before 1 April 1998, Mogae had 'prevailed upon General Khama' to relinquish his army command 'in the interests of the nation and the [BDP]'. He was initially 'reluctant to do so', and President Mogae had 'promised' that when Party stability was restored, and the administration was running smoothly, 'I would grant him the break he had planned' to attend to 'his duties as Chief and to his personal and other interests'. The President continued: 'he believes that time has now arrived'. As Vice-President, General Khama 'has served with distinction for over a year'. He would, in addition, resume his functions and duties on his return, and would 'remain holding the substantive office of Vice-President during his leave of absence'.[100]

Michael Dingake, leader of the BCP, said that this was 'an unheard of practice in the annals of constitutional democratic government', and it was 'absurd' to grant such leave to a Vice-President. Mogae's advanced justifications were flimsy: the recruitment of Khama into government leadership had, in fact, 'exacerbated the tensions within the BDP as well as the public service'.[101] The editor of *The Gazette* asked what other decisions the President and Vice-President might have made which neither the public nor the ruling BDP knew about. If Khama had approached the Vice-Presidency as merely a temporary position 'the people of Botswana have been seriously deceived'. Mogae's decision represented a dangerous constitutional precedent.[102]

Elitism and presidentialism are accompanied, supported and extended by low levels of political participation by voters. Turnout was a creditable 68 per cent at national elections in 1968, and it reached an all-time high of 77 per cent in 1994 when the Botswana National Front had run an effective opposition campaign under the slogan of 'Time for a Change'. But only 56 per cent took part in the country's founding elections in 1965, 30 per cent did so in 1969, and participation fell as low as 21 per cent in 1974.[103] When referenda were held in October 1997 to approve a range of important and overdue electoral reforms – to establish an Independent Electoral Commission, lower the voting age to 18, and accord the vote to citizens resident outside Botswana – just 16.7 per cent of those eligible took part.[104] After Ian Khama Seretse Khama went among his subjects in the by-election in Serowe North, 37 per cent of the eligible electorate voted.[105]

The national elections of 1999 saw the extinction of an effective parliamentary opposition in the country, with only about 42 per cent of those with the right to vote doing so.[106] Within the age group 18 to 21 there were approximately 21 300 young people who had gained the right to vote for the first time, but only 5 per cent of these bothered to register; similarly, out of an estimated 17 400 newly enfranchised absentee voters, just 1395 registered.[107] No mediation usually exists between the citizen-voter and the state: parliament too is inactive and self-interested, and civil society weak and undeveloped. President Mogae's understanding of democracy accords closely with this quiescent citizenry 'We're very proud of how dull our elections are', he said in late 1999, 'It proves that our democracy is working'.[108]

Accountable to themselves

With a constitutional elitism legitimized further through the practice of electoral politics with a largely inactive citizen mass, the way is open not only for unchanging government – under formally democratic conditions – but for non-accountable government as well. Cases abound. In the early 1990s there were gross irregularities in the supply of teaching materials to schools; illegal land transactions in peri-urban villages outside Gaborone, in which senior ministers Peter Mmusi and Daniel Kwelagobe were involved; and extensive malpractice in the management of the Botswana Housing Corporation, involving, among other incidents and people, a serious conflict-of-interest situation on the part of an Assistant Minister for Local Government, Lands and Housing – those responsible characteristically denied all wrong-doing sometimes with vehemence.[109] There was also the near collapse of the National Development Bank (NDB) under a burden of unredeemed loans.

The Minister for Finance, Festus Mogae, had described the NDB in 1991 as 'a pillar of our financial system'.[110] but by 1994 many leading ministers were heavily indebted to this institution for which they themselves were collectively responsible. Some were in default for more than six months. Among others, Minister Kedikilwe held an outstanding loan of P640 000, of which P260 000 was in arrears; the Minister for Labour, Patrick Balopi, was indebted to the Bank via a company he owned to the extent of P1.1 million; Johnny Swartz, a prominent BDP backbencher, owed the NDB P1.12 million; and President Masire owed P546 000. The President's brother, Basimane Masire, figured in the top 15 of the Bank's debtors near the end of 1993 with a loan outstanding of P1.2 million that appeared never to have been serviced.

This came to light through a leaked document. The many ministers concerned prevaricated, they blamed the Bank itself, but provided no explanation on how such loans were obtained, on what collateral, and how repayment was frequently deferred. Anonymous sources inside the NDB stated that ministers and other MPs had repeatedly sought loans for which they did not qualify. Their collective debt to the Bank which the government administered was an estimated P30 million.

Ministers suggested that they were farmers like other people who sometimes got into difficulties in repaying loans. President Masire declared that it was 'unethical' to question the role of the ruling elite in the near bankruptcy of the NDB, adding that 'the media should refrain from this witch hunt'.[111] He also indicated later that he saw agricultural production in Botswana as being an inherently risky pursuit, for which access to bank credit was essential. 'The people who venture', he declared, were 'the hope of our society'.[112] He seemingly assumed, and implicitly admitted, that he perceived it natural for government leaders to act simultaneously as venture capitalists; he did not enlarge on this linkage between government and business, and he was not asked to do so.

No serious rebuttal or revision of the released figures was forthcoming throughout the several weeks of commotion in early 1994. University students and concerned citizens held two lively protest demonstrations in Gaborone, but the governing elite was not pressed for further information. Yet it was at the elections eight months later that voter turnout and the Opposition's parliamentary strength reached all-time highs.[113] Citizenship could develop in Botswana, it seemed to follow, if the people had organization, leadership and a realizable possibility of betterment.

Non-accountability was similar when it was revealed in April 1999 that the ruling party had received a donation from an undisclosed foreign source totalling P2.4 million ($500 000). The purpose of the gift was to assist the BDP to contest the forthcoming elections. The BDP's treasurer, Satar Dada, who was also a large car distributor and multimillionaire, confirmed this to *Mmegi's* Prof Malema: 'The money will be used for the election campaign and to buy vehicles', Dada said. The governing party had apparently anticipated receipt of the gift, and had been buying cars over the previous seven weeks: it had bought 40 vehicles, one for each constitutency, from Satar Dada's Motor Centre, reported Malema. Dada declined to give the source of the money. A spokesperson in the Office of the President, Ross Sanoto, said equivocally that the government does not 'really' condone foreign funding. Only four people were said to know the source of the gift and the conditions attached: President Mogae; BDP chairman, Ponatshego Kedikilwe; BDP secretary-general, Daniel Kwelagobe; and Dada. Malema also revealed that the money had moved by a circuitous route from Zurich through New York to Gaborone, where it arrived on 17 March.[114]

In late May it was reported that Dumelang Saleshando had been sacked from Wesbank, accused of leaking the news of the BDP's gift. It was further suggested that the P2.4 million 'originated from a subsidiary of De Beers'. Satar Dada was named as being a member of the board of Wesbank. Saleshando, it was further noted, was fired 'after pressure on the Bank from the BDP leadership'.[115] The BDP executive secretary, Botsalo Ntuane, affirmed in May that his party 'is not telling anybody the source of its funding because there is no reason to do so'.[116] Kedikilwe, shortly after, accused journalists who were investigating the foreign gift of having a hidden agenda, and he reiterated that the BDP did not owe anybody any explanation on the matter.[117]

The BDP had actually received a total of P3 346 852 in donations from undisclosed sources during the first half of 1999, its own financial statements indicated. Addressing a ruling party Congress in July, Treasurer Dada said that he preferred to describe the source of these funds as 'friends and business communities'. The party, he declared, appreciated their continued support. He explicitly declared that their largesse would not be wasted: 'As their choice is a wise one, we can assure them that they will not be disappointed'.[118] The nexus directly attested to again.[119]

The ruling elite maintained their refusal to disclose the source of these donations. They were oblivious to the ethical involvements – the public's right to know, and the unfair advantage conferred upon the predominant governing party and denied to a weak opposition in the national elections.[120] But the Party Treasurer was not disappointed either. Among the four nominated MPs named by President Mogae thereafter was Satar Dada.

The public learnt of the elite's abuse of their privileged access to NDB loan money, and of the big donation to the BDP, through the initiative of whistleblower employees,[121] and investigative reporting by the independent press. The rulers responded by attacking those who would dare to question them, and with a rigid refusal to explain. Charged with abusiveness and witch hunting, the media too quickly fell silent. Outsa Mokone, editor of *The Guardian*, saw Botswana afflicted by 'the battered wife syndrome' – 'each time we are short changed by our leadership, we try to make excuses for them, for fear of appearing disrespectful'. Silence, and the resulting forgetfulness, was possibly an even greater problem in Botswana than South Africa. 'Lest we forget', said Mokone, 'the media [here] is the last line of defence against excesses committed by the government, NGOs and the business community. Botswana...is a one party dominant state. The political opposition is fragmented and weak. The parliamentary watchdog role has been eroded... [and] the civil society is small and still developing.'[122]

Elitism and presidentialism have stifled the development of citizenship in Botswana, and rendered democracy a legitimizing ceremony for government. The low turnout in October 1999, and the increased support for the ruling party, was the more outstanding for coming so soon after the gift of the P2.4 million, and on the heels of Mogae's egregious decisions a month before the poll.[123] A characterizing feature of Botswana's democracy is the symbiosis between its ruling elite and business. The cases above suggest that it, and the historically sanctioned elitism in general, is the probable source of non-accountability in government.[124] Democratization and increasing popular participation was closely correlated with a reduction in corruption in nineteenth-century England.[125] 'Kohl's shame', after being Chancellor of Germany for 16 years and his party's chairman for 25, was ultimately his 'arrogance', his 'straightforward contempt for democracy', his disbelief in the people's right to know.[126]

But the silence of the rulers is arguably greatest of all in Botswana in another area, that of policy towards and the treatment of the indigenous San (to be discussed in the following chapter). Poverty and the dependency of the San are not issues for public discussion and decision; elitism and non-participation maintains this silence, and the San's long subordination. If there are skeletons in the cupboard of Botswana's democracy, despite the fulsome praise of world leaders, none are nastier than the routinized injustice which they experience.

2
Routinized Injustice: The Situation of the San in Botswana

Not the least of the difficulties faced by the San is that they are a 'people without history', without a single self-given name, and with no accurate information in Botswana even of their numbers.[1] Their history was appropriated by conquerors, and their names are those of their masters and governors; all to varying degrees terms of abuse. Popular and official usage in recent decades is reliant upon Basarwa, supplemented since 1974 by the government's special construction, Remote Area Dweller, abbreviated commonly to the dismissal acronym 'RAD'. Stigmatization and discrimination are in-built. Most San children grow up in Botswana knowing that the name by which they and their people are known is a swear word for others. Deep subordination follows emotional abuse over time. Willemien le Roux quotes a San woman in the Western Sandveld saying: 'I know I am a Mosarwa but I do not know why. It is probably because I am poor'.[2]

The 'RAD' depiction represented a purposeful avoidance of ethnic recognition and, by corollary of possible indigenous status; but at the cost of additional obscurantism and distortion. The different names San, Basarwa, Bushmen and Remote Area Dweller all refer to much the same people, and as social categories closely overlap.[3] But the supposed geographical distinctiveness of the new term does not stand up either to demographic inquiry or to socio-political scrutiny. Gulbrandsen and associates reported in 1986 that the large 'RAD population' of Central District, for example, was found in all five sub-districts, including such established centres as Serowe, Palapye and Mahalapye. They believed that 97 per cent were of 'Basarwa origin'; that there was also 'a number of impoverished Bamangwato ... living far from serviced villages'; groups of Bakgalagadi and Baherero, and 'more mixed groups in the Boteti'; and that in 'several settlements in Nata ... Bakalanga and Basarwa share the same living conditions'.[4] According to Hitchcock two years later, 'groups identified as RADs' could be found in Kanye, Francistown and the capital Gaborone.[5] Similarly, Campbell and Main found that in the Western Sandveld of Central District in 1990–91 they 'could see no apparent difference between the lifestyle of San and other RADs'. In addition, 'all San sp[oke] dialects which ... [we]re mutually understandable'.[6]

If serious and experienced observers tend to use the names San and Remote Area Dweller well-nigh interchangably, and if the latter term has no precise geographical content, then what Remote Area Dweller – and the status of San – actually connotes is not physical but economic, and political remoteness from power. Noting that the 'great majority' of Remote people in the Sandveld were San, that 'numerous single men, emanating from a wide variety of groups' have married into San and other Remote communities, and have in effect 'become RADS' themselves, Campbell and Main state that 'we commenced with one conception of a RAD, but had to change this as work progressed'. They finally defined a Remote Area Dweller as:

> A person who has no home in a village where there is a recognised *kgotla*, has no claim to land which is recognized by [a] Land Board, and has no claim to the use of water without expectation of conditions being imposed ... [7]

Thus, the lack of recognized political leadership, and the absence of secure land and water rights, constitute the salient baseline characteristics of San in Botswana in the 1990s; they hold with greater or lesser severity in different places, and each feature is subject to what is usually slow, even miniscule change.

Since the Botswana government collects no demographic statistics on an ethnic basis, no census data for San exist. What is available is a variety of informed estimates for time and place. For 1990, Hitchcock believed that there were 63 000 San plus 59 000 other Remote people in Botswana.[8] Ghanzi District is an important home area for San, where significant demographic change appears to be occurring. As noted below, the total number of Remote people in the District was officially put at 10 122 in 1988, constituting then 42.2 per cent of the total Ghanzi population. At the end of the 1990s, however, the San population on Rein Dekker's estimates was 16 000, representing then around 55 per cent of all the people in the District.[9]

In 1993, Hitchcock and Holm had noted that the San formed 4 per cent of the country's total population.[10] But if there is no sharp distinction but rather considerable overlap between the categories of San and other Remote Dwellers, and if the two totalled together at least 120 000 on Hitchcock's other estimate in 1990 – neglecting his earlier higher figure of up to 180 000 – then San could represent around 10 per cent of Botswana's total population of 1.6 million at the end of the 1990s.[11] What appears to emerge from the existing statistics is that the population of San–Remote people in Botswana is probably larger than is conventionally thought; that they represent a significant minority in the country's total population, much higher, for example, than the Saami in Norway who, at about 50 000 people, constitute only around 1 per cent of all Norwegian people;[12] and an increasing majority in a region like Ghanzi.

Aside from the special usage Remote Area Dweller, three main concepts are appropriate to an analysis of the position of the San in Botswana:[13] the indigenous people; the impoverished; and the underclass. All three are relevant, and there are no necessary incompatibilities between them. While the first is of historical, international and comparative legal importance,[14] it is possibly the second and third which are analytically and politically more significant in a developmental, long-term sense. The San are the indigenous people of southern Africa in simple, historical fact; David Lewis-Williams has dated their rock paintings to as much as 27 000 years BP (Before the Present).[15] They are simultaneously among the most impoverished in Botswana; and their structural poverty and subordination is so deep and long-lasting as to have relegated them to the position of an underclass in society, both historically despised and propertyless.

The approach below focuses upon the identification of trends and tendencies, and on the clarification of change, or the lack of it, regarding access to incomes, land, cattle and other productive resources, and political representation. Socio-economic change is perceived as a process over time, which occurs in a milieu of constraints and limitations which must also be recognized and assessed. That all San settlements – that is, government-established reserves or locations – in Ghanzi District possessed recognized and elected San *kgosi* in 1999 was, for example, a decided step forward, even though those leaders now faced considerable constraints on their freedom of action.

The inheritance and the continuity

In the 1880s, on the eve of the establishment of the Protectorate, the future Botswana already possessed 'strong, centralized, and highly stratified' state systems, the largest of which was Bamangwato, today's Central District. Wealth in Tswana society was based on the ownership of cattle, and status was related to birth. Economic, political and ceremonial power all lay in the hands of the ruler, a king or *kgosi*. He was surrounded by an elite composed of the extended royal family and rich commoners. Below them were ordinary commoners, and below these were non-Tswana subject and servile groups who had been absorbed as the kingdoms expanded. The 'principal' servile group was the Basarwa (San/Bushmen).[16] It was a society of pervasive inequalities, wherein 'no man was another's equal', and where economic and political power dovetailed.[17] Khama III, ruled from 1875 until 1923, oversaw the establishment and consolidation of the Protectorate, and was the largest cattle and serf-owner in the country.[18]

Serfdom was the condition of the San then and later. The power of individual Tswana masters over San serfs (*malata*) increased after 1875, as San became private property. With the spread of the pastoral economy whole San families were forced to become the unfree dependents of cattle owners. They were unpaid except in kind, moved and transferred at will, inherited between masters, and subjected to arbitrary punishment. This was made patently clear in the trial of the aristocratic Simon Ratshosa in 1926,[19] and at another trial in 1931 following the seizure and beating of three San, one of whom died after receiving over 300 wounds. Murder charges were not sustained against the Bangwato perpetrators, but testimony revealed that San were frequently flogged and conventionally inherited.[20]

Forced to act on these publicized revelations, a colonial inquiry (the Tagart Commission) confirmed that many Basarwa were tied to masters for whom they worked without payment as agricultural labourers, servants and hunters. Their children could be taken from them to work in the houses or on the farms of their masters. Property rights for Basarwa existed only on the whim of the master, who was usually quick to seize whatever they might arduously acquire. Tagart also reported that Basarwa 'almost unanimously' declared that they wanted freedom, and many called in addition for the cattle, land and ploughs that would be necessary to ensure their independence.[21]

A further survey, by J.W. Joyce in 1936–37, enumerated 9505 Basarwa in Bamangwato with 'another 1000 or so' out of reach and uncounted. Those living east of the railway along the Shashi and Motloutse rivers had 'virtually emancipated themselves' chiefly through access to outside wage-labour – they ploughed their own lands and held cattle. But in more inaccessible areas, west and southwest of

Serowe, Basarwa were tied. There was little evidence that they received any remuneration other than milk, and punishments like flogging were still inflicted on the spot. Joyce identified 213 masters, of whom at least 141 were Ngwato and 38 Kgalagadi. The largest serf-owner was Tshekedi Khama, with 1395 San dependents, while 24 others 'owned' between 100 and 400 San each.[22]

Overall, San servitude essentially represented 'virtually free labour' for the elite of the big cattlemen in the country. It was a highly functional, developmental system, and it 'lay at the very roots' of the successful Tswana political economy through the first-half of the twentieth century.[23]

When Botswana gained independence in 1966, 'the great majority' of Basarwa in the reserve, on the assessment of Miers and Crowder, were 'worse off' than they had been three decades earlier. Ngwato cattle owners were depriving them of stock systematically, and dispossessing those who still had any control over land or water resources. The expansion of cattle production was turning San into 'a landless, cattle-less proletariat'. This affected the poorer strata of Ngwato too, but the San suffered the 'additional disability of being socially despised'.[24] Other observers took a similar view. Lord Hailey had written in 1953 of the continuance of Basarwa serfdom then, and Silberbauer and Kuper offered a detailed account of its existence in southwestern Ghanzi district in 1966.[25] Thus, for the San then and later, there existed structural long-term poverty,[26] plus stigmatization, enduring discrimination and sometimes a consequent self-hatred and relegation to the very bottom of the social hierarchy.

Silberbauer, in association with the colonial Population Census Officer, assessed the Bushman population of Bechuanaland at 24652 in 1964, noting that this figure was probably 'twenty percent inaccurate'. They were widely distributed. 'Some four thousand' were counted on the then white-owned ranches in Ghanzi, 6000 were described as 'wild' Bushmen, while 'the remaining fourteen thousand-odd' lived 'permanently, or for most of the year at Bantu villages or cattle-posts, or in close proximity to them, as labourers or clients of the Bantu.'

But Silberbauer, the Bushman Survey Officer, contributed influentially himself to the distortion of the San's history and experience in favour of their Tswana expropriators and dominators, writing in the same place of

> these peaceful [Bantu] pastoralists and cultivators [who] entered a country so thinly populated that there was room for both them and

the Bushmen. When they met at places for which there might have been competition, e.g. waterholes, peaceful agreements were concluded which proved beneficial to both parties.[27]

The special features of Botswana's elite democracy place fundamental constraints upon the position of the San. As noted in Chapter 1, regular, competitive elections exist where the government has never changed, constitutional power is concentrated in the executive, popular participation in voting is low, and public discussion on the problems of the San hardly occurs.[28] San poverty and ethnic subordination exist as problems, but have not yet become issues for public debate and remedial decision-making. Well-founded recommendations to government from reputable observers on the situation faced by the San have been routinely ignored. Proposals for the reform of the Remote Area Development Programme, supported by San representative groups, the Norwegian government and elements within the bureaucracy itself, arising in the early 1990s, seem to have been quietly stifled at cabinet level over subsequent years.[29]

Drought relief and food aid

Botswana is a country of recurrent drought, but broad-based drought-relief programmes acquired increased scope and effectiveness through the 1980s. Supplementary feeding systems were expanded to assist vulnerable groups. These included children, lactating mothers and pregnant women, and also official destitutes, totalling 41 000 beneficiaries in 1986 – up from some 35 400 two years previously – as well as Remote Area Dwellers numbering 19 000, down from 20 000 over 1984–85.[30] Despite a harsh climate, state action ensured that drought did not lead on to famine and to deaths, the linkages which caused two to three million people to perish in the 1970s–80s in Ethiopia and Sudan, in the Sahel and Bangladesh.[31] Yet comparative national policy effectiveness did not mean that there were no specific or regional problems. During the drought of 1979–80, for instance, 'much' of the centrally distributed food aid either 'did not reach those in need, was wasted on the way or was slow to arrive'.[32] In the Western Sandveld in 1990, Campbell and Main found serious weaknesses in the distribution of food to Remote people. At some settlements in June everyone received rations, children and adults, whether employed or not; in one case, only men received food, and in another all adults but no children were fed. When food issues recommenced in December similar incoherencies occurred, but the diversion of the aid also took place. Campbell and Main found 'RAD food bags' in the homes of people who owned considerable numbers of cattle but had no Remote Dwellers working for them. Issues were also 'extremely irregular' through to February 1991, and 'many people' said they had received only one issue in three months.[33]

Most significantly, continuing reliance on food aid created dependency in itself. As Campbell and Main noted in the Sandveld, food relief had become vital for the Remote people 'and now they cannot manage without it'.[34] By the late 1980s the impact of food relief on the San and other Remote people was both wide and deep. Gulbrandsen and colleagues reported that 'the RADs [we]re up to 90 per cent dependent [on food handouts] for their subsistence',[35] and Mogwe, quoting from Remote Area Development Programme figures, similarly noted that almost all Remote people were reliant on relief over the whole period 1982 till May 1990.[36] Drought relief operated on an on – off basis, and Hitchcock and Holm observed shortly after that San tended to remain on RAD settlements – which usually had no income-generating capacity of their own – as long as they functioned as a food distribution centre.[37]

While no famine occurred in Botswana even as domestic food production fell,[38] dependency was deepened and maintained among impoverished San. However, a more beneficial cash-for-work scheme began to be introduced towards the mid-1980s, as an addition rather than as a replacement for food distribution. The Labour-Based Relief Programme (LBRP) constituted cash for the able-bodied, initially P2 per day, in 1985–86, when some 70 000 jobs were provided for very limited periods, commonly two months. The work was labour-intensive and, on such things as the building and upgrading of roads, airstrips and dams, was socially useful and potentially productive. In 1986–87 the daily rate was P2.25. Neglecting the fact that this pay was for rotational, short-term work only, it was considerably more than what a San cattle-herder received, and greater too than the most lowly paid of urban workers such as domestic servants.[39]

The Monitoring Programme presented detailed figures on the incidence and significance of LBRP over six RAD/San Settlements – one in Southern District, four in Kgalagadi and another in Ghanzi in 1990. In Thankane 37 respondents out of an estimated Settlement population of 355 were employed on the LBRP in 1990, and they received an average monthly income during part of the year of P60, while in Monong five people out of a population of 110 worked in LBRP and earned some P48 per month when doing so.[40]

Labour-based relief projects were 'often the most important income earning opportunity' in Kgalagadi Settlements and villages in the mid-1990s, according to the findings of Corjan van der Jagt. But this work was obtained by only 8.5 per cent of the potentially active population, some 225 people in all. The wage had then been recently raised from P4.50 to P6 a day, and employment under LBRP was 'normally two months at a time'. An employed man or woman might therefore bring in a total amount of P184 – P92 times two – to his or her household of perhaps some seven people in a year.[41] Some 8 per cent of households were 'entirely dependent' on such income. Which has to be considered in the light of the fact that '49 per cent of the potentially active population' held no source of income-earning activity whatsoever.[42]

Quinn and her associates state that LBRP 'aim[ed] to increase the income earning potential of the village'.[43] It constituted cash for people who otherwise obtained little or none. LBRP represented the most positive aspect of Botswana's drought relief programme, but it operated sporadically and drew in only a small percentage of San and other Remote people.

The low wages policy

The absence of an explicitly stated programme does not mean that a policy or official position does not exist.[44] Liberal democratic governments may not wish to elaborate on the positions they adopt towards, say, minority rights and the poor, but if governmental statements are only partial and implicit, the consequences of the underlying policy are likely to be evident and examinable. The lineaments of the San's subordination are etched into the political economy of Botswana and are not easily efaced by official amnesia or anodyne references to assimilation and good intentions.

The low wages policy acquired a firm though terse endorsement in 1990. The Presidential Commission on the Review of the Incomes Policy noted in March that 'a very high proportion' of workers in domestic service and in agriculture received an income well below the minimum wage in sectors which were covered by the statutory minimum wages Act. They referred specifically to a sample of agricultural workers who got a cash income of less than P30 a month – the equivalent, they further said, of the amount allocated for food rations for destitutes. The Commission therefore recommended that the domestic service and agricultural sectors should be brought within the provisions of the Employment Act 1982, both with regard to uniform wages and the regulations governing working hours and leave.[45]

The government firmly 'rejected' this proposal. The recommendation was 'unenforcible, and thus impracticable'. The government adhered to the principle that it should not introduce laws or regulations 'which it cannot implement, or has no intention of implementing. To do so would raise workers hopes unnecessarily ... '[46]

A fairly comprehensive attitude was expressed in this important White Paper. Poverty should be one factor for consideration in fixing minimum wages, along with such others as 'productivity levels and prospects in the Botswana economy'. The government believed that the current system of minimum wages differentiated according to occupations and industries should continue; but in another area, the remuneration of the highly paid, significant change was readily and speedily embraced. Recommendations for a new salary structure with an 'appropriate salary differential between scales at the middle and senior levels', were described as 'essential', underscored with the declaration that they 'should be implemented without delay'.[47]

San farm labourers' wages

When San acquire waged employment, farm labourer is the job they are most likely to obtain, and various studies have testified to the extremely low wages and poor conditions which they experience. Gary Childers in 1976 found a total of 4512 San living on the Ghanzi freehold farms as squatters and farm labourers mostly in very unsatisfactory conditions. They earned on average P6.13 a month, plus food rations of milk, tea, sugar and tobacco. But a worker might go two or three months before receiving his food rations.[48] While Ghanzi farmers, supported by rising cattle prices, 'ha[d] become noticeably wealthier' since the end of the 1960s, the San '[we]re becoming even poorer than they were in previous years'.[49] They faced 'oppression and discrimination' on a wide and constant basis.[50]

When Mogalakwe visited the district ten years later, he found that 61 per cent of the San farm workers he surveyed were receiving wages of between P5 and P30 a month. They were often paid 'irregularly', with 'unwarranted deductions' made in some cases from their wages. 65 per cent of those sampled were not paid for overtime worked, and 56 per cent had never been given annual leave. They had no rest on public holidays, and most of them, he said, 'work[ed] from sun rise to sun set, every single day that passes'.[51]

The Gulbrandsen report was on the operations of the Remote Area Development Programme nationally. He and his associates said that many Remote people sought regular or seasonal employment as labourers with cattle or in arable farming. The relationship of the labourer to the [cattle] owner was in general one of 'utter dependence' and injustice. When women were employed in arable farming, the majority got work only during peak seasons, as weeders or bird scarers. Lack of minimum wages protection in the agricultural sector was 'particularly detrimental' to the workers' interests.[52] Their findings with regard to the Ghanzi farms were consistent with those of Mogalakwe. Cattle ranchers paid San and other Remote people 'rarely more than P15–P20 per month'.[53]

The 1991 study of Remote Area Dwellers in the Western Sandveld in Central District found San cattle labourers getting average wages of 'about P25 per month' with milk and food. This was an improvement, they said, on 1977, when the wage had been 'between P2 and P5 per month' – thus, even lower that what Childers had observed in Ghanzi at much the same time. Campbell and Main noted, however, that in 'national terms' the 1991 wage 'remain[ed] incredibly low'.

That was not all. As in Ghanzi, many owners and their agents are 'extremely irregular' in their visits to cattle posts, and workers' pay is often delayed. 'Gaps of 3–4 months are common, up to 8 months not uncommon and delayed payments of as much as a year or more were recorded.' One individual reported that 'he had not been paid for four years'. There were still cases, Campbell and Main said, 'where people work only for food'.[54] The giving of food rations 'as part of the payment package', they noted, 'is not regulated in any way and is subject to the same vagaries' as payment of wages. Not only did the quantity and quality of the food vary considerably, but 'normally, months go by before food is delivered. Some employers deliver rations only once a year.' Deepening dependency, as Gulbrandsen had earlier suggested, was integral to such a wages system. Workers recognized that the delayed payment of wages tied them firmly to their workplace. And, as one San labourer explained: 'If we complain over our pay, we get fired.'[55]

The 1990–91 Monitoring Programme reported on employment for Remote people, mostly San, across the country. Work on such things as road-building paid much better, briefly, than the stereotypical San role of herdsman. They found average monthly wages for labour in Thankane in Southern District of P70: in Groot Laagte in Ghanzi P60; and in Molong in Kgalagadi P40. However, these earnings were obtained by only a small minority of Settlement households, 14 to 24 per cent in these three, where household size averaged between five and eight members. The period of employment was between four and eight months in the year.[56] The Gulbrandsen/Mogalakwe/Campbell Main top figure of around P30 per month may not have been much exceeded.

The achievement of high per capita growth and incomes has been one of Botswana's major successes. GDP per capita in 1992, for instance, was P5886, when the Pula was worth US$0.48. But there was also the historically based low wages policy for unskilled labourers and, after 1990, a highly differentiated salary structure for the well paid. At the end of 1992, the gap between the top public service salary (P8216 a month plus sizeable allowances) and the statutory minimum wage (P237 a month) represented 34.7 : 1.[57] Childers emphasized the fact that in Ghanzi in the 1970s the rich cattlemen were getting richer while the San and other Remote people were getting poorer. By the 1990s the difference between the top bureaucratic earnings and those of the San labourer was more than 270 : 1.

New light was cast, in March 1999, on the Botswana government's claim of 1990 that statutory minimum wages for domestic and agricultural workers would be unenforcible and impracticable, when the South African government announced its intention of moving in just that direction. The Labour Minister, Membathisi Mdladlana, said that domestic and farm workers would benefit from the Basic Conditions of Employment Act which came into effect in December 1998. New procedures were expected to be in place covering these two sectors within the next year. A representative of the Domestic Workers' Union, Selina Vilakazi, said that they would ask for a minimum wage of R800 a month, rising through R1200 for a full-time worker engaged in cleaning, cooking and child-minding.[58]

Cattle production and the absence of land rights

A number of policies and policy positions have focused upon the development of cattle production, especially its intensification since independence. Their deeper roots lay in turn in the process through which San lost access to land, possibly their control over cattle, and their freedom in preceding centuries under the impact of expanding Tswana elites and embryonic state structures.

Though much remains obscure, evidence suggests that the San were not always and everywhere simply primordial hunters and gatherers. For Edwin Wilmsen and James Denbow, the San across the Kalahari

were producers of salt, ceramics and ornaments over the previous mil-
lenium, settled communities were established, and some engaged in
long-distance trade.[59] They were also pastoralists controlling in different times and places herds of big-horned cattle. The evidence is wide
but not entirely substantial: for example, limited archaeological findings; eye-witness travellers' accounts; and linguistics;[60] and not least
important, the continuing resurgence of cattle-keeping by individual
San over recent decades in Botswana, against the opposition of ranch
owners and state policies favouring the owners.[61] Until around the
turn of this century, they might also have possessed their own political
organizations and leadership; long-distance trade, of course, required
some degree of organization and hierarchy to function.

Their dispossession began slowly then accelerated, but it seems difficult to underestimate its importance – the land, cattle and labour
power and skills which the San lost control over were effectively utilized by rising Tswana elites. Miers and Crowder noted that the system
of San servitude, by the 1920s, lay at the roots of the Tswana pastoral
economy, allowing the masters to build up large herds while freeing
them from onerous tasks, and enabling them to engage in politics,
trade and other profitable activities.[62]

Wilmsen and Rainer Vossen have pictured foraging, as it existed perhaps a century ago, as an option open to the San to escape dependency
within the Tswana political economy, but at the cost of being further
marginalized as the unchanging Bushmen of conventional ethnogra-
phy.[63] But the viability of even this possibility was soon closed with
the spread and intensification of cattle production. By the 1970s there
were 176 freehold farms in Ghanzi with a further 38 awaiting allocation, and the increasing cattle were 'destroying much of the indigenous veld food that [was] so valuable to the Basarwa'. Some 4500 San
living on 207 farm settlements were 'impoverished'.[64]

Introduction of the tribal grazing land policy

The rapid spread of commercial ranches under the Tribal Grazing Land
Policy (TGLP) threatened most Remote people. Announced in 1975,
the policy was quite attractive to an ambitious cattle-owner. Rents on a
ranch of 4900 to 6400 hectares, at the beginning of the 1980s, were set
at a sub-economic level of P256 a year, and the non-payment of even
that sum was not a condition for lease-termination. Tenure was a
50-year lease, which was renewable, inheritable, subleasable and subdi-
vidable; as near to freehold as one might get. No limitations on stock-
holding were imposed, and none were introduced on overgrazing in

communal areas.[65] Implementation of the programme, said Hitchcock, went 'relatively quickly', and by 1988 the 'goal of establishing 700–1000 ranches ha[d] already been achieved' nationally. There were, he estimated, 'over 20 000 people' who resided in the commercial ranching areas.[66]

While attempts were made from some quarters to accord some limited protection, or at least compensation, to existing San residents, the Attorney General's Chambers ruled them illegal. The view that Remote Dwellers were landless nomadic foragers held full sway; ranch lessees were to obtain full rights to the land, and 'anyone caught trespassing would be liable to removal and criminal prosecution'.[67]

Places such as Cgae Cgae (or Xai Xai), Dobe and Nqoma had been occupied by the San over centuries in the past, and other places such as Ukhwi in Kgalagadi and Thankane (or Thankana) in Southern District were known to have 'a long history' – more than a hundred years – of habitation by San in the contemporary period.[68] Land occupied by Remote people, according to Campbell and Main, was allocated for ranching 'without regard for RAD needs'.[69] By about 1988, 'the whole of the Western Sandveld had been occupied by cattle-owners'. San and other Remote people, they made plain, 'ha[d] no real land-use rights and c[ould] be told to move by anyone who ha[d] been awarded such rights by [a] Land Board'.[70]

In Ghanzi initially, then elsewhere, San were transformed through the growth of cattle production into ill-paid labourers, beggars and poachers – a virtual return to the subservient underclass position which was entrenched in the 1920s and 1930s and lingered on much later.[71] Serious observers do not mince words here. Gulbrandsen and colleagues stated that Basarwa were 'forced into serfdom' by ranch owners. Most of them, for instance, 'strictly forbid' Basarwa to keep cattle on the ranches[72] – in itself powerfully perpetuating their weakness. Campbell and Main found that cattle-owners 'treat RADs as servants', and 'in the state of mind to which [they] have been reduced ... some still even talk about being "owned"'.[73] Hitchcock and Holm concurred, saying that the social status of the San 'remains to the present little better than that of a serf'.[74]

The Settlement programme

The Settlement programme began in Ghanzi, where cattle were already concentrated and where the numbers of San and other Remote people were particularly high relative to the total district population. Childers had enumerated some 4500 impoverished Basarwa on the farms, of whom 1475 were 'squatters' in the view of the farm-owners although, as he noted, they were usually 'resid[ing] on land which was originally theirs by fact of occupation'.[75] The containment of surplus labour was a very strong factor in the origins of Settlements as conceived of by Ghanzi cattlemen.[76]

But there were also other aspirations in the minds of some sympathetic officials like Childers. West Hanahai was the first of four Settlements originally planned in 1976 under the District's Land and Water Development Project for the Ghanzi Farm Basarwa.[77] The 'primary need', according to the Basarwa themselves, was to 'have their "own place", with an adequate water supply', where they would 'have an alternative to their [present] status as squatters and discontented labourers' on the freehold farms. The Settlement was a way of providing the Basarwa 'with access to land and water which would enable them to work for their own livelihood'. It was also seen as offering access to government services like health and education that were then unavailable to Basarwa.[78]

A borehole was equipped at West Hanahai in 1978 and 400 square kilometres of land around it were allocated to the Settlement 'for use by its inhabitants'. In early 1979 about 150 Remote people moved from several areas of the farm block to the site near the borehole. Another was then being drilled at a second Settlement at East Hanahai, and one was planned for Groot Laagte in the north-west of the Ghanzi farms – the number of the District's Settlements expanded fairly quickly. East Hanahai's population grew slowly, and in January 1982 it was some 300 people.[79]

Childers, Stanley and Rick also noted that, despite the strict prohibitions of the ranchers, 'over half of the households' which had settled at West Hanahai 'arrived with their own cattle (normally 2–8 head)'. They also showed an 'impressive' interest in arable farming. By January 1982 there were over 200 cattle on the Settlement, with 'over half of these belonging to two residents'. The District Council had a livestock support system under which it had provided 18 cattle to nine non-cattle owners since 1979. 'Nearly all households', in 1982, were engaged in arable farming on plots averaging 2.5 hectares.[80]

But some of the serious problems which have afflicted the Settlements programme were already evident. Although they were created for occupation by San and other Remote people, the government still had no specific policies on who should be allocated land for residence or allowed to graze and water cattle there. Outside owners of large cattle herds had moved on to West Hanahai, causing 'numerous problems' for its Basarwa residents including 'over-taxing the low yielding water supply and denuding the surrounding veld area'. A worse situation 'seriously affected the RAD community at Kagcae': 'Several thousand cattle' from two neighbouring boreholes were destroying the veld and much physical infrastructure on the Settlement. This problem had existed over six years already, but 'nothing ha[d] been done' to remedy the matter.[81] Despite the interest in farming, there was also a 'lack of food' at West Hanahai, and 'hunger [was] a common condition'.[82]

An important underlying reason for these failings was the existence of a 'leadership vacuum' in most Settlements. Childers and colleagues, like Gulbrandsen and other observers shortly after, recognized that San on the freehold farms had been deeply conditioned historically for dependency. They nevertheless detected 'a strongly expressed need for leadership at the RAD Settlements'. The lack of organization and leadership was highly debilitating, but it seemed not to originate primarily with the San; the government acted to perpetuate their organizational weaknesses. In West Hanahai, in Kagcae and in Bere, the government had 'taken over the role of leadership' in the Settlements. Generally, government and Council officials approach the San 'as children who are not capable of making or implementing decisions on their own'.[83]

The physical capacities of the Settlements were seriously inadequate. By the early 1990s eight officially permanent Settlements existed in Ghanzi. The number of Remote people, mostly San, was then 10 122 – representing 42.2 per cent of the District's population – of whom about half were living on the Settlements. These averaged 20 square kilometres in size, located in either Communal Grazing Areas or Wildlife Management Areas, and on what was actually 'marginal infertile land', within 'ecologically fragile' areas. Browsing and grazing resources were 'extremely fragile' on all of them, and the possibilities for arable farming were 'very limited'. Remote people's 'access to land, water and other resources' had in fact 'diminished considerably over the past years'.[84] Gulbrandsen's team had earlier 'repeatedly stressed' in their report that RAD Settlements had 'few or no productive resources' even for subsistence.[85]

What was grossly inadequate was also deeply inequitable. The area allocated to Remote people in 1988, according to the Ghanzi land-use zoning plan, totalled 2400 square kilometres. Thus, 42 per cent of the District population had access to, but did not have exclusive rights or even adequate control over, 1.7 per cent of the District's land. A little earlier, on Hitchcock's figures, some 19 000 square kilometres was zoned for commercial farming in Ghanzi – 17 000 square kilometres of this was freehold – and acquired by roughly 250 individuals and syndicates. These together had ownership of good land eight times greater in size than 10 000 Remote people.[86] The expansion of the ranching programme was continuing.

Villagization

From their origins in Ghanzi in the 1970s, Settlements functioned as zones of concentration where marginalized, impoverished people could be provided with infrastructural and welfare services, like water, clinics and schooling, more efficiently. This was effectively a villagization strategy, though one which could be deemed 'reasonably successful' in this infrastructural aspect.[87] Productive and income-generating resources, the bases for self-sufficiency, which Childers seemed to have envisoned, were bad to absent. This was manifested through most of the 1980s when, as noted, 90 per cent of all Remote people were dependent for their subsistence on food relief. Where grazing and water resources existed, these were usually appropriated by outside cattlemen with the tacit or explicit consent of government, under the rubric of a citizen's freedom of movement in Botswana.

The allocation of small plots, as arable fields or 'backyard gardens', commonly a hectare or two in size, to individual Settlement residents, does not represent secure individual tenure. Korfage stated that 94 such plots had been allocated in Ghanzi, of which only 29, by 1992, were 'developed'. Their soils, like those around them, were generally poor, with crop production very limited.[88] But there were indications that the government was not entirely happy with even such nominal land allocations to Remote people. The Minister for Commerce and Industry, George Kgoroba, said in parliament in August 1998, that where Settlements were established within areas designated for livestock production, his Ministry 'would not advise the land board to register... backyard gardens'. Referring to the residents of Mmea, Makgaba, Lekoba and Jamakata in Central District, he stated that 'arable farming [was] not encouraged in this area to avoid land use conflicts'.[89]

The government's livestock distribution programme initially offered selected households two heifers, well below what was necessary to establish a viable, sustainable herd.[90] Allocations have been increased through the 1990s to around five cattle per beneficiary. Like Childers, the evaluators from the Chr. Michelsen Institute (CMI) recognized that 'many RADs... have good knowledge of livestock keeping', and they judged cattle distribution as 'the most successful' of the official income-generating activities among San.[91]

But if the infrastructure was sometimes reasonably good, and the allocation of cattle far more positive than, for instance, the making of furniture for non-existing markets, Settlements remain places of impoverishment. Basarwa poverty is 'constantly reproduced', according to the CMI evaluators, because they and other Remote people lack access to basic productive resources like land and water. The long food-relief programme, for example, functioned to alleviate the effects, but not to address the causes, of the impoverishment.[92]

Absence of land rights and leadership

The Monitoring Programme found no exclusive land rights in existence in any of the Settlements they studied, that is, no 'formal and exclusive communal land allocations to RAD communities'.[93] Landlessness is closely interrelated, as Childers apparently recognized, with political leadership. Gulbrandsen's team saw that Settlements without officially-recognized headmen had no legal protection against the depredations of outside intruders.[94] By the mid-1990s the consequence was that 'fairly sizable number[s]' of cattlemen had moved into RAD Settlements seeking the infrastructure they sometimes contained, turning domestic water sources into cattle watering points, and the Settlements into 'the equivalent of cattle posts'.[95]

Important changes occurred through the latter 1990s while underlying causes of poverty remained, in practice, the same. In Ghanzi, where the San possessed their highest demographic leverage in the whole country, all Settlements had acquired gazetted headmen or women – 'kgosi' – by 1999; both Chobokwane and Groot Laagte had San women kgosi that year. This was a big step forward, borne on the increased political participation by San in national elections in 1989 and 1994, and the government's seeming awareness of its significance. But through a variety of stratagems the new political momentum appeared to have been effectively contained. When Basarwa representatives attempted to raise issues of land rights on the District Council – where the governing party retained its majority – they were apparently told they were 'lying'. Various means were used to block San candidates at elections,[96] and the elected and gazetted Settlement leaders also faced tight limitations. Neighbouring cattlemen went straight to the Land Board, bypassing a San kgosi, when they wished to reside on a Settlement. The position of the active or outspoken kgosi could be undermined, and he or she even removed – as was said to have happened in Groot Laagte – in favour of someone more amenable to the status quo.[97] Near the end of the decade, conditions on the

Settlements were 'worse than before',[98] and no secure land rights had been obtained.

But, again, some movement forward was being made. Three Settlements, those of Chobokwane, Groot Laagte and West Hanahai, were perhaps acquiring control over neighbouring leasehold extension farms, those of 164NK, 154NK and 173NK, respectively. It was a long, slow and convoluted process. Ghanzi District Council had decided upon the allocations in 1989,[99] but 'apparently as the result of pressure from Gaborone', the transfers were blocked – a non-governmental consortium which was assisting the San was asked to withdraw for proceeding incorrectly, and the leases eventually issued contained an addendum that if the farms were not 'developed' by 1996 they could be reallocated.[100]

Senior government members were the source of the pressure. These included, according to *Africa Confidential*, Johnny Swartz, long-sitting governing party member for Ghanzi; Patrick Balopi, Minister for Labour and Home Affairs, and owner of a farm adjacent to 173NK; and Anderson Chibua, previously District Commissioner in Ghanzi, and head of one of the commercial farming syndicates with an interest in the farms. In the process, Michael Tshipinare, Assistant Minister for Local Government and Lands, told Ghanzi Council in March 1991 that the idea of transferring farms to Basarwa had come from expatriates interfering in domestic affairs. Swartz, for his part, denied personal interest, but declared publicly that the properties should not go to the San.[101]

Government leaders apparently recognized the precedent involved in transferring valuable leasehold farms to Basarwa, and the matter was held up for more than a decade. The Norwegian government, generous foreign donor to the Remote Area Development Programme, saw the monoeuvering and prevarications emanating from Gaborone as important too. As the CMI evaluators stated: 'the events [of the Ghanzi Farms issue] caused doubts to be raised about some of the most fundamental preconditions for the programme to succeed'.[102] This played a role in Norway's eventual withdrawal of support for the RADP.

The further intensification of cattle production

Improvement in conditions facing the San over recent years have been on a piecemeal basis, subject to limitations and containment in many cases. But where cattle ownership is concerned, fundamental problems seem to exist. By 1991, established government policy, according to Richard White, had 'led to a rapid increase in the concentration of livestock in the hands of a small minority'. Though cattle remained the major source of rural wealth, 74 per cent of rural households, by that year, had no access to them.[103] The historical trajectory in the intensification of cattle production was against the smallholder, whatever his or her ethnicity, and government planning seemed directed towards the quickening of the process. For the prevention of disease and for the better quality of beef, herd management was being stressed, and government-sponsored schemes existed to assist farmers here. There was, for instance, the Services to Livestock Owners in Communal Areas (SLOCA), but in order to benefit a farmer had to have 25 cattle or more, and display what was called total commitment to the project. Another, Livestock Water Development (LWD), was generous in offering infrastructural assistance, but appeared aimed at syndicates with at least 60 stock among their members. A Mokwena farmer, Monthelesi Lopang, said that as a small-scale farmer he could not even think of putting up a fence, and schemes such as SLOCA and LWD '[we]re meant for farmers with large herds'.[104]

Specific innovations in herd management appeared particularly invidious to the small and middle-scale peasant. Much of the country's beef exports went under very favourable terms to the European Union (EU). On grounds of quality control, in 1999–2000 the EU was promoting, in cooperation with the Botswana government, a system of identification, registration and trace-back of all cattle in the country, utilizing electronic tagging; labelled export packs of deboned beef-cuts, it was intended, would be traceable to the individual animal and farming unit of origin.[105] Stepped-up management standards represented acute problems for all small cattle owners; he, or less likely she, might soon become an historical anachronism – as smallholders in the United States, once the bedrock of the American Republic, had been rendered statistically invisible by the early 1990s.[106] But if the quickening trend continued in Botswana, it would bear most heavily, given the historical record, on those San who had gained access to livestock.

Land rights in South Africa and Australia, self-government in Canada

But South Africa was also showing that restitution could be made with regard to land rights for the San, as well as in the provision of minimum-wages protection for unskilled workers. After two years of negotiations, the South African government had finalized the purchase of land from white farmers, and in late March 1999 handed over 25 000 hectares, south of the Gemsbok park, to the Khomani San community. The land represented a 'potentially lucrative source of tourism income'.[107]

Presiding at the handover, Vice-President Thabo Mbeki said that the San were among the country's 'worst victims of oppression', and affirmed that 'this [was] a step' towards restitution and rebirth.[108] The transfer occurred with sincerity and warmth. When Derek Hanekom, Minister for Land Affairs, met David Kruiper, leader of the community, the previous December, they were reported to have 'greet[ed] each other like old friends, shaking hands and hugging'.[109] Two months later, the Schmidtsdrift San received tenure to the farm of Platfontein.

Some 15 per cent of Australia's land, by 2000, was owned and controlled by the country's first people.[110] In Canada, around the same time, the indigenous Inuit, numbering 25 000 people, acquired a self-governing homeland, Nunavut, covering one-fifth of the country's total land area. It was described as being North America's boldest step in aboriginal self-government.[111] Botswana's immobility on indigenous land and political rights was made more starkly incongruous.

Relocation and dispossession: repeated experiences

As already suggested, relocation and dispossession have been experienced by the San in relation to a number of closely interrelated forces – the rise of Tswana state institutions since the early nineteenth century; the commercialization and subsequent intensification of cattle production, especially since 1975; and, in association with the RADP, for what might be called bureaucratic convenience.[112] Hitchcock stresses the fact that this has been the repeated experience of San and other Remote people over generations in Botswana: on his broad schema, a first wave of dispossession came with the creation of freehold farms on Ghanzi Ridge at the end of the nineteenth century; a second and broader dispossession came with the TGLP after 1975; and another has occurred over recent decades on the very Settlements ostensibly established to accomodate the San,[113] to note only the most outstanding stages in the long process. Hitchcock and Holm wrote of the 'sometimes devastating consequences' of dispossession for the San as follows: 'the invaders run wells dry, overgraze range land, decimate *veld* foods, destroy field crops and even ruin homes'. In 'almost every case', they said, 'the central government has been unwilling to intervene'.[114]

The fragility of human rights

Relocation and dispossession are continuing and constant threats to which landlessness and their lack of effective political leadership exposes the San. The Panos Oral Testimony Programme reports that Settlements in Botswana are not unusually 'places of despair and social disintegration', where 'drunkenness, promiscuity, early teenage pregnancy, and family violence are rife'.[115] Trauma, a near refugee-like status in one's native country, and renewed servility, as Campbell and Main saw in the Sandveld, are further consequences.[116]

Relocation appears as an icon of a near absence of human rights. It has been the fate of indigenous people under specific political conditions, usually extremely exploitative domination, of a colonial or quasi-colonial kind; such as in apartheid South Africa, in French Algeria, in Australia, and during the Highlands Clearances in Scotland when, it was said, 'sheep ate people'.[117] Campbell and Main, it should be re-emphasized, came to see Remote people as those without a recognized claim to land, and in 1990 they noted, 'all RADs' in the Western Sandveld were threatened by removal.[118] What was done by the sheep in the Highlands is being done by 'cattle' – by government policy and market forces facilitating their production – in Botswana. Tswana cattlemen utilize the resources that might be present on Settlements because they possess constitutional rights of free movement and residence; but the same rights are effectively denied to San each time they are dispossessed and relocated.

The origins of the Central Kalahari Game Reserve

The removals from the Central Kalahari Game Reserve (CKGR), which went on in earnest through 1997, are the latest example of this practice. Botswana has chosen to set aside two-fifths of its land area as parks and reserves devoted to wildlife and tourism activities, supposedly the second-largest allocation of this type in the world. The CKGR is the country's largest reserve and, covering more than 52 000 square kilometres, the second largest in Africa. Established in 1961 on the recommendation of the Bushman Survey Officer, Silberbauer, its original function was to provide land where the San could continue to pursue hunting and gathering; in the words of the Proclamation, 'to protect wildlife resources and reserve sufficient land for traditional use by hunter-gatherer communities of the Central Kalahari'.[119] At the same time the area was declared a game reserve under the Fauna Conservation Proclamation, which reserved hunting and gathering to those whose 'primary subsistence was derived from wild plants and animals'.[120] Regulations laid down in 1963 governing entry into the Game Reserve extended the legal protection provided for San as follows: 'No person other than a Bushman indigenous to the [CKGR] shall enter the said Reserve without having first obtained a permit in writing from the District Commissioner, Ghanzi.'[121]

At the time of its inception, the population of the CKGR was around 4000 people, whose ancestors, Pedder considered, had probably occupied the area for around 2000 years.[122] By the mid-1980s, however, the number of residents had declined to around 1300, most of whom were concentrated in a few specific Settlements in the south of the Reserve under the administration of Ghanzi District Council and the RADP located there. At Xade there were, in 1985, 860 people; next largest was Gope with 200, and at Mothomelo there were at most 150 residents.[123] Xade had acquired a borehole and other facilities, and the establishment of permanent water, Pedder observes, 'had a dramatic impact' on the lives of the residents. The population at Xade, for example, had risen from some 40 people in 1965, to 860, and then to 1200 by 1995.[124] The people of the CKGR were from a number of different ethnic-linguistic groups, for instance, Bakgalagadi, Gannakwe, and Gwike. But many of them, as San or as other Remote people, felt that they had much in common. Ditshwanelo reported that in Kukama in 1996 both Basarwa and Bakgalagadi said that 'they had lived together for so long that they considered themselves to be Basarwa', while in Kikao they were told 'we are all Basarwa because we live on this land'.[125]

Development and the CKGR

Towards the mid-1980s, the government had begun to reassess its policies towards the Reserve. In 1984 the European Union had indicated that it might stop buying Botswana's beef if, as Pedder states their position, it continued to be produced at the expense of wildlife. Three years earlier, Falconbridge began prospecting at Gope, in what later became a joint venture with De Beers. The numbers of San residents rose in the hope of jobs, and for the piped water that had become available.[126]

In 1986 the government made a number of important decisions. Social and economic development at Xade and other Settlements in the CKGR were to be frozen; sites would be identified outside the Reserve to which the existing residents would be 'encouraged to relocate'; incentives would be identified to promote these removals; the Department of Wildlife and National Parks (DWNP) would act immediately to tap the Reserve's tourism potential, and increase its staff and logistical capacity to this end. Recommendations made by the government's own Fact-Finding Mission of the previous year, that San could continue to reside in the Reserve in association either with community-based tourism activities, or as game guards employed by the DWNP, were rejected. The stress was upon the Reserve's tourism potential, and on the protection of the wildlife to realize it. Further, a quarter century after the CKGR's foundation on contrary principles, wildlife and human settlement were no longer seen as compatible.[127] That the humans concerned were also the indigenous inhabitants of the region appeared immaterial.

Implementation was initially variable, though the government's stated objectives remained firm. Patrick Balopi, Minister for Local Government, Lands and Housing, told parliament in December 1995 that services for Basarwa would only be provided outside the CKGR because building schools and clinics inside '[would] not be compatible with maintaining the pristine environment of the game reserve'.[128] He and George Kgoroba, Minister for Commerce and Industry, briefed councillors and land-board members in Molepolole on the relocations two months later, when the latter stated that tourism could become Botswana's number-one income earner if, he emphasized, wildlife was conserved and game reserves made attractive to tourists.[129] While all services aimed at assisting San residents had been stopped since 1986, the construction of roads for the Wildlife Department was proceeding in the CKGR, as was the development of the prospective diamond mine at Gope.[130] No suggestion emerged from the government that the Gope mine threatened either the Reserve's 'pristine environment' or its tourism potential.

Implementing the removals

Official attitudes rigidified as John Hardbattle and other San representatives sought international support against the relocation.[131] When Balopi met CKGR residents on 17 February 1996 he told them: 'I have not come to address any other question with you except that you must move ... you must be out by June'. A Ghanzi District Council representative was also explicit when he spoke to residents later: 'The Government will bring development to those who move outside the Reserve ... Those who would like to be given development [*sic*] would migrate, and those who do not want to get it ... would remain.'[132] The government was issuing threats, but it was also offering inducements to those who might choose relocation – among the latter, according to Ditshwanelo and the *Okavango Observer* of Maun, were variously offers of money, five cows, 15 goats, eight donkeys, and a plot of land for ploughing.[133]

The Ditshwanelo mission learnt that what the government had effectively said to the residents was: 'if you do not move, you will have to look after yourselves – you will be denied water and medical care – and you will remain with the soldiers', on patrol in the area. Or in the words of another person: 'Those who are moving are doing so because of government policy...they are not doing it freely.'[134] Outsa Mokone may have summed up the situation when he reported 'relentless' pressure upon San residents in the Reserve: 'sometimes it is a display of force by government officials, more often a word whispered to residents to scare them'.[135]

Much criticism was also directed at San leaders like John Hardbattle and Roy Sesana; their motives and behaviour were repeatedly questioned and their position badly distorted. Hardbattle was proceeding in an ungentlemanly way, according to the Permanent Secretary in Local Government and Lands in April 1996; they were only advancing 'their own personal interests', a press statement declared;[136] and in June, President Ketumile Masire criticized Hardbattle for supposedly choosing to see him outside Botswana. The President further claimed the same month, that while his government was open to criticism, it 'would reject sentiments expressed by people who are opposed to any form of development of Basarwa'.[137]

By mid-June 1997, Xade was empty of its residents. They had been moved to New Xade, 60 kilometres away. Here there were few trees, no potable water and no permanent buildings. A school was in a tent and a clinic in a shed. Winter was beginning and, 'contrary to promises', says Christian Erni, 'the people were not provided with any building material'. A group of senior government officials arrived in the tent village with promises of spending P10 million on development, and Minister Balopi specifically denied that the government was unfairly pressuring Basarwa to move.[138] Later, in mid-1999, New Xade remained 'a wasteland'. A 'drunk man demand[ed] that Paul [Weinberg] photograph him and as we dr[ove] through kids ran out screaming "sweets, sweets". There [was] an air of listlessness and despair, a feeling that this is the end of the road.'[139] Compensations made to the relocated people, said Pedder, were actually 'piecemeal', while Ditshwanelo found no indication that the government was 'seriously considering the issue of compensation in both its narrow and broad definition'.[140]

Samora Gaborone was closely involved in the future of the CKGR. He stated in May 1998 that the government had speeded up its resettlement campaign following the sudden death of John Hardbattle on his return from overseas the previous year. The First People of the Kalahari had indeed written letters to Minister Balopi and to his successor at Local Government and Lands, Margaret Nasha, but these were neither acknowledged nor responded to. Gaborone believed that the responsible Ministry '[does] not want to enter into negotiations with Basarwa'. No consultations had occurred with the residents – if there had been, he believed, no one would ever have moved.[141]

Diamonds and tourism

The government made conspicuously little reference to the Gope diamond mine when it stressed tourism and environmental protection throughout this time. The 1961 proclamation was superseded by the Wildlife Conservation and National Parks Act of 1992 which made no mention of the specific reasons for the establishment of the Reserve. Over the years, 'much prospecting' for diamonds, oil and uranium had taken place,[142] and detailed exploration for diamonds had gone on at Gope in south-eastern CKGR since 1981, and test mining was undertaken in 1997. For the Department of Wildlife itself, the mine which could result from this was assessed as being very large indeed – 'as big as that at Letlhakane'. The Gope mine would be 'so large and permanent that there would be no realistic chance of rehabilitating the area for a very long time'.

Here was a threat to the Reserve's 'pristine environment', and seemingly to the realization of its tourism potential, much greater and more immediate than that represented by a thousand or so San. The responsible Department's position was, nevertheless, notably sanguine. If the feasibility study recommended development, their management plan said, 'it would be undesirable and unrealistic to try to oppose it, given the importance of diamond mining to the economy'.[143] In the distorted and decidedly limited public debate on relocation, into which the government leadership had reluctantly and only partially entered, no reference was made to these significant factors.

After Guy Oliver published a story in a Johannesburg paper that prospective diamond mining by De Beers was connected with the evictions from the CKGR, the government responded with a number of firm but untrue statements.[144] E. Molale, the Permanent Secretary at the Ministry of Local Government, writing in the same paper, declared that '[Basarwa] have not been and will never be dispossessed of any land'; that, after '15 years' of 'consulting and negotiating', some Basarwa had agreed to move 'of their own free will'; and that it was 'the desire [of the government] to promote the dignity of Basarwa as human beings'. He specifically affirmed that: 'There are no mines coming up in the CKGR.'[145]

Severe doubt was cast on the government's proclaimed actions and intentions earlier by Festus Mogae, then Vice-President and Minister for Finance and Development Planning. Speaking when the removals were about to begin, he said: 'How can you have a Stone Age creature continuing to exist in the age of computers? If the Bushmen want to survive, they must change, or otherwise, like the dodo, they will perish.'[146] Such views were incompatible with any belief in the human dignity of the San, but they would have constituted a powerful spur to what was actually underway. Harsh sentiments were also expressed by the Director of the Department of Wildlife and Natural Resources, Sedia Modise, when the removals from Xade were in progress in June 1997: 'There is no future for the Basarwa', he reportedly affirmed, 'They must join the modern world now.'[147]

Official estimates indicated that around 3100 people had been removed from the CKGR through 1997–98 and relocated near Kaudwane in the south. Another 1200 had gone from Xade to New Xade at the same time. But denting the official claims that all had moved of their own free will, with adequate arrangements made for their reception, about 400 San had moved back without governmental assistance from Kaudwane and New Xade to Mothomelo and Molapo inside the Reserve.[148] When Weinberg and Weaver arrived at Molapo in 1999 'a small crowd gathered, all very young or very old. Slowly, carefully, younger men and women beg[a]n to emerge as the word spread that we [we]re friends, not foe.' In contrast with the squalor of New Xade, Molapo, they found, was 'a vibrant, buzzy community'.[149]

The removals and the hardships of the San were the costs of the diamond mine. Only in July 2000 was it officially admitted that mining was planned at Gope. Speaking to the Ghanzi District Council, the Minister of Minerals, Boometswe Mokgothu, explained that explorations had so far cost Falconbridge and De Beers around P100 million, that the planned mine would cover an area of 46 square kilometres, and it would have a lifespan of 18 years. A definite decision on developing Gope would be made in terms of the profitability of the investment. The government, it was still claimed, would protect the fragile bio-diversity of the Reserve; 'only a mine camp will be established at a conveniently determined site, and the workers will come into and out of the camp rotationally on a two-week basis.' In the interests of the whole nation, Mokgothu was reported as saying, the small communities currently occupying the mine area will be asked to move.[150]

The director of the Hotel and Tourism Association Botswana (HATAB), Modise (or Modisagape) Mothoagae, said that their doubts that Basarwa were relocated from the CKGR for tourism and wildlife considerations were now vindicated. He found the new revelation shocking, especially as regards the length of time that it took for the government to come into the open. The rights and principles of the Basarwa had been compromised. 'If Basarwa are moved because of a [mining] development, then it brings in a question of compensation. They must be compensated accordingly', he said. The information officer at the Botswana Christian Council, Letlhogile Lucas, took the same view. The government must ensure that Basarwa benefit from the mine, because 'there is no doubt that the place is theirs'. But he was troubled, too, by the lack of accountability and responsibility: 'I believe the government should go back to the community and apologise. It should also apologise to the nation.'[151]

Hunting and tourism

According to Egner and Klausen in 1980, the country's wildlife resources had always been administered 'only minimally in the interests of the poor', and the introduction of unified regulations had had 'disastrous effects' – they placed greater discretionary powers in the hands of officials, and capital-intensive hunting with costly firearms became the 'preferred form'.[152] A Special Game Licence (SGL) was available to San and other Remote people for the hunting of particular animals – to a specified number, for a stipulated area and duration, for subsistence purposes – the actual issuance of which has depended upon the energy and judgement of a small number of game scouts.[153]

Hunting and criminality

Hunting has tended to become an enterprise of peril and proto-criminality for the San and the illiterate rural poor in general. In the passing of a few years, San and other Remote residents in the Thankana area of Southern District became virtually enclosed by ranches, and hunting was 'nearly terminated'. Exclusive hunting rights became the prerogative of ranchers, and the residents were perceived as potential poachers.[154] A special licence must always be carried and its terms adhered to regardless of the availability at the time of game. Between 10 to 30 per cent of Remote people in the six Settlements covered by the Monitoring Programme claimed during 1990–91 that they had been charged with an offence by police or game scouts, mostly involving poaching or stock theft. In Groot Laagte, 82 per cent of those so charged received prison sentences averaging 4.5 months.[155] Repeated allegations have been made of the physical abuse of San at the hands of police and Wildlife Department officers.[156]

According to Richard White in 1992, the administration of hunting was a 'shambles'. One result of such real or apparent confusion was that 'large numbers of rural people who need licences to support themselves and their families [we]re unable to obtain them'. At the same time, however, 'many influential people benefit[ed] from the present inequitable hunting system'.[157]

Withdrawal of SGLs

Aerial census data collected by DWNP have suggested that the numbers of wildlife had declined substantially by the mid-1990s. Many factors had contributed to this, including population growth, habitat change, and the intensification of cattle production with its emphasis on fencing for disease control and herd management. Despite this array of causes, 'suggestions ha[d] been made', Hitchcock noted in 1995, that 'one way to reduce the rate of wildlife decline would be to do away with [SGLs]'. While he recognized, of course, that relatively few Remote people were totally dependent on foraging for subsistence, it remained the case that many groups continued to hunt for meat and skins, and collected items like ostrich shells for jewellery-making, an 'important source of income for sizable numbers of RAD households'. Wildlife played 'a significant role' in the lives of many Remote people, and the abolition of SGLs could have negative impacts on the rural poor.[158]

In a study of resource management in Western Botswana a little later, Chasca Twyman noted that wildlife resources might in fact have been underutilized in parts of Ghanzi District, and a prevailing 'confusion' over the retention or otherwise of Special Licences.[159] No full records existed in the Ghanzi Wildlife Office of the numbers of SGLs allocated yearly, but estimates suggested that the figures ranged from '50 to 200' a year between 1990 and 1995, and 'about 300' in the District in 1996.[160]

Hitchcock has stated that, in 1996, the Dept of Wildlife decided that SGLs should be abolished, although 'no formal announcement of this decision was made' to anyone.[161] The loss of the licences appeared thereafter to be underway. According to the same researcher in 1998: 'Three years ago [the government was] giving 1000 [SGLs] a year to Remote Area Dwellers' in Botswana. 'Last year they gave at most 100 for subsistence hunters'.[162] This seemed in accord with government intentions, even if the public in general and Remote people specifically were uninformed of what was afoot. As the senior government minister, Daniel Kwelagobe, stated in parliament in March 1997: domestic hunting should be strictly controlled and the period reserved for hunting should perhaps be shortened. A ban on hunting might even be considered. 'People are nowadays fed on drought relief schemes', he complacently claimed, 'and I see no reason why there should be an excuse for people supplementing their food rations with wildlife meat'.[163] Twyman quotes the Principal Game Warden as saying that 'SGLs are not so important', and that those affected 'will be willing generally to forgo their SGL'. She concluded that 'the envisaged scenario' is clearly 'a cessation of individual hunting rights'.[164]

Controlling crafts

The controls and restrictions extended, in fact, well beyond individual rights to hunting. An important and reasonably lucrative craft industry fashioning ostrich shell into necklaces and bracelets existed among San and other Remote people in Ghanzi and the Kgalagadi;[165] it had been an element in their exchange systems for a very long time.[166] But Botswana introduced a new Ostrich Management Plan Policy in 1994 which stipulated that a licence must be obtained, on payment of a fee, from the Dept of Wildlife before ostrich-related products could be obtained, bought or sold. Shells could only be collected, it also stated, in the four-month period from April to August. Proto-criminality now came into being for San craftspersons here too – someone without a permit and in possession of ostrich products was liable to arrest for violating conservation laws. A further restriction existed in that a person holding a Special Game Licence could not hold another permit simultaneously, and so could not legally engage in ostrich-shell collecting.

The new Management Policy seemed intended to take a natural resource out of the hands of individual gatherers and craft-makers and place it in those of commercial or other organizations. Groups must, in this case, establish premises where the shells are kept, and which must be open to inspection by Wildlife officials on a regular basis. Collection quotas are allocated, and women's groups must first be organized and recognized officially before DWNP will grant a collecting quota. This process seemed fraught with problems and delays, and the worry of arrest in the interim for the women. Those in West Hanahai in Ghanzi attempted to form an ostrich-user group, but it took them two years to obtain a quota and the licence to exploit and sell ostrich products. Even then, suggested Hitchcock, the possibility of being deemed guilty of poaching still appeared to exist. The shells which the San collected were often hatched egg pieces, but the Dept of Wildlife nevertheless considered even these to be trophies, on a legal par, say, with elephant tusks or a lion skin. This could mean that women are potentially law-breakers even in their licensed crafts groups.[167]

Controlling natural resources

Other natural resources which the San have historically utilized for subsistence and income-generation purposes were also being drawn under the government's control mechanisms. Devil's Claw (or grapple plant) is an important medicinal tuber and probably the most important veld product in the 1990s in its money-earning capacities.[168] Its harvesting by this time required a permit from the Agricultural Resources Board of the Ministry of Agriculture.[169] Much the same was perhaps in store for mopane worms, and for the palm fronds vital in the making of the baskets which represent Botswana's distinctive art-form. Resource access was being collectivized, commercialized and organized. Where hunting was concerned, San in future had two options, thought Hitchcock;[170] a person might apply for a citizen's hunting licence, but the possession of a relatively costly firearm was prerequisite and beyond the reach of most San, and the permissible type and number of animals would be restricted. Alternatively, they might form community trusts or companies to qualify for the allocation of wildlife quotas. But for reasons noted above, the San were not well-placed to pursue the latter and better alternative effectively. Control over the area of residence was necessary if access to its natural resources was to be ensured, and information on new and complex procedures was almost equally essential and highly difficult to acquire due to the secretive nature of government policy-making.

Tourism and big business

Government policy was firm, enshrined in National Development Plan 8, that tourism should be 'one of Botswana's engines of growth'.[171] Well-organized commercial operators were already acting on this principle. One such was John Mynhart, chairman of the Cash Bazaar group of companies, described as having extensive interests in hunting and the safari sector in Chobe, including ownership of Hunters Africa which operated hunting and photographic safaris. Competition for the exploitation of valuable natural resources was intensifying in 1999, even for a solid concern like Mynhart's. He said he had invested heavily in facilities and infrastructure for tourists, but when the concession areas came up for tender he lost the area where he had invested. One of the companies which was understood by *The Botswana Gazette* to have won the tender for the area previously held by Mynhart's company was

Linyanti Investment, co-owned it was said by ex-President Masire's younger brother, Peter Basimanyana Masire.[172]

Commercial activity was stiffening as tourism became the third-largest contributor to Botswana's gross domestic product, growing at an average of 10 per cent through the 1990s, and reaching a growth rate of 11.1 per cent in 1998/99.[173] It was in part between 'settler' and 'citizen' commercial interests, and some were strong and experienced in the field.[174] But it was also between national and foreign tourism interests, and very prominent people were involved. Louis Nchindo, managing director of Debswana Diamond Company, complained that most safari tours were being marketed outside Botswana, and the money involved never entered the country. 'We are being cheated by foreigners', declared Nchindo; 'In Botswana the foreigner is king'. Millions of Pula in tourism remittances, it was claimed, were remaining in foreign hands. George Kgoroba, Minister for Commerce and Industry, shared Nchindo's sentiments, Outsa Mokone reported.[175] A 'protracted battle to control the [tourism] sector', according to the latter, was underway.[176] Kgoroba was further concerned that expatriate workers were being employed by tour operators, and imported handicrafts and souvenirs were being sold to tourists to the detriment of local products and producers. The Minister had taken his concerns to HATAB, and their director, Mothoagae, had responded firmly by stating that his organization had no control over companies operating mobile safaris from outside Botswana, and that it was the responsibility of government – specifically the departments of Labour and Immigration – to ensure adequate citizen participation in employment in the industry.[177]

Other interests and leading politicians were engaged through the broad issue of land use. Here there was a division between, on the one hand, big cattle and land owners, the marketing agency the Botswana Meat Commission (BMC), and a big lobby like the Hurwitz group which supplied around 15 per cent of the cattle which went through the BMC each year; and, on the other, a broad coalition of new leaders, environmentalists and tourism interests. Among the established pro-cattle grouping were Ketumile Masire and ex-Minister Patrick Balopi, and Martin Mannathoko of the BMC. Not only did he head reputedly Africa's largest abattoir, but he had his own investments in 'farming and other businesses' and had 'no intention to dis-invest from the livestock sector'.[178]

President Mogae, however, stood in firm opposition to the taxation policies and other assistance which the cattle interests historically enjoyed.[179] General Khama was linked to the environmentalist cause from his time as BDF commander; HATAB had given him its highest tourism award in Maun in 1996, and he was patron of the Kalahari Conservation Society. Sharpening his engagement, he was also understood to have 'a business interest in the tourism industry'.[180] Louis Nchindo was another 'ardent environmentalist', and according to Mokone he was additionally Mogae's 'other closest friend, advisor, and fellow Oxford University alumni'.[181]

Anneleng and others judged that the government was in effect implementing a tourism policy which promoted Botswana interests in hunting and safari operations in areas like Chobe and Ngamiland.[182]

Tourism and small business

While the exploitation of natural resources offers a potentially important way forward for the San through jobs and income creation, gaining access to them was facilitated neither by their many weaknesses, nor by the intensified activity among the rich and powerful within the tourism sector. The mechanism which the government has offered the small and the weak is that of Community Based Natural Resource Management (CBNRM), and the Joint Venture Partnership (JVP). Originating within the Ministry of Local Government and the Department of Wildlife, it is the latter which is the implementing agency. A community must organize itself, establishing in particular a representative and accountable management body. If it fulfills criteria laid down by the Department of Wildlife and National Parks (DWNP) it receives and manages a hunting quota for its area. Success here is dependent upon a community having experience in enterprise management and the support of local government and other agencies.

While a consultative approach is stressed by Wildlife, it is one which, in the view of Twyman and Maitseo Bolaane, is highly focused and end-orientated. Various meetings are held, but the JVP option, wherein the community leases all or part of their quota to a commercial safari company, is 'the *only* one [that is] fully explained and the *only* one seen to be in the communities' best interests'.[183] For Bolaane, JVP is 'made the norm', and the state has 'only one set of rules for one option'.[184]

Sankuyo and Khwai

Bolaane compared the experiences of the communities of Sankuyo and of neighbouring Khwai in the utilization of natural resources. Both are located in Wildlife Management Areas in Ngamiland, adjacent to Moremi Game Reserve. Sankuyo's population was mainly Bayei, totalling about 400 in the 1990s. The village economy was based on arable agriculture, veld produce and small stock – no cattle was allowed in the area. It had a government-provided primary school, clinic, kgotla structures and a Village Development Committee. Sankuyo quickly became the second area in Botswana where CBNRM was implemented. Its Management Trust, Sankuyo Tshwaragano (STMT), was registered in November 1995, and soon after acquired leasehold over Controlled Hunting Area NG/34 through the Tawana Land Board. As speedily, a tender was awarded to the commercial operator Game Safaris in January 1996. The subsequent lease, from 1998–2001, was with Crocodile Camp. The Wildlife Dept, the district council and other agencies provided the Trust with technical assistance and training throughout this time.

Khwai is on the edge of Moremi. Its population is of San origin, people who were originally relocated there when the Game Reserve was established in the 1960s. They numbered about 300 in 1999, although many youth were absent, seeking employment in Maun. It was still not a gazetted village, and it had no primary school or clinic. The local economy had stressed hunting and gathering for subsistence, but three safari lodges – Tsaro, Game Trackers and Machaba – had been established nearby, and the Khwai people, indicating possible self-help capacities, had redirected their activities to cutting thatching-grass for sale to them. It had constructed a management group and registered a constitution, but approval from the DWNP was awaited in early 1999. The Khwai community were, however, 'reluctant to go into a joint venture partnership with a commercial safari operator', and they were uncertain about the 'rules, incentives, and benefits' of the JVP model.[185]

In the operations of CBNRM, land boards may grant leases of 15 years based on three renewable five-year periods. Hunting quotas are annual and specify the number and type of animals. The winning bidder for a contract, the partner in the joint venture, emerges through public meetings where the community, associated with other so-called stakeholders, asks questions of the safari operator. The National Resource Management Project at Wildlife, assisted by the United States Agency for International Development, has provided extension services for CBNRM. The tendering process can prove profitable for a community – Bolaane states that in some areas the value of the annual concession fee has increased three or four times at each round.[186]

But limitations are nevertheless tight. A community cannot make an agreement with a company or other third party without the approval of a land board and Wildlife. The commercial safari operator is not obliged to inform the community about its profits or losses, and the community has no involvement in the marketing of the joint venture. It is not a joint partnership in a real sense, believes Bolaane, but rather a contractual relationship between the resident group and the operator. The rules of the model essentially operate to allow safari companies to gain access to land and its wildlife through the contract with the community.[187]

In 1997 there were nine registered CBNRM organizations in Botswana. The Chobe Enclave Community Trust and Sankuyo Tshwaragano appear to indicate that, in an area rich in natural resources like the Ngamiland environment, CBNRM generates significant revenue for organized local residents. In the same well-endowed area the CgaeCgae Tlhabololo Trust has performed well since 1992. XaiXai is a community of some 400 people of whom 70 per cent are San and 30 per cent Babanderu; the community's chief, nonetheless, is non-San. The Trust's 10-member Board is elected by the community, and in 1998 its composition was 50 per cent San. The marketing of crafts and cultural eco-tourism brought the Trust some P80 000 in 1998.[188] But mistrust generally persists between the communities and their venture partners.[189] 'Tempers flared' at a meeting in Maun in early April 1999, with Kgosi Mathiba of the Batawana calling on safari companies to 'leave my country as it was'.[190] Bolaane believes that community's like Khwai, which are skeptical of the merits of JVP, are probably distinguished by two features, positively and negatively: they already have links with tourist lodges and such, and they have a 'historic alienation from ancestral lands'.[191]

Tourism in the CKGR

The tourism development now underway in the CKGR seems intended to bypass or exclude the past and present San residents. According to a representative of the people who had returned to Molapo either late in 1998 or early in 1999:

> We get no money from the government for the tourists coming through here. We get tourists coming who want to … walk in the bush, or see some dancing or buy some crafts, but the government tries to stop it. We want to work with tourists, and the government must understand that this is a good thing for this park.[192]

But the problem was not one of simple misunderstanding. According to the management plans of Wildlife, five tourist lodges were intended for the Reserve in 1999 – all are far from any officially-sanctioned San settlement, and by May 1999 no past or present San community had been involved in this planning.[193] Mathambo Ngakaeaja, coordinator at the Working Group of Indigenous Minorities in Southern Africa (WIMSA) Botswana, believes that the CBNRM projects at Tshodilo Hills, Zutshwa, and XaiXai, are serving to remove the San even further from land and resources rightfully theirs. With the quota system of natural resource utilization, it is 'the most influential people [who] will get the quota, and they will run the show'.[194]

The inheritance of deprivation and discrimination

Twyman presents a detailed breakdown of the CBNRM initiatory scenario as envisaged by DWNP, contrasted with the more laboured and limited developments which usually take place. The stages where progress is slowest and most fraught are the vital later ones: registering the community's Trust; acquiring lease over the land; and the joint venture procedure. She states that, while 'the language and images of policy implementation' are presented by Wildlife as 'participatory and empowering', they are found in reality to be 'subordinating and dictatorial'. The government has adopted an approach in western districts that pays little attention to the diversity and inequalities in Botswana society.[195] San communities are often in a weak position to profit from the CBNRM–JPV model; in mid-1999 Khwai villagers were believed to have had their application for a concession area turned down because they wanted membership in their community trust reserved for Basarwa.[196] Secure land rights and recognized political organization are prerequisites for a community's effective participation. The Ghanzi District Development Plan 1997–2001 states that 'the rights of the Basarwa to land are, in general, rather tenuous'.[197] San and other Remote people in western districts, Twyman concludes, 'feel [that] they have been deprived and excluded from the management of their wildlife resources and ... cheated now that populations have declined'.[198]

Welfare: destitutes programme and pensions

The poor have been a large and deprived section of Botswana society since the beginnings of the pastoral economy, and the San have been prominent among them for the same time; poverty, and impoverished San, exist as a structural factor in the country's political economy.[199] The highest rates of permanent destitution in Botswana were found in 1995/96 in Ghanzi and in Kgalagadi – respectively, 59.9 and 46.2 per 1000 population. Destitutes are officially understood as being 'the poorest of the poor', and Remote people are recognized as one of their main components.[200] In sharp contrast with the other aid and welfare programmes, Labour-Based Relief and the new old-age pension, the destitutes allowance is provided in kind only. This in itself represents an impediment upon their normal activity – access to cash income is a necessity of meaningful citizenship.

The ration basket of food which they receive is itself inadequate in nutritional terms; constructed in 1980, it was on BIDPA's assessment 'extremely frugal', providing only 'an extremely limited variety of nutritional inputs', which fell 'short of a minimal food basket to provide for healthy subsistence'.[201] The money allocated to the destitute's allowance was similarly well below the actual cost of the food basket in recent years. In 1995 the destitute's allowance had an assigned value of only P82.80 per month in rural areas, and P61.59 in the towns; when the actual cost of the items in the Ministry of Health's basket was, according to BIDPA, P120. National aid to destitutes was introduced only in 1980, when the allowance was a flat P8.50, it had subsequently been increased on four occasions, but its real value had 'remained fairly constant' over the preceding decade. In the western districts, transportation and food costs were higher, and the value of the rations was lower still. Typically, the actual basket which administering council staffs provided to Remote people, represented 'significantly lower proteins, vegetable and other nutritional components'. BIDPA's interviewees in those areas said that the rations they received were even 'too low to meet an individual's survival requirements'.[202]

The numbers of destitutes have been rising rapidly. When Botswana's total population grew by about 60 per cent between 1980 and 1996, the number of permanent destitutes increased threefold, from 5000 to 15 597. Nevertheless, these figures are probably underestimates – 'the original selection criteria', says BIDPA, have become 'outmoded', with the result that 'many people' who are destitute may not qualify for support. The official definition of a destitute, devised by the Ministry of Local Government in 1980, presupposes a bereft, isolated individual, but 'often' there are other unregistered destitute people in a household or 'the entire household is destitute'.[203] It is also stigmatizing: he or she must be seen to be 'without any form of asset and ... have lost or being deserted by family and kin', and be 'physically or mentally incapable of working'.[204]

Parsimony towards the very poor was not borne of some policy lapse or failure to update or fine-tune existing programmes. The report of the Presidential Commission on incomes policy in 1990 recommended a reassessment of support for destitutes: current practice, it noted, that no more than one individual in a household was declared destitute at any one time, was unrealistic, and the support provided should reflect the actual cost of providing basic food and shelter in the area concerned. The government, however, amended this proposal severely. Changes to the poverty datum line 'should only be used as a guide' in specifying a 'strictly limited' support basket. 'It should be emphasised', the White Paper declared, 'that destitute amounts should always be lower than the lowest minimum wage so as to ensure that such welfare payments do not discourage work efforts'.[205]

In the circumstances which actually prevailed, it was even more parlous. Given the government's effective wages policy, the existing lowest minimum wage for San in western districts was around P30 a month, if a person was fortunate enough to acquire paid employment. In fact most San were very unlikely to obtain any work, other than LBRP, in those areas.

The pension

The Botswana government introduced an old-age pension in October 1996 worth P100 per month, raised to P110 in April 1998 and available, significantly, in cash. Although this was superior to the handout offered to the very poor, it was extremely mean in regional and in national terms. The South African pension at much the same time was R520 a month, roughly 400 per cent greater, while in Namibia it was worth slightly more. The cost of Botswana's pension if, say, about 60000 people were to gain from it was some P6 million, negligible in comparison with government spending elsewhere – that on the military, for instance, having risen from some P214 million in 1992 to P625 million in 1995.[206] Elderly destitutes ceased in 1996 to receive the destitutes allowance, but after April of the following year they became eligible for both that and the pension.[207] Johnny Swartz, Member of Parliament for Ghanzi, said that the majority of the Basarwa community who qualified for the pension did not receive it, as of March 1998, because of their inability to establish their age satisfactorily.[208] The following year Kuru board members said that San still had difficulties obtaining the pension due to the proof-of-age difficulties, illiteracy and their general remoteness.[209]

The difficulties faced by the rural poor in gaining access to the pension were starkly displayed in mid-1999. On 23 July Mmekhwe Meagowe died a pauper in a shack on a cattle post in the vicinity of Letlhakane, east of Orapa. She had no identity card and could get neither the destitute's allowance nor the pension. The government only acted after a photo of the visibly aged and impoverished woman, lying on her side on the ground, appeared in *The Guardian* in March. But Meagowe's official identity and back-dated pension payment totalling P2850 was sent out to her some five days after her death.[210]

Welfare for survival

Welfare policies for the poor in Botswana are intended for the physical survival of a qualified person only. A new poverty datum line (PDL) was published in 1991, current into the new century. Constructed on the knowledge that the incidence of rural poverty, on official statistics, had risen from 45 per cent of households in 1974 to 64 per cent in the mid-1980s, it was purposefully designed to be of 'a minimal nature'. As in the government's White Paper, severity and denial pervaded the work. The kind and quantity of food was calculated on the basis of the 'minimum necessary to maintain physical health', and the clothing similarly assessed in the PDL was in terms of 'legality', 'decency', and practicality. Household furniture embraced no bed, mattress, table or chairs. Nor were any knives, forks, plates or cups and saucers included in the calculations. The exclusions were carefully stressed: 'all cosmetics (except vaseline)'; for entertainment, 'there is nothing. No toys ... books or magazines; no allowance for writing materials, stamps ... ' And 'most importantly, there is no allowance for travelling'.[211] Participation at funerals and weddings is part of normal social life for most Batswana, and successful work efforts have frequently resulted from a readiness to travel.

In Namibia, however, wages and welfare policies have a broader and deeper focus. The Namibian Constitution contains a chapter entitled Principles of State Policy, with the sub-heading 'Promotion of the Welfare of the People'. The government is thereunder obliged to ensure that workers are paid 'a living wage', one which is 'adequate for the maintenance of a decent standard of living and the enjoyment of social and cultural opportunities'. The pension which the elderly were 'entitled' to receive was understood in exactly the same socially enabling terms.[212] Notions of a living wage, and of welfare as the right of the poor or elderly to the active enjoyment of their lives, are still novel in government in Botswana.[213]

The Remote Area Development Programme (RADP): governmental keystone

The RADP, introduced in 1974 with the short-lived title of Bushman Development Programme,[214] was intended as an initiative towards rural development. When the RADP was evaluated by the CMI research team 22 years later, it was the essential incoherence in the approach that was stressed: 'it is a decentralised programme with a series of disjointed components that receive little central direction'. The 'predictable result' had been towards 'a steady operational preference for the more straight forward but expensive infrastructural activities', to the neglect of more complex components such as production and income-boosting endeavours, monitoring and research.[215] There was also a strong orientation towards Ghanzi. National expenditure under RADP, 1979–84, totalled P634 945, of which Ghanzi received easily the largest district component with P281 953. Hitchcock adds that a bias towards the western districts was 'built into the programme [from] its exception'.[216]

RADP had overall supervision for policies dealing with the San, but it was neither prestigious nor large. Established within the Ministry of Local Government, it was never more than 40 staff officers – of whom perhaps some three were San – and for most bureaucrats a posting to the programme, say Hitchcock and Holm, was seen as an undesirable career move. The support which it attracted from politicians was similarly small,[217] reflecting the equivocal and distrustful attitudes existing in the upper echelons of government towards assisting the San.

While 'money itself', the CMI evaluators usefully stressed, 'ha[d] not been a problem' for the RADP,[218] the effective utilization of money was. Most funds, Hitchcock and Holm believed, were directed towards building hostels for schools, permanent water sources and official salaries. RAD officers tended to 'concentrate on the one service they c[ould] perform easily'. In 'most cases' this meant in fact transporting and supervising San children in boarding schools.[219] In the mid-1990s, as the CMI learnt, the RADP was just one of the Ministry's 24 or so projects. The primary concern there was 'how effectively the funds [we]re disbursed. Not enough attention [was] given to policy matters...' The Botswana government, the researchers said, had 'done reasonably well with the infrastructural components of the RADP', and 'rather badly with all the rest of it'. The 'major shortfall' was in income generation. The causes of the failures were fairly clear: necessary improvements depended on 'the political and administrative will of government and Councils', and this had been 'distinctly lacking'. The RADP's problems and failures were not, in relatively wealthy Botswana, due to an absence of money and resources, but to the lack of 'political commitment' to the goal; the RADP's status in government was 'low'.[220]

Proposals to extend, in fact virtually to transform, the programme's ambit to include land rights, political organization and productivity for the San, were emphasized by community groups and the Norwegian aid agency in the early 1990s. The Ministry of Local Government announced, in October 1992, that it had completed a review of the RADP that was, in the words of the Permanent Secretary, Pelonomi Venson, intended to shift the emphasis away from infrastructural development and towards 'culture, land issues, leadership, and community development'.[221] Terje Vigtel, senior Norwegian representative in Botswana, added that his country wanted 'priority consideration for land requirements and land rights, cultural identity, [and the] representation of RAD's in advisory/decision-making fora'.[222] These path-breaking initiatives were seemingly negated silently at Cabinet level; the Ministry's review is thought to have reached Cabinet about October 1994, but it was sent back to them on the grounds that it contained proposals that went outside their jurisdiction.[223] This decision or non-decision was an important indicator of the government's priorities.

Some officials felt, Hitchcock states, that 'there is no longer a need' for a RADP. The poorest people in Botswana will be covered by existing welfare programmes.[224] These are, however, demonstrably inadequate, and the wealthy ruling elite of Botswana, now and earlier, is more characterized by its acute meanness to the poor than by its generosity. Adequate welfare is a necessity, but it remains aside from the developmental concerns of the San for secure land rights, control of resources, autonomous political organizations and an end to discrimination.

Since the withdrawal of Norway's assistance, and the government's failure or refusal to enunciate a credible new programme towards the San and other Remote people, the RADP is in abeyance. The government's involvement, notes Saugestad, has 'reverted to a low-intensity continuation of the infrastructure components'.[225]

Routinized injustice: subordination in schooling and law

Hitchcock and Holm believed that the RADP contained 'a de facto objective' of promoting the assimilation of San children through schooling. The social infrastructure of the programme was 'a carrot' to induce the San to locate in government-controlled settlements. Within the family, 'parents are asked to allow their children to become cultural Batswana'.[226] Roy Sesana said that RADP 'takes children' for education, often far from their homes;[227] if they return to the household they are sometimes estranged from their parents and from San culture. Those with fortitude, however, may nevertheless acquire access to educational resources. Kamana Phetso, Kuru Board Secretary, was sent to a secondary boarding school 1000 kilometres from home; he reports constant discrimination from his teachers, that the RADP was frequently late in supplying San pupils with soap and uniforms, and he missed his family. His grades declined and he performed poorly, but he eventually became the first in his family to complete schooling to Senior Secondary level.[228]

Schooling is a critical phase in which young San learn that they have a history of being primitive people from the bush, of being serfs; it is when, according to Willemien le Roux, discrimination and subordination is brought home to them partly through wide-ranging abuse. It begins with the rupture from family and home. While school hostels ranged in standard across the region from the very poor to the fairly modern, the system itself represented overwhelming 'trauma and anxiety' for both parents and children.[229] Hostels embodied the previously unknown forces of routine and confinement. Emotional abuse is such that San children sometimes change their identity – endeavouring to register themselves, after about three years at school, as a member of the 'closest other language group', for example Bakgalagadi in Botswana or Coloured in South Africa. Abuse is verbal and physical – corporal punishment is applied almost everywhere in schools – and San girls are especially prone to sexual abuse on the expectation of a servile people's 'duties to their masters'.[230] Le Roux summarizes the process as follows:

> the younger children in school suffered because of the separation from their parents, as well as physical abuse by bullying and lack of care in hostels. The teenagers suffered more … discrimination, stigmatisation, boredom and physical and sexual abuse.[231]

Events in 1999 demonstrated the accuracy of this analysis. One night in February at Otse school, west of Mahalapye in Central District, 221 San children left the neighbouring RAD hostel to walk back to their parents on distant cattle-posts. When they were found later next day they had covered around 40 kilometres, but an eight-year-old girl left behind during the night due to tiredness was dead, on discovery or shortly after, and her body partly eaten by animals. The authorities had prior warning that problems existed at the school which eventually led on to the mass exodus. Earlier in the month, some 20 boys had boycotted classes, and complained to the school principal, Spencer Lecage, of verbal and physical abuse inflicted on them by the matron.[232]

It seems unlikely that generalized improvements in schooling for San resulted from this tragedy. In November of the same year 'indiscipline' was reported as rife in the primary school at Tshwaane, a RAD settlement near Motokwe in Kweneng District. Teachers were being subjected to disrespect, according to head-teacher Martha Visage, who reportedly vowed to stamp out the rot. Five Basarwa boys, aged 16, had already been flogged. Visage depicted widespread lawlessness at the school – breaking of doors and window panes, vulgar graffiti, absenteeism, theft, love affairs among adolescents – and attributed the cause firmly to Sesarwa culture. She complained that 'Basarwa don't yet appreciate the importance of education'.[233]

The law too easily displays a harsh and unyielding attitude to the problems of the Basarwa, and the exigencies of the impoverished get scant recognition. In 1997, Tlhabologo Maauwe and Gwara Brown Motswetla, subsequently described by Justice Dudley Reynolds as being 'illiterate, suffer[ing] from difficulties of communication', and 'without resources', were sentenced to death for the murder of a cattle farmer, Bashingi Majeremane, north of Nata village in 1995; he was in pursuit of Maauwe and Brown, after finding that they had killed and eaten his cow, when he was allegedly struck on the head. No evidence was put to the court of the poverty of the accused before passing sentence. Their execution was set for 16 January 1999, when Ditshwanelo won literally a last-minute stay of execution. President Mogae had already signed their death warrants, and the graves of the two men were dug and awaiting them.[234]

Experienced advocates acting for Ditshwanelo later established that the state-appointed defence lawyers in the original hearing and the appeal were incompetent and did not represent their clients properly. Maauwe and Motswetla had not understood court proceedings, which were conducted in languages they did not properly comprehend. When the two accused had a letter written on their behalf to the Registrar of the High Court, stating their dissatisfaction with their lawyers and asking that they be replaced, it was not acted upon. Phandu Skelemani, Attorney General of Botswana, argued for the state that Ditshwanelo should not even be allowed to appear, that the poverty of the Basarwa was unproven, that it did not in any case affect the guilt of Maauwe and Motswetla, and that the defence lawyers for the two, as Skelemani chillingly said, according to *The Guardian*, did what best they could in the circumstances. Justice Reynolds ruled at the end of October that the accused 'were not afforded a fair hearing', and ordered a retrial at a later date.[235] Without the initiatives and resources of Ditshwanelo, the deprived illiterate San would have been nine months dead by then.

Representations

Government policy has had success in specific areas only – the Labour-Based Relief Programme has assisted a small number of people, providing them with a cash income on a short-term basis; the increased cattle distribution of recent years to individual beneficiaries; the still-awaited transfer of freehold farms to three Settlements in Ghanzi, after long delays and procrastination; and, again in Ghanzi, the election of recognized San *kgosi* in all Settlements. Against these piecemeal but not unimportant gains, the dispossession continues, even widening and deepening as regards the San's precarious access to natural resources. On the basics of secure land rights, incomes and autonomous political organization little or nothing has shown improvement over three decades of independence.

Poverty is an historically structured and highly pervasive element in the political economy of Botswana. If its amelioration is to be achieved, only the most direct, planned and prioritized strategies would suffice. Nothing of this kind has yet emerged from the Botswana government, where development to date has focused upon growth, and the good rewards that flow in consequence to those who make the biggest contribution to that growth.[236] For farm and household labourers, the destitutes, the aged and the bulk of the San, it is emphatically survival alone that is attended to.

The government has shown no openness to change, either on the broad issues or with regard to detailed policy proposals from reputable sources. Campbell and Main noted, significantly, that 13 years after Hitchcock's report on the Western Sandveld, 'not a single recommendation [he made] ha[d] apparently been implemented', while in the actual direction of development land once available to Remote people had been taken over by cattle-owners.[237] Inaction by the Botswana government also resulted from the recommendations made at a series of regional conferences on the San in the 1990s in Gaborone and Windhoek. The Botswana government steadfastly refuses to recognize even the indigenous status of the San; the country would not celebrate the International Year of the Indigenous People, Chapson Butale, Minister for Local Government explained in 1993, since all Batswana are indigenous to the country.[238] Saugestad's work has focused upon this sustained denial of the San's indigenous status by the government.[239] Despite their relatively high numbers, the San in Botswana are in a far weaker position, socio-economically and politically, than, say, the Saami in Norway or the Inuit in Canada, or the San in South Africa today. The contrast between Thabo Mbeki's warm and supportive views expressed to the Khomani San, and Festus Mogae's depiction of the people of the CKGR as stone-age creatures or dodos, could hardly be sharper. Removal, relocation, and dispossession have been their repeated experiences, for bureaucratic convenience and for national developmental exigencies. In failing to recognize the basic human rights of San, Botswana necessarily fails to extend them in material and political areas.

Affirmative action towards the amelioration of poverty has no support within the upper levels of government. Speaking at his inauguration as President in 1998, Festus Mogae hoped that his compatriots would agree that 'one cannot strengthen the weak by weakening the strong and enrich the poor by simply impoverishing the rich'.[240] The analysis of the origins of poverty, the identification of the agencies and factors which brought it into being and might serve to maintain it now, has little value either. At his budget speech in 1999, the new Minister for Finance and Development Planning, Ponatshego Kedikilwe, recognized that poverty and unemployment were twin problems, but immediately added: 'It is neither proper, nor helpful, to blame the Government or any other institution alone for shortcomings in addressing problems of poverty'.[241] The long record suggests that if poverty continues to be approached simply as a poorly-funded welfare matter, rather than as one of justice and entitlement and broad economic strategy, the structural impoverishment of the San will not be reduced.

Elitism, low popular participation and the subordination and impoverishment of the San form an interlinked triad in the political economy of Botswana. The subordination of the San was carried through by the rising Tswana ruling elite, and the weakness of democracy subsequently – presidentialism, public indolence, secrecy and low accountability – has facilitated its continuance. Injustice meted out to around 10 per cent of the population is in the foundations of this system. The engendering of participatory democratic forms in the future, similarly, is unlikely to be achieved without the concomitant emancipation of the San. Botswana's democracy will remain dysfunctional as long as their poverty endures.

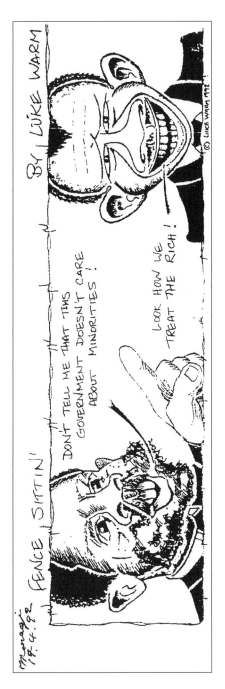

Figure *left* is Festus Mogae, *right* is Ketumile Masire.
Reproduced with the permission of the managing editor of *Mmegi*, *'Sechele Sechele'*, 17 April 1992.

Part II
The USA

3
The Liberal Capitalist Paradigm: Elitism and Injustice in the United States

While all established democracies today are located within capitalist systems, not all democracies, now or earlier, are or were the same. In liberal (or representative or electoral or elite) democracy, the predominant form of the twenty-first century, it is hard to address inequalities and poverty as issues demanding attention. Where that system is associated with *laissez-faire* capitalism, as is usually the case, it is more difficult still. The United States is the leading liberal polity, and it is the home, and global progenitor, of an extensively deregulated market economy. This new flexible capitalism creates inequalities and injustice which the liberal polity, with its largely alienated, non-participatory electorate, is unable to address. The richest liberal capitalism is also the most inequitable in the advanced capitalist world, where injustice is the lot of the proliferating underclasses of blacks, Hispanics and poor whites.[1] Other contemporary democracies, such as social democracy in Western Europe, have notably lower levels of inequality and fewer people in poverty. Participatory democratic forms, in actuality in Athens 508–322 BC, and in the mass movement in South Africa in the 1970s–80s, were significantly different again. But the ascendant American liberal capitalism threatens both its own citizens and more egalitarian systems elsewhere. The evidence suggests that where deregulation, flexibility and downsizing are uncritically embraced, the quest for equality and justice is abandoned. A large helot underclass has been 'ballooning' in the United States, 'disciplined by fear and scarcity, [and] subject to endless surveillance'.[2]

American capitalism

The United States near the end of the 1990s was wealthy and highly productive – on the assessment of the brokerage firm Merril Lynch it

71

was 'Paradise Found: The Best of All Possible Economies'.[3] Within this apparent prosperity, however, the situation of most working people was bad and worsening. The average weekly earnings of the 80 per cent of ordinary working Americans fell by 18 per cent between 1973 and 1995, from $315 a week to $258 a week,[4] and this latter figure represented a rather inadequate sum. According to Andrew Hacker, a three-person family living on $235 a week – the federally defined poverty threshold in 1995 – earned just enough to provide for subsistence in rural, but not urban, areas.[5] $25 000 a year, or $480 a week, was a more plausible estimate, he felt, of the minimum income a family would need to survive intact and open some opportunities to their children. One-third of all full-time jobs in America paid then less than $20 000 a year, and half of the jobs for male workers paid below $28 000, barely enough to provide a minimal standard of living for a family.[6]

While the United States has been the only advanced society in which productivity was steadily rising over the past two decades, the incomes of eight out of ten of its people 'have stagnated or fallen'.[7] Output per person of all non-farm workers in the private sector rose by 5 per cent between 1973 and 1995, while the real hourly earnings of production and other non-supervisory workers fell by 12 per cent.[8] The poorest fifth of the population saw their share of aggregate household income fall, from 1975 to 1995, from 4.4 per cent to only 3.7 per cent. And the share of the fourth quintile also fell (from 10.5 per cent to 9.1 per cent), as did that of the middle fifth (17.1 per cent to 15.2 per cent), and the second fifth's as well (from 24.8 per cent – their highest share ever over the 60 years from 1935 – to 23.3 per cent).[9] The large majority of the population were steadily, remorselessly losing out. On Hacker's figures, some 64 per cent of wage earners in the mid-1990s received incomes of less than $25 000 per annum.[10]

The terms of trade for the acquisition of social basics like housing and families were worsening too. In 1970 the price of an average new house had represented twice a young couple's income; towards the late 1990s it was four times that sum. In 1970, 66.3 per cent of Americans lived in detached single-unit homes, but by 1990 only 59 per cent did so; those living in trailers or mobile homes had more than doubled over the time to 7.2 per cent. Car prices, in the land of the automobile, had risen too – a new one was 38 per cent of a new couple's income in 1970, but with in-built high-tech refinements it required about a 50 per cent outlay two decades later.[11] According to Hacker, 'the chief accommodation' that most workers have made to a reliance on incomes of $21 000 or less per annum is to 'postpone marriage and

having children' – raising them had become to be seen as 'too expensive'.[12] No advanced country had a weaker system of child-care; the
poor were left with 'family daycare', notes Kuttner, taking in each
other's children; a sick child easily meant a job crisis. Health had got
scarcer too. More than 70 per cent of Americans had access to health
insurance through their jobs at the start of the 1990s, but only about
61 per cent did so at its end.[13]

Not all of course were worse off. While the vast majority were getting
poorer, a small minority in this highly productive society were getting
markedly richer. The household income of the top or best-off fifth had
risen, 1975 to 1995, from 43.2 per cent to 48.7 per cent. Better-off still
were those within the top 5 per cent of households, whose income share
had gone up from 15.9 per cent to 21 per cent. At the very top there was
both room and great riches. About 68 000 families, near the end of the
1990s, had incomes of $1 million a year, five times as many as in 1979
(inflation adjusted for).[14] Moreover, while there were 13 billionaires in
America in 1982, there were 170 of them in the late 1990s.[15]

Hacker's 68 000 families included, in 1995, some 2500 corporate
chiefs, 1500 men and women in Wall Street securities firms, and
smaller numbers of lawyers, athletes, film stars and a few physicians.
Of these, 'Wall Street money managers' and certain chief executive officers (CEOs), had done extremely well; in the early 1980s they had each
obtained as much as $6 or $7 million annually. By the late 1980s and
early 1990s, some were acquiring $100 million and eventually $1 billion in a single year. One such was George Soros who made $1.5 billion
in 1995. A single year also saw Michael Eisner, chairman of the Walt
Disney company, paid $203 million;[16] another, 1997, brought him
remunerations worth $400 million.[17]

At the end of the 1990s the good fortunes of the 2.7 million people
who by then comprised the richest 1 per cent of American households
were such that their total after-tax income was the same as that
received by the 100 million people with the lowest incomes combined.
The topmost group controlled 13 per cent of after-tax income, owned
39 per cent of national wealth, and half of all stockmarket shares. The
net worth of Bill Gates alone was equal to that of the bottom 40 per
cent of the population. Wealth by then was 'more concentrated among
the top 1 per cent and top 20 per cent of American households than at
any time since the Depression'.[18] The share of total income received by
the upper quintile reached 49.2 per cent in 1998.[19]

The inequalities accompanying the acquisition of this great wealth
are huge; when Eisner acquired his $203 million, the state of Texas

provided an annual welfare stipend to a mother with two children of $2130. The inequalities are also worsening. The pay-cheques of corporate chairmen in 1975 were 40 times larger than that of a typical worker, but in 1995 the same differential had reached 190.[20] Estimates of inequalities differ in details. Another found that the average CEO of a *'Fortune* 500' company earned 41 time more than a factory worker in 1960, but gained 157 times as much in 1995. Figures provided by trade unionists showed that the average manager obtained 326 times more than the average factory worker near the end of the 1990s, while the same ratio had been only 44:1 in the 1960s.[21] An 'overclass' had arisen, and the gap between rich and poor in the American paradise was matching Brazilian levels.[22]

Between 1995 and 1997 the income received by the poorest fifth of families fell by an average of nearly 7 per cent or $580 per family. Among the very poorest single-mother families the drop was even greater; the bottom 10 per cent saw their incomes fall by almost 15 per cent over this time. Their losses were partly due to lower incomes, but most were caused by a big cut in government means-tested assistance in the form of food stamps and housing subsidies. President Bill Clinton signed the 1996 'welfare reform' bill into law despite professional advice that a million more children would be impoverished in consequence.[23] The number of poor children getting food stamps, for instance, dropped by 18 percentage points, 1995–97.[24] Near the end of the 1990s, at least 10 per cent of households in 18 states were actually hungry, or without access to adequate food; in New Mexico, 15.1 per cent of households were either hungry or threatened with hunger.[25]

The meaning and significance of the figures was not in question. Among the world's advanced capitalist countries, the United States had 'the most glaring income gaps'.[26] Britain, too, in the 1990s was a 'far more unequal society than 20 years ago', and the country had been divided into 'a handful of economic "giants" in a sea of poverty-stricken "dwarves"'.[27] But other comparable capitalist countries were markedly different from the United States and the 'Anglo-American model' it shared with Britain. In Japan, the ratio between a CEO's earnings and those of a factory worker – as with the above – was 17:1.[28] The top quintile of income earners in capitalist South Korea received only six times what the bottom fifth obtained. On an index of income inequality in 14 largely European and North American countries, Finland was first – the most equitable – Sweden was second, and the United States was ranked 14th. The United States was the worst for double, cumulative reasons: as Hacker says, 'partly because its rich receive more than their counterparts in other countries, and mostly because those who are poor get so much less'.[29]

Inequalities are not deep and deepening in the United States because of a capitalist 'hidden hand'; Finland, Sweden and Japan, for example, were both capitalist and democratic, and newly-industrialized South Korea was democratizing. Specific policies were chosen and implemented by American corporate and political elites to bring Simon Head's 'new ruthless economy' into being. Hacker points to 'the [underlying] structure and the culture of the nation's economy', and to tax-breaks granted to the very wealthy near the beginning of the Reagan presidency.[30] Head notes that a 'huge transfer of wealth from lower skilled, middle class American workers to the owners of capital assets and to a new technological [elite]' had occurred.[31] John Gray identifies contemporary American capitalism as characterized by 'hire-and-fire', 'slash-and-burn', and 'winner-take-all' values and techniques.[32]

Widespread deregulation has been followed, outsourcing (of supplies, services and production processes) and downsizing strongly emphasized. Outsourcing tends to have the effect, according to Head, of lowering the skills-level of a firm's core workforce, reducing their wages and undermining trade union organization.[33] Downsizing is most obviously directed towards taking jobs and wages from that 80 per cent of the American population – the creation of 'disposable work and disposable workers'.[34] Estimates of the numbers of American workers who have been downsized, from 1980 to 1995, according to Sennett, vary from a low count of 13 million to as high as 39 million.[35] IBM had practiced a paternal capitalism with lifetime employment and loyalty between employer and employees into the 1980s, but a newly recruited chief executive slashed the workforce from 406 000 in 1986 to 219 000 in 1994.[36] In the first-half of 1993 alone, a third of its employees were sacked in three plants in New York, and the company downsized operations wherever possible; 'corporate loyalty', declared a management consultant quoted by Sennett, '[was] dead'. A 'climate of fear', in the words of an executive, was generated during the same process at AT&T, when 40 000 jobs were precipitously cut.[37]

Downsizing is a key element in American corporate reengineering, and it has, Sennett states, 'a direct connection to growing inequality'. Only a minority of redundant middle-aged workers, he notes, found new jobs at the same or higher wages.[38] It also has had the effect of transferring a large part of what was saved in wages and salaries to the corporate chiefs. The CEOs of the 22 biggest downsizing American firms in 1995 saw the combined value of their share options upsized by

$36.6 million on the day their layoffs were announced.[39] Dunlap, the CEO of the Sunbeam Corporation, became known through the mid-1990s as Chain-Saw Al for the way 'he downsized thousands of workers while earning millions of dollars for himself'.[40]

Downsizing and outsourcing were the newest supplementations to existing legal mechanisms that discriminated against the worker-losers. Lazare notes that entire categories of workers, often the most vulnerable and exploited, are effectively barred from unionizing. Even in the 1990s, thousands of workers were still fired each year in the United States for endeavouring to form trade unions.[41]

Deregulation and globalization were broad reasons for the stagnation or fall of most Americans' incomes and economic prospects. The induced decline of labour unions was another and, according to Finnegan, the associated growth of a low-wage service sector was a third. Political decision-making had influenced all three. It is, he affirms, 'governments that decide to regulate' or deregulate, 'to accommodate capital rather than labour, to tax one constituency and not another'. Inequality and poverty in the United States 'is a matter of political economy, of deciding how wealth will be distributed'. In the world's richest country, scarcity has no longer anything to do with it.[42]

American liberal democracy

The ruthless economy is contained within what Abraham Eisenstadt accurately defines as 'the paradigmatic liberal polity'.[43] Liberal democracy is essentially a system which is emphatically value-free. It aimed, at its origins in the first great wave of democratization when socialism and social democracy were on the agenda in Europe, at incorporating the masses into politics, as Weber pertinently put it, in an orderly way – not through 'irrational', participatory interventions like demonstrations and strike action, but in voting for competing elites in periodic elections.[44] The old democratic ideals of justice and equality were shorn-off as dangerously ideological, while Lockean beliefs in the rights of individual property ownership remained. The former were in any case irrelevant to what democracy represented in Schumpeter's influential terms, simply a 'political method', an 'institutional arrangement', for determining the governors.[45] Weber's 'law of the small number' readily prevailed.[46] Elitism accompanied by popular passivity, as Lipset clearly observed, distinctively characterized the main tendencies within the liberal form of democracy.[47]

American democracy, elitist, non-activist, value-free, is the extreme form of the liberal democratic variant.[48] Its law is 'essentially the law of property relations',[49] and its 'civil servants, judges, and politicians' have at times 'regarded the economy as an object for extortion'.[50] While universal suffrage for white males was introduced early in the western states, 'the majority of the [country's] population did not place any value on an honest administration, or... never collectively manifested this'.[51]

Consistent with the winner-take-all principle, the society 'prizes winners and despises losers'.[52] Injustice easily results. When most countries in the European Union imprison fewer than 100 persons per 100 000 inhabitants, the United States incarcerates more than six times this number, rivalling at the end of the 1990s only Russia for the world's highest imprisonment rate.[53] America's rate of incarceration in 1994 was 14 times greater than Japan's, and was rapidly growing. The numbers of people locked up near the end of the 1990s was three times greater than the total of 1980; by mid-1995, an estimated 1.1 million people were in jail, and by 2000 the prison population reached two million.[54] Bondage in America has historically embraced a wide range of unfree people, variously, according to Scott Christianson, slaves, indentured servants, bonded labourers and prisoners; as such, he notes, it has played a central if unrecognized role in building the Republic throughout its history. The motives of profit and of punishment mutually propelled this process, and popular support for mass incarceration over the centuries has been strong and constant.[55]

In 1993 the Governor of Illinois announced a 'sweepstakes', with the winner to become the site for the state's newest and harshest prison, a place of punishment for convicts who assaulted guards in other facilities, for prison gang members responsible for the death of other inmates, and for men who repeatedly tried to escape. Thirty-four communities entered the race, with the residents of the small and declining town of Tamms enthusiastically welcoming the judges with school music groups and fire-truck cavalcades. 'Everyone pulled together', it was reported, with the local high-school students sending handwritten letters to the director of corrections pleading that he choose their town. No one doubted that this maximum-security prison – a 'supermax' – would constitute the rebirth of their town.[56]

America's rate of violent crime is extremely high,[57] and punishment is more than proportionate. America alone in the Western world 'enthusiastically endorses the death penalty'.[58] It is currently executing people, says Lazare, at the rate of one every five days,[59] at an average cost, given the lengthy appeals process, of $2.5 million per execution.[60] It is one of only six countries which enforces the death penalty for crimes committed under the age of 18 years.[61] American prisons are extraordinarily barbaric places 'where homosexual rape and sex slavery are considered by the authorities and a complaisant public to be appropriate, if unregulated punishment'.[62] On top of the existing motivations of profit and punishment, the 1990s, says Gray, saw recourse 'to a policy of mass imprisonment as a surrogate for the controls of communities which unregulated market forces have weakened or destroyed'.[63]

Certain categories of prisons, exemplified by the super-max, have 'the avowed goal of harming people', according to Jean Maclean Snyder of the MacArthur Justice Centre at the University of Chicago. Inmates at Tamms are kept in solitary cells, measuring 8 feet by 10 feet, into which their food is injected through a slot in the door three times a day. Individual prisoners might be allowed, alone, into bare concrete exercise pens for at most one hour per day. A very low convict–guard ratio of two to one at Tamms is supplemented by high-tech security. Visitors are rare, and phone calls forbidden. Prisoners are 'kept from any human contact', in effect, says Bergner, 'safely entombed'. The prison's seminal idea, he believes, is 'absolute isolation'.[64]

Snyder says that the super-max inflicts cruel and unusual punishment on the many prisoners who arrive with serious mental illnesses and on those who develop psychiatric problems due to the intense isolation. About 10 to 20 per cent of inmates, she estimates, are too mentally ill to control their actions under the oppressive conditions; self-mutilations and attempted suicides occur under the complacent observation of the guards. The prison responds to these and other offences with the denial of normal food, the removal of the prisoner's clothes and of his mattress. Those who refuse to conform are left naked in their concrete cell with only their hands to eat with day after day. Not a single prisoner, in the 18 months since the super-max opened, managed to work his way out and back to a regular prison.[65] 'Howling', audible outside, 'begins most afternoons around three. The outbursts are constant and guttural, then sporadic, fading. If there are words, they are impossible to make out.' The town's residents claim to have become accustomed to it, but admit that it disturbs the first-time visitor. Bergner states that the building and running of a super-max represents an 'extraordinary expense'. Nevertheless, some 20 were built nationally during the 1990s.[66]

Mass, totalitarian imprisonment is backed up by intense policing targeted at the urban poor, especially the numerous black poor. The Street

Crimes Unit in New York tripled in size between 1992 and 1998, and its officers began to search people, 'preety much at random and often with little cause, on the streets, in housing estates and in apartment blocks'. Young black men were 'constantly frisked'. Over the two years from 1997, the Unit searched 45 000 people and arrested 9500 of them. The killing of the West African, Amadou Diallo in February 1999 when New York police burst into the foyer of his apartment building and shot him 19 times, was an incident in this programme of harassment and suppression.[67] The policy of so-called intolerance of crime and that of mass imprisonment necessarily reinforce each other.[68]

The militarization of policing – in tactics, weaponry and police mentality – was also rapid throughout the 1990s, especially as Congress and successive Presidents pursued their 'war on drugs'. The number of Special Weapons and Tactics (SWAT) teams grew steadily until, on the assessment of the criminologist Peter Kraska, 90 per cent of police departments in cities of more than 50 000 people had SWAT units. They are heavily armed paramilitary troops; SWAT personnel typically wear body armour, camouflage outfits, face masks and helmets. Their weapons are Beretta pistols, submachine guns, M-16 assault rifles, grenade-launchers and 12-round shotguns known to their users as 'street sweepers'. Some units possess armoured personnel carriers, and many have been trained by the army's special forces. Most are used in search of drugs and drug-dealers – police have the added incentive that they can often keep the cash and other assets confiscated in such raids.[69]

The nation's war on drugs might be more accurately understood as war on the users of drugs, especially those of the urban poor. Hitchens notes that the mere possession of cannabis can fetch a life sentence, and sentences for possession of crack cocaine, 'a poor people's drug', are 10 times harsher than those for possession of the powder cocaine 'consumed by the rich'.[70] Yet according to the code of the street, understood by poor urban blacks, 'slinging' dope is about 'as morally neutral as working behind a post-office counter'.[71]

SWAT units, according to a number of researchers, represent the routine use by police of heavy and totally disproportionate military force. There are supposedly no firm statistics on the numbers of shootings or killings by SWAT teams, but there was the Waco catastrophe in 1993 in which 80 people died and, for instance, the killing of a 64-year-old farm worker in Dinuba, California, when a SWAT team crashed through his front door supposedly looking for a stolen gun.[72] According to a study prepared by Jean Weber: 'These units are going into housing projects, into black neighbourhoods, as if they're hostile territory': Kraska reports that SWAT units are regularly deployed to serve drug warrants or for routine patrols of particular districts. Their use is growing, he affirms, not because of rising crime, or because there is any evidence that they reduce it, but because the police want such units and tactics – many police, he says, from direct observation, find the paramilitary experience, at home in the towns and cities of America 'intoxicating'.[73]

Imprisonment in the United States not only functions to contain and punish, but also serves to deprive weak and vulnerable people of their political rights and voice. In mid-1994, says Christianson, nearly 7 per cent of all black men nationwide were imprisoned. In New York State simultaneously nearly one in four young black men were under the control of the criminal justice system. Because incarcerated persons were universally prevented from voting, and the laws in 13 of the most populous states stripped felons of the vote, a disproportionately large share of African-American men were, by implication, disenfranchised.[74] Other estimates deepen and extend the political disempowerment. In total, 14 states ban convicted felons from voting for life; 29 ban them while on probation; and 32 ban them while on parole. The result was that some 3.9 million Americans, at the end of the 1990s, were temporarily or permanently disenfranchised, of whom 1.4 million were black men.[75]

Young says that the American criminal justice system expanded in the 1990s to an 'unprecedented level', focused with an 'unparalleled intensity' on the underclasses of the ghettos.[76] Police regularly sweep through poor neighbourhoods stopping and searching whomever they like; yet the Supreme Court, David Cole observed, has repeatedly refused to require the police to advise people of their constitutional right to refuse to submit to an unlawful search.[77] The legal representation offered to the poor is also grossly inadequate.[78] These and the associated imprisonment practices are, for Cole, systemic parts of American liberalism. Constitutional protections cherished by the majority barely exist for most poor and black people. Furthermore, it is only by denying basic rights to poor and black Americans that prosperous whites can enjoy the comprehensive constitutional protections which are supposedly available to all. If everyone enjoyed the same legal protections against search, seizure and arrest, the police would find it difficult or impossible to do their job.[79]

The economic losers are treated with scarcely greater concern. Experts of corporate reengineering, such as Michael Hammer and James Champy, write with frankness about the 'abject terror' and the 'total inner panic' of workers about to learn of their redundancy. But they nowhere recognize that employees have interests which should be subject to negotiation and compromise. Nor do they write of pay and, if it is discussed, says Head, it is in isolated, bilateral encounters with the employer where the latter 'generally has the upper hand'.[80]

Inequitable and unjust as this situation is, it is not the worst of it in liberal capitalist America. 'What all black kids do know, in their bones', according to Finnegan's experience, 'is that racial inequality has always been the American rule, and that for as long as they *can* remember, life for the poor has been getting harder'.[81] The situation of the young Hispanic underclass is not so different, and he writes of 'the dark spiral of downward mobility, of children growing up [today] to find themselves worse off than their parents'.[82] Youth in general are being hard hit. 'Society requires both parents to work', he quotes Pearl, one of his informants, as saying. 'Single parents also have to work. So kids are left to raise themselves...There's no one to teach them how to care...how to *live*. So they form these [gangs] and, right or wrong, these are their families'.[83] Finnegan also emphasizes 'the official and political neglect of children, particularly poor children', which includes a 'brutal squeeze on public school funding in much of the country', most spectacularly in large and rich California.[84] Recent surveys indicate, he says, that American society is developing a fear and loathing for young people generally. Finnegan lived closely with poor white, Hispanic and black youth across the country, and he says that 'kids sense that class lines in America are hardening'.[85]

Capitalist America, for Adam Przeworski, is 'an inhumane society', interlinked closely with its paradigmatic liberalism.[86] Its highest inequalities and huge prison populations are supported by one of the lowest voter participation rates in the world. 'Barely a third of [eligible] voters turnout for most elections.'[87] The Great Communicator Ronald Reagan, for example, received votes from only 28 per cent of those eligible in 1980, and Bill Clinton entered the White House in 1992 with 24.5 per cent of the electorate supporting him. The Republicans led by Newt Gingrich won an historic mid-term Congressional victory in 1994 with 39 million voters behind them, 35 million voting Democrat, and with another 112 million eligible Americans staying home.[88]

The political influence of wealth in circumstances of high inequalities and low popular participation easily becomes dominant and decisive. In the 1998 election cycle: 'the candidate who outspent his opponent emerged victorious in 95 per cent of House [of Representatives] races and 94 per cent of Senate races. In more than 60 per cent of House districts, the winner outspent the loser by 10 to 1.'[89] A majority of today's Senators, observes Lind, are millionaires.[90] In the 1998 congressional elections, spending on television advertising reached a high of $531.9 million, and voter turnout was 36 per cent.

These two aspects of American liberalism are not unconnected. Most TV commercials were designed to turn voters against a candidate, not to persuade voters or to discuss issues seriously. Each of the major parties aimed at discouraging the other's voters from going to the polls, and 'prefer[red] to leave the race to the hard-core partisans on both sides'. Voters, and especially the young, see access to power being sold to the richest interest groups, and conclude that their single vote is worthless; 18 to 26-year-olds in particular 'do not believe that Washington works for them'.[91] It is hardly intended to do so. Politicians 'spend their lives dialling for dollars', concentrating on 'the 100 000 or so people who give virtually all the money and the smaller group who have their telephone numbers'. Political candidates spend around a third of their time 'trying to raise money from rich people'. Well-funded groups like the National Rifle Association, the Christian Coalition or the American Association of Retired Persons have influence.[92] Big corporations have power.[93]

Manipulative elites and nihilistic liberalism

The essence of American politics, according to Hitchens and Huey Long, is

> the manipulation of populism by elitism. That elite is most successful which can … present itself as most 'in touch' with popular concerns; can anticipate the tides and pulses of opinion; can, in short, be the least apparently 'elitist'.[94]

The New Democratic presidency of Bill Clinton, 1992–2000, exemplifies the perfection of this tendency, especially in his hallmark strategy of 'triangulation' – the achievement of a balance between those who support you, and those whom you support – and his concentration on 'transactionalism' or the making of deals.[95] The scuppering of health insurance proposals through 1993, the 1996 pre-election 'welfare reforms', and the gay-baiting Defence of Marriage Act were designed both to garner support from Republicans and to commandeer their issues. The Democratic party was simultaneously guaranteed, as David Frum put it, control over the executive branch, and it condoned, in return, the President's campaign-funding abuses and his perjury; the liberal left 'swallows the soft promises of Clinton', and the right 'demands, and gets, hard guarantees'.[96]

As Clinton beat a steady retreat from the progressive positions of predecessors like Roosevelt, deception and manipulation were constantly utilized. The polling business, says Hitchens, is 'the essential weapon in the mastery of populism by the elite'. It provides them with an idea of what the mob is thinking, and of how that thinking might be changed, or 'shaped', allowing for 'fine callibration' and for 'capsules of "message" to be prescribed for variant communities'.[97] Donors provided much of the necessary funds. Some 80 major fund-raisers and donors were invited into the historically hallowed rooms of the White House – the Oval Office, the Lincoln and Roosevelt rooms, the Map room – as either rewards or inducements, and asked for money. Steven Grossman, president of the Massachusetts Envelope Company and of the America–Israel Public Affairs Committee, for one, contributed at least $400 000 to the Democratic party and to Clinton's election campaigns.[98]

A high-priced banquet at the Hay-Adams Hotel, in February 1996, saw President Clinton thanking his benefactors and boastfully describing the manipulative techniques their funds facilitated:

> In the last quarter of last year … we spent about $1 million per week to advertise our point of view to somewhere between 26 and 42 per cent of the American electorate … The lead that I enjoy today in public opinion polls is about one-third due to that advertising … I cannot overstate to you the impact that these paid ads have had.[99]

Dick Morris declared that every word in such advertisements was closely supervised by Clinton, and recorded his delight, as Hitchens tells it, at 'finding a way through the legally imposed spending limits', 'dumping a fortune into early TV spots', and 'stealing the Republican's clothes'. Morris bought a commanding lead in the polls, and obtained 'his personal cut of the take amounting to almost $1.5 million' during 1995–96. The Clinton elite, moreover, was consistently able to rely upon Republican understanding and discretion when it came to problems with campaign contributions.[100]

The manipulation and the abuse of public office reached its probable depths regarding the President's relations with Gennifer Flowers, Paula Jones, Kathleen Willey and Monica Lewinsky; the attempted portrayal of Jones as someone with the greed and scruples of 'trailer trash', and of Lewinsky as 'a stalker', the latter trick only undermined when the FBI confirmed in August 1998 that her blue dress was stained with the

President's semen. President Clinton lied under oath in a civil disposition, to a criminal grand jury, to the people, and to the Congress.[101] As the evidence of abuse and turpitude built up, Clinton endeavoured, rather successfully, to promote liberal support from within his own constituency with the claim that what was at issue was not his own deep wrongdoing but a 'right-wing conspiracy'.

Two other important ploys were attempted, according to Hitchens. 'The privacy defence' claimed that his consensual relations with Lewinsky, a very young and highly impressionable person employed in his own office, was of concern alone to himself and herself, and to his wife and daughter; if the latter did not condemn him, no one else could.[102] This touched on the nihilism within contemporary American liberalism, and the elevation of an amoral tolerance.[103] The 'popularity defence' had been used by Ronald Reagan, but it was at the core of triangulation. Clinton's populism always suggested to the people that he was one of them; the powerful on a par with the powerless, the ultimate elitist con, feasible only in a non-participatory democracy. When President Clinton lied and cheated, therefore, he was merely fallible and human as the people were too; critics who pointed to his actual crimes were moralistic and sanctimonious. His claims were strengthened by polling which consistently accorded him an approval rating of some 60 per cent. With popular opposition to his impeachment even stronger,[104] the actual process was 'amputated and perfunctory'. Abuse of office, and lying under oath by a president were condoned by the people and the Senate. The 'demeaning of the presidency [was] considerable', and probably unended.[105]

Clinton eventually paid Paula Jones $850 000,[106] and in April 1999, federal Judge Susan Wright in Arkansas cited the President for contempt of court and found him guilty of wilfully providing false testimony under oath in 1998 when he denied a sexual relationship with Lewinsky. She declared that he had obstructed justice, that he had in fact 'undermined the integrity of the judicial system'.[107] Judge Wright's decision found the President guilty of some of the original charges in the failed impeachment. Clearer light emerges on what the Clinton presidency represented: the demeaning of the highest elective office; the elevation of manipulative elites over atomistic masses; and the opening of opportunities to future crooked presidents.[108]

Poverty and inequalities are not easily discussed in such a non-functioning democracy. Popular discontent, notes Gray, is mainly expressed in movements on the fringes of political life, that is, beyond the purview of the established elites. For Merrill Lynch, Francis

Fukuyama and many others, the free market is synonymous with the American paradise and its liberal polity. The huge costs of the free market, widening and deepening though they are, are 'taboo subjects' in the national discourse.[109] Citizenship, it might be thought, is about as vibrant in contemporary American liberalism as it is in the Botswana variant. The techniques of elite domination differ, but not the subordination of the weak and powerless.

Regulated/'stakeholder' capitalism and social democracy

Though American triumphalism suggests otherwise, there are different forms of capitalism as there are historically different democracies. These differ from the American model significantly, not least on the issues of the ends of the capitalist endeavour, the role of the state, and on who participates in corporate policy-making. 'Stakeholder' (unlike shareholder) capitalism is a generic shorthand term which embraces distinct though overlapping models – chiefly Britain's postwar welfare state, Scandinavian social democracy, the German social market, and the East Asian interventionist strategy. Some of what these have in common has been summarized as follows:

> What goes under the name of capitalism varies a lot from country to country, even among rich economies. A big difference is in attitudes to public companies; in particular, in views about their duties and responsibilities beyond their obvious objective of producing goods and services... In Japan and much of continental Europe... firms often accept broader obligations that balance the interests of shareholders against those of other 'stakeholders', notably employees, but including also suppliers, customers, and the wider 'community'.[110]

Sennett refers to the 'Rhine model', in existence in the Netherlands, France and Germany for more than a century, where trade unions and management share corporate power, and the state provides pensions, education and health benefits.[111]

Much of the distinctiveness of European social democracy was in the breadth of its aims and aspirations. Its core demands in Germany in 1891 were the democratization of society, a welfare state, and regulation of the labour market.[112] The Social Democratic Party in Sweden through the 1930s laid the foundations for the postwar West European model of social democracy – the compromise between labour and capital, as Sassoon describes it, and the establishment of successful institutional structures for permanent negotiations between employers, trade unions and government on labour and social policies.[113] What was being attempted was the melding together of what liberalism and liberal democracy separates and frees – the economic and the political dimensions of society; the regulation of capitalism in the interests of a more effective democracy and of the poor. British Labour's historic mandate in 1945, says Sassoon, was to introduce a fairer society where excessive inequalities would be removed, while those that persisted would not deprive anyone of basic social rights such as employment, health and education.[114]

In 1938 in Britain, the top 10 per cent of the population had received 34.4 per cent of all post-tax income, while by 1949, partly as a result of wartime egalitarianism and partly through Labour's priorities, this ratio had been reduced to 27.1 per cent. Sassoon stresses that what the social democratic welfare state promoted was an equality of the highest standards, not one of minimal needs.[115] From around 1945 to 1975, the European form of capitalism afforded social democracy a key role. With growth and full employment, a large proportion of the surplus produced was allocated by political means, not by market forces, to health, education, public transport, child-care and old-age protection. These measures served to stabilize capitalism and, he adds, enabled acceptance of regulation on minimum wages, paid holidays and similar provisions which legislation, backed by trade union demands, imposed.[116]

The German social market, social democracy, and the East Asian model today have different socio-political arrangements for accommodating the interests of CEOs and shareholders with those, most notably, of workers, but the outcomes of such participative and consultative processes are distinctively different from America.

Inequalities of income, as noted already, are unusually low in Japan, Taiwan and South Korea, and Sweden has the second most equitable income distribution on Hacker's index. On data presented by Przeworski, the percentage of people in poverty after taxes and transfers, in the late 1980s, in Norway was 4.8; in Sweden 5.0; while in Britain it was then 12.1; and in the United States it was 16.9.[117] The German social market, states Gray, 'enfranchises stakeholders – employees, local communities, bankers, sometimes suppliers and customers – in corporate governance'. Workers in firms with over 800 employees were assured of representation on supervisory boards; its capitalism accorded a lower weight to share values than do American and British free-market economies. When workers lose their jobs, as they now do, they receive about two-thirds of their working incomes in unemployment benefits (cf. about one-third in Britain, even less in America). He quotes the chairman of the leading electronics firm Siemens, Heinrich von Pierer, once saying: 'The hire and fire principle does not exist here and I never want it to'.[118] The state, in the German model, has the constitutional obligation to assist in reducing social inequalities, thus creating a more just social order. State social policy, adds Mahnkopf, supports a productivity pact of labour and capital, particularly in terms of pensions, health and humane working conditions.[119]

Yet the values and institutions of stakeholder capitalism, in Europe and East Asia, are now under serious threat from the slash-and-burn, hire-and-fire, winner-take-all techniques emanating from the United States: Global flexible capitalism, notes Gray, 'is an American project'. Social democracy and social market capitalism 'are inherently incompatible', he asserts, with unrestricted global free trade. For full employment and decent wages, a government needs to develop socio-economic policies specifically designed for that end;[120] as the welfare state's experience has indicated. Growth reduces poverty only if the pattern of that growth is from the outset intended to benefit the poor, either directly through increased employment and incomes, or indirectly through taxation and the good social services which they provide.[121] Earlier free-market capitalism did not foster social justice,[122] and unregulated globalization fiercely opposes it.

Ruthless capitalism on a global scale threatens the institutions and values of the Rhine systems, but they survive where corporations, the state and a functioning democracy wants them to. In the Netherlands in 1998 'employers, trade unions and government cooperated closely'. Unemployment was a relatively low 5.5 per cent – though with the proportion of part-time workers twice that of Germany's – and observers spoke of a 'Dutch miracle' characterized by both 'growth and social cohesion'.[123] When Prime Minister Goran Persson introduced his budget in September 1999, he promised that 'Sweden will consolidate its position as a leading welfare nation'. The economy was emerging from a long period of sluggishness into an apparently strong transformation. Industries were being extensively deregulated and new high-technology companies established, while the government continued to finance health, education and many social services. Growth was around 3.4 per cent, and was forecast to reach 3.9 per cent in 2000, and unemployment was down to 5.4 per cent in February of that year.

Regulated capitalism survives where people are unattracted by gross inequalities in incomes, and where they possess the organizational and institutional means to act on their preferences. The decline of trade unions and the absence of collective bargaining arrangements facilitated the rise of the flexible, ruthless capitalism in the United States, and their retention supports social democracy and regulated capitalism in Europe.[124] Three of the oldest systems, Germany, France and the Netherlands, have had falling unionization, but rising coverage of collective-bargaining arrangements nonetheless. In other European countries, Sweden, Finland and Spain, Freeman reports, both unionization and collective bargaining have increased in scope. The Rhine model and social democracy are more egalitarian, not necessarily less productive than the flexible Anglo-American system, and the engulfment of the former by the latter is not an inevitability.[125]

The American spectre

America's flexible capitalism produces 'disposable work and disposable workers', a process directly connected to the acquisition of immense wealth by the few. Amidst inequalities that are uniquely high in the advanced capitalist world, and of political participation which is similarly low, American liberalism is notable for the predominant influence of wealth and the wealthy. Voting is largely for the 'hard-core partisans' of the two established parties, and actual dissent is chiefly a fringe activity. The demolition of jobs and working lives under extensive downsizing has led, as Sennett argues, to the destruction of trust, loyalty and commitment not only in corporate workplaces, but in human relations extensively. Acceptance of the economic slogan 'no long term', in society and the family, means 'keep moving', no commitment, and no sacrifices to or for each other[126] – ultimately an erosion of morality that seems evident in many spheres: in the multiple injustices to which the poor and youth are subjected; in that 'dark downward spiral' on which many of them are embarked; in the inbuilt distortions of the criminal justice system; in the constant amoral manipulations of the populist political elites; and in the inability of the passive people to come to grips with the reality of elite domination, specifically, with the outstanding abuses perpetrated by President Clinton.[127]

This is the advanced form, the epitome, of liberal capitalist democracy. It represents itself as the future for other capitalist democracies. The long-established social and stakeholder democracies can only hope to defend their notably more egalitarian and fairer systems today through a broad-based defence and adjustment of their policies and programmes. Germany's Rhine model, Mahnkopf says, 'has proved very successful to date'; nevertheless, its survival, partly through new notions of 'innovation competition', was not guaranteed.[128] South Africa is in a weaker position internationally than Germany or Sweden, its democracy is weakening under pressure from a predominant ruling elite, and that elite seems unaware of or unconcerned with what advanced liberal capitalism represents. They speak easily of the opportunities supposedly offered, but seem dangerously complacent about the inequalities and injustices it entails. But the country also possesses a strong trade union movement, and its rate of unionization, 1985–95, was one of the highest in the world.[129]

Part III
South Africa

Prelude to South Africa

The following three chapters focuses on the elite–mass dichotomy in the African National Congress and in South African politics as the country moved towards majoritarian rule and the leading nationalist party gained political predominance. The theme throughout is of a relatively small elite acquiring and endeavouring to extend power, under what has been, since 1994, liberal democratic conditions. The bulk of the final chapter is on the same process from the opposite, the bottom-up, side when, in the 1970s and 1980s, a large, popular, democratic movement developed in opposition to state power and elite domination.

This does not purport to be a general political history of contemporary South Africa. Things that would be important within that broad account are excluded here – the achievement, for example, of a rights-based constitution which rejects the death penalty, and entrenches the rights of gays and lesbians. Notable gains for gender equality in politics and government since 1994 are unmentioned,[1] and the integrity of the imprisoned Nelson Mandela is neglected party because it is self-evidence and is attested to elsewhere. The work of the Truth and Reconciliation Commission, one of the highlights of post-apartheid politics, is considered in specific areas only, chiefly as light was cast upon elitist privilege, presumptions and power. The cruelties and injustices of apartheid, furthermore, are not dwelt upon, since it is the new South Africa which is under examination – not just that or President Mandela in and after 1994 – but as what was ushered in by the trade unions, students, and civil society from the early 1970s. *This* new South Africa – lower-case 'n' – takes the priority, because it bore and still bears closely upon the future of the country. It was not only the antithesis of apartheid but also, in its aspirations and capacities, of present-day elitism.

Note

1. Around 1998, 24 per cent of seats in parliament, for instance, were held by women, placing South Africa sixth on a list of 37 countries in this regard. *The Economist*, 26 September 1998, quoting UN data.

4
Elitism's Place in the ANC

Elitism has a firm place historically, structurally and procedurally in the African National Congress (ANC), the country's leading nationalist party. In its formative years between the two world wars, the party leadership, according to McKinley, 'rejected organising amongst the mass of Africans'.[1] When a so-called national defiance campaign was embarked upon in the early 1950s, 'little effort was made' to mobilize the black urban working class, though they represented the most readily organized section of the people. A key aspect of the action, moreover, was for protesters to court arrest through public acts of civil disobedience, a step which many ordinary workers simply could not afford to emulate. The party leadership, he believes, 'recoiled from mass mobilisation'.[2]

Elitism also stemmed from the illegality imposed by the apartheid state, and the clandestine life which resulted. When the ANC's closely associated organization, the South African Communist Party (SACP) reformed underground in the early 1950s, a small group of people established a cell structure to provide secrecy and security. The party soon became less open and democratic, and dissent among a limited membership was discouraged;[3] leadership easily became out of touch with the masses and the realities facing them. Operation Mayibue saw Joe Slovo and Govan Mbeki promoting an elaborate, detailed plan for guerrilla war by 7000 men in four regional operational areas in South Africa. Non-existent weaponry referred to in their plans included 210 000 hand grenades and 48 000 anti-personnel mines. Further elaborations stated that a 40-foot-high furnace, a mid-sized factory and a workforce of 200 would be required to manufacture the arsenal. All this was 'embraced with fervour by most other members of the High Command', as Slovo and Mbeki proclaimed that 'the time for small thinking is over', and 'history leaves us no choice'.[4]

Black political resistance in South Africa had been 'crushed' by 1964, according to Bonner and Segal.[5] In the early 1970s the only functioning components of any ANC organizations were in exile, and these were consumed with factional fighting.[6] But the external presence soon after was vast, including thousands of Umkhonto weSizwe (MK) cadres in regional camps, an administrative headquarters in Lusaka, and a diplomatic presence in over 30 countries, with London as their hub.[7] Strategy focused upon an externally-generated armed struggle under such abstractions as 'arming the masses' and 'people's war', though the party had no internal structures with which to generate, let alone sustain, 'mass uprisings'.[8] Pretoria's response in the form of 'total war' and regional destabilization further promoted authoritarianism in the ANC, as MK endeavoured to root out all collaborationist cadres, real and imaginary, from its midst.

A security department, Mbokodo, 'the stone that crushes', interrogated suspected cadres in regional centres in Africa. An ANC paper, quoted by Shubin, declared: 'Our guiding principle must be that every new individual is suspect until proven innocent'.[9] Extreme measures readily occurred. When MK troops in Angola issued democratic demands in 1984, their protests were crushed, first by the Angolan Presidential Guard, then by public executions at Pango in northern Angola and the imprisonment and torture of their leaders.[10] Another detention centre was Quadro (or Quatro), where suspected MK personnel were placed in freight containers without ventilation: 'A place where if they give you bread, you think its cake. The whole cell ha[d] to share a cup of water.'[11] Leading ANC members could be swept into the net. In the mid-1980s, Pallo Jordan was arrested and held for six weeks in Lusaka, without being told why, then or later. He was on the left of the ANC and critical of authoritarian trends in the SACP.[12] A senior MK commander, Thami Zulu, was detained in the same place for 17 months, and died of poisoning just five days after his release in November 1989.[13]

Till well into the 1980s, the ANC struggled 'virtually in vain' to establish a political or military presence inside the country, while the exiled leadership remained divided over policy and dogged by favouritism, regionalism and tribalism.[14] The ANC in exile acted as a 'secretive, autocratic organisation'. Decisions were taken by a council and passed down the chain of command with little room for dissent.[15] Trewhela's judgement is sharper: the ANC in exile, 'especially in Africa', behaved 'like a one-party state. Dissent of any kind was not tolerated.'[16]

When change began to occur in South Africa, first as independent trade union action in the early 1970s, then as resistance to Pretoria from students and youth in the middle of the decade, and as popular democratization from the school, community and workplace up in the 1980s, it came independently of the ANC, and the exile group was incapable of a positive response. The mirage of armed insurrection represented the totality of its thinking. In 1984 Thabo Mbeki declared on Radio Freedom: 'We must destroy the enemy organs of government...render them ineffective and inoperative...In every locality and in all parts of the country, we must fight to ensure that we remove the enemy's organs of government.'[17] In London, Lusaka and elsewhere, Mbeki was aware that the Black Consciousness Movement (BCM) was beginning to radicalize young black men and women, and he perceived this, not as a creative harbinger, but as a potential undermining of the supposed vanguard role of the ANC. He started to identify the leadership of the new movement, working towards their incorporation into the established party.[18]

The formation of the United Democratic Front (UDF) in August 1983, was a path-breaking step in South African history and politics. It saw millions of ordinary people striving to improve and gain control over their living and working conditions in a process which combined protest with democratization. It was neither generated nor controlled by the ANC,[19] and it was barely understood by them either. It 'came as a shock to [Mbeki and] the rest of the ANC leadership'.[20] Organizational dominance and elite power and position seemed threatened. A 'tightly knit clique' had made all the ANC's decisions for more than 20 years, and they had 'no intention of letting their authority slip away'.[21]

The route of external armed struggle had promoted elitism and secrecy, while the domestic popular struggle of the 1980s was entirely opposite. Nelson Mandela was enabled to meet UDF leaders in the period between December 1988 and his release from prison in February 1990. But he was not at ease, Meredith believes, in their exuberant environment, where his independent leadership was under potential challenge. He possessed a 'strong authoritarian streak and a preference for taking action on his own responsibility, for dealing directly with other leaders'.[22] The UDF was a coalition of hundreds of community, youth, student groups and trade unions – it represented some 565 affiliated groups around 1984, and around 700, amounting to more than two million people, at its peak.[23] It developed a political process which was 'highly democratic and decentralised, based on constant contact and discussion...and collective decision-making.' It was a political mode 'entirely alien to the Lusaka exiles'.[24] Mandela's behaviour in talking to the government in 1989 was hugely debated in the UDF.

According to the Reverend Allan Boesak: 'People were worried, because they didn't know what Mandela was talking…about…He had not consulted, and there was no greater sin in the UDF.'[25] He came out of prison, according to Meredith, with his tendency towards 'aloofness' hardened, and he 'evaded intimacy'. He quickly became close again to the ANC's old guard.[26]

Talks and non-accountability

Negotiations with the National Party government of P.W. Botha and then F.W. De Klerk began in the mid-1980s, and were characterized by elitism and secrecy. Nelson Mandela in prison, and Thabo Mbeki in various towns and cities, initiated and led this process. Mandela, according to Waldmeir, 'kept his Lusaka colleagues in the dark about everything', and gave 'no details of the hundreds of hours of talks' which went on in Cape Town, for instance, around 1986. He himself 'had to ask [Justice Minister Kobie] Coetsee for details of Mbeki's 1986 meeting with Pieter de Lange' in New York. Mbeki had been engaged with Pretoria through intermediaries since a Quaker professor, Hendrik van der Merwe, visited him in Lusaka in September 1984. Over the next three years he had spoken to 'cavalcades' of white South Africans, 'almost continuously'. He had set out to win the friendship of these influential, sometimes powerful men and, as a result, Gevisser adds, understood, as others in the ANC leadership could not, how discredited apartheid was becoming in the eyes of its very upholders. He knew that the enemy was ready to talk.[27]

Mbeki led about a dozen meetings between ANC officials and members of the Afrikaner elite near Bath, between late 1987 and mid-1990, and only 'the most senior' of ANC leaders were informed of these talks.[28] They had the support of President Oliver Tambo, but they were not accountable to the party's representative bodies, the National Executive Committee (NEC) and National Working Committee (NWC). Mbeki's contribution, Gevisser generously suggests, was that he 'nudged the ANC away' from its long and sterile fixation on armed struggle; but he reinforced its tendencies towards secrecy, duplicity and non-accountability while engaged in this supposed nudging. Joe Slovo, Chris Hani and Pallo Jordan were among his critics, on the specific grounds, Gevisser states, that it could have been done differently. 'It's not that we were opposed to the fact that Thabo was talking to the enemy', one of them said, 'it's that we were opposed to the fact that he was *not* talking to us!'[29] As Mandela, too, did not consult the UDF in Cape Town in late 1988–89.[30]

Gevisser observes that Thabo Mbeki had always been earmarked for senior leadership in the ANC. By the 1980s he was already on the SACP's central committee and the NEC when he became head of the ANC's department of international affairs, and Oliver Tambo appointed him as his political secretary, as his de facto proxy. He had arisen along 'two parallel routes': alongside Oliver Tambo, and in the SACP, which was simultaneously the perceived intellectual and organizational vanguard of the liberation movement in exile, the commander of MK, and the conduit for the financial and other support emanating from the Soviet Union and its East Bloc allies.[31] Mbeki actively utilized both these distinct paths to power throughout the 1980s. The capacities he earlier utilized, on Trewhela's recollection, were a 'strict, unquestioning Stalinism combined with serious attention to organization'.[32] As he was talking with leading Afrikaners, acquiring new friendships and trust[33] and insight into their thinking, he was still propagating, for example at the Seventh Congress of the SACP in Havana in 1989, mass insurrection. After 1990, Mbeki made the decision, Gevisser says, to let his SACP membership lapse – it went back to 1962 – and he has not spoken publicly about his leadership role in the party.[34]

At the ANC's national conference in Durban in July 1991, Nelson Mandela replaced his ailing friend Tambo as president, but a former UDF leader, Patrick Terror Lekota, strongly criticized Mandela for his tendency to try to impose his will on the party's decision-making, and received a 'huge cheer' in so doing.[35] Cyril Ramaphosa was a former student activist who had built up the mineworkers' union from a membership of 6000 to 340 000, and helped launch COSATU, one of the primary forces for democratization in South Africa. He was unsympathetic to the old-guard principle that length of service was the main qualification for party office, and had publicly stated, before Mandela's release, that the latter should not expect to walk out of prison and take over the ANC. He was one of the new generation of political activists, and one of the few in the party leadership who had tried to control the depredations of Winnie Madikizela-Mandela in Soweto and in the democratic movement in general. In elections to the NEC, many of the old guard were swept away and replaced by former UDF leaders 'whom Mandela and Winnie had previously tried to exclude'. The post of secretary-general went to 38-year-old Ramaphosa, 'despite Mandela's strenuous efforts', and to intense applause from delegates.[36] Madikizela-Mandela was also elected to the NEC.

Thabo Mbeki had returned to South Africa in 1990 after an exile lasting 28 years, one year more than Mandela's period of imprisonment.

When he led the Lusaka delegation to a meeting with government on 2–4 May 1990 at Groote Schuur in Cape Town, where representatives of the UDF-Mass Democratic Movement (MDM) were included,[37] he introduced himself with blended truth and insincerity as: 'I'm Thabo Mbeki. I carry the bags for my leaders.'[38] He had then, according to his biographers, little time for real contact with the ANC's grassroots;[39] Gevisser's account is of a man unwilling or unable to seek the confidence of the mass membership.[40] Hadland and Rantao note that in London in the 1970s 'people feared' Mbeki because of his 'knowledge'.[41] Joe Slovo had become a vocal critic of Mbeki's approach to the crucial issue of talks – among others, says Gevisser, was Mac Maharaj – and as these entered the formal stage of negotiations with the government, Slovo was 'one of the key people' behind the replacement of Mbeki, as ANC chief negotiator, by Cyril Ramaphosa.[42]

The mass membership of the party, not its top leadership, appeared to want a more open and representative negotiations process. The ANC's July conference had 'reiterate[d] our standpoint that negotiations shall not be secret'. It had directed the NEC 'to ensure that a comprehensive representative [negotiations] team' should function 'under the supervision and direction of the NEC'.[43]

Elite immunity and non-accountability

A number of different events at the end of the 1980s and in the early 1990s influenced the transition to majority rule and helped to ensure that it would assume a conventional elite-democratic form. The position of Winnie Madikizela-Mandela was, then and later, a crucial exemplar of the elitism and non-accountability at the top of the ANC. Her 15-room mansion ('Winnie's Palace') in Orlando West was burnt down by high-school pupils on 28 July 1988, as residents watched in silence. The arson attack was precipitated by the reign of terror which she and her vigilantes waged in the community, as she enjoyed a lavish lifestyle while proclaiming her populism, militancy and high status in the liberation struggle and nation. Informed of the events, Nelson Mandela was obliged to react, and a Crisis Committee of community leaders was set up in September 1988 chiefly to limit further damage.

But her Mandela United Football Club was not disbanded, and its activities continued in and out of her new residence in Diepkloof. Members of the Crisis Committee, Aubrey Mokoena, a UDF executive member and Dr Nthatho Motlana, were unable to secure the release of four abducted youths – Lolo Sono, Stompie Seipei, Pelo Mekgwe and

Thabiso Mono – from Madikizela-Mandela's hands in early 1989.[44] With further publicity and the involvement of Bishop Peter Storey of the Methodist Church, with both Oliver Tambo and Nelson Mandela informed of the brutality and disappearances, the Committee held a meeting in Soweto on the night of 16 January. Mekgwe and Mono – released that day following an earlier instruction from Nelson Mandela – informed the participants of their abduction and beating, first by Madikizela-Mandela, then by gang members. The Committee thereafter resolved that Madikizela-Mandela should be isolated from all progressive organizations, and that she should 'desist from creating an impression that she speaks on behalf of the people'. A further report was conveyed to Tambo in Lusaka confirming that Madikizela-Mandela had participated in the beatings at her house. It said too that 'she seems to think that she is above the community. She shows utter contempt for both the crisis committee and the community.'[45]

Dr Abu-Baker Asvat was shot dead in his surgery on 27 January, and later the body of Stompie Seipei was identified.[46] These killings were flagrant, interconnected and but two among many other barbarities with which she was associated. Asvat had been summoned by Madikizela-Mandela to examine Stompie on 1 January, after the boy had undergone a prolonged period of 'Break Down' in her hands – the victim was repeatedly thrown into the air and allowed to fall to the floor – and the physician pronounced him in dire need of hospitalization; immediately afterwards she and her accomplices decided to dispose of the boy.[47] Though public concern escalated, and the police, slowly and partially, began to act, Mandela herself 'remained curiously immune from police interrogation'.[48] Murphy Morobe, a leading figure in the UDF–MDM, flanked by UDF co-president Richard Gumede and COSATU president Elijah Barayi, issued a statement in the name of the MDM on 16 February which directly linked Madikizela-Mandela to Stompie's killing, and explicitly declared that the football team and 'the reign of terror' which it carried out was 'her creation'. He went on: 'We are not prepared to remain silent where those who are violating human rights claim to be doing so in the name of the struggle'. She had 'abused the trust and confidence of the community', and the MDM therefore 'distance[d] itself from Mrs Mandela and her actions'.[49]

Meredith observes that Nelson Mandela wanted all of this to be dealt with inside the ANC; the avoidance of further embarrassment to the organization and its leadership was paramount. He wished to avoid an open examination of her actions, and the public denunciation of her gross wrongdoing by the MDM. The UDF–MDM had placed a particular stress on the accountability of the leadership to the led in a meaningful process of democratization, and criticism of leaders was held to be an essential element in this process. Morobe was already on record as saying: 'We do not believe that any of our members are beyond criticism; neither are organizations and strategies beyond reproach'.[50]

This approach to leadership and democracy was in opposition to the elitist traditions of the ANC, and to its policies as they had been developing in the hands of Mbeki and Mandela, towards Pretoria. Krog observes that there clearly was 'close contact' between the Madikizela-Mandela household and the police. There was also a 'broader contact between the judicial system and the politicians, who knew how things stood', in the tentative negotiations between the ANC elite and the government. 'Some Attorney-Generals' at the time refused to prosecute her.[51]

Both Mandela and the ANC leadership in exile felt that Morobe's press statement had gone too far.[52] Nelson Mandela acted as if none of these enormities had happened, and through 1990 he assisted her 'at every opportunity', says Meredith, to gain high office in the ANC. She proclaimed that the state's reluctant and bumbling efforts to prosecute her represented nonetheless a campaign to discredit the ANC, and Mandela took the same view. He went further and 'threw his full weight into getting the ANC to declare publicly its support for her'.[53]

Her trial in the Rand Supreme Court began in February 1991, with the ANC presenting it as a political, not criminal, trial, and with an inadequate prosecution mounted by the state. George Bizos opened his defence by saying, 'You are the wife of the Deputy President of the African National Congress?', and led a virulently homophobic attack on Methodist Minister (now Bishop) Paul Verryn who had given refuge to some of her victims. Prosecutor Jan Swanepoel was 'thorough in the areas he covered', but also 'left many alone'.[54] He later maintained accurately that he was hampered by the poor quality of the police investigations, and was never given the wherewithal to disprove Winnie Mandela's alibi effectively.[55] On the incomplete and partially false evidence presented to the court,[56] the findings of Justice Michael Stegmann were nonetheless telling. He found her guilty but only on four counts of kidnapping and as an accessory to assault. But she had, he said, shown herself to be 'a calm, composed, deliberate and unblushing liar'. Madikizela-Mandela, he stated, 'fundamentally misunderstood or ignored the responsibilities which came with [her] position as leader'.[57] Nelson Mandela portrayed this as a vindication of her innocence, and 'he continued to support [her] drive for power and office'.[58]

Elite consensus, elite control

Another event of long-term significance occurred in March 1991 when the UDF was formally disbanded, and the ANC succeeded in exerting its organizational dominance over the independent popular movement. Lekota even endorsed the ANC leadership's view that 'the purpose for which we were set up has been achieved', that by latter-day assertion the UDF was just a surrogate for the exiled ANC.[59] Marais notes that the move evoked 'widespread but impotent disgruntlement at rank-and-file level'.[60] Other organizations which had helped to drive the movement of the 1980s, like those of women and youth, were disassembled and incorporated into ANC structures. They were then assigned basic and dependent tasks supportive of the ANC like fundraising and membership drives,[61] or utilized by individual party leaders, notably Madikizela-Mandela and Mbeki, as mass electoral supports for themselves. Demobilization proceeded, and the way was smoothed for the ANC old guard to assume control.[62] Once-lively civics were transformed in half a decade into non-governmental organizations, appendages to state programmes and initiatives. COSATU, by strong contrast, retained its distinctive social base and its organizational strength and independence.

The aims and role of political action also changed. The tendencies and movements for popular power, which the UDF and its affiliates represented, were quickly diverted away from democratization and refocused on 'mass action'. This was a tactic to be turned on and off by the ANC leadership – 'tap mobilization' – to wrest concessions from the NP government and strengthen the position of the ANC's leaders and negotiators.[63] The method was worst displayed at Bisho in September 1992, when Ronnie Kasrils led a group of marchers in direct confrontation with the Ciskei Defence Force. Kasrils and other ANC leaders survived, but 28 other marchers were killed, mostly shot in the back as they fled.[64]

The notion of consensus, as in particular an agreement among leaders, was already important in the ANC, and was to become even more so as a palliative to electoral competition in and after 1994. In November 1991, an inter-elitist strategy was accepted in the ANC as the means towards the achievement of a government of national unity. Negotiations would satisfactorily proceed, it was believed, if the government and the ANC reached bilateral agreement on contentious issues before other parties in any multiparty forum were included.[65] While this was a realistic notion in the actual conditions of military and state power at the time,[66] it contributed further towards depoliticization and the marginalization of popular forces. NEC member Pallo Jordan said that the ANC was elevating negotiations to the level of strategy, and it was in danger of losing what had been won on other fronts. Senior SACP member, Blade Nzimande, also said that Slovo and the negotiators were developing a scenario in which 'the masses are absent'.[67]

In the specific form of 'sufficient consensus', this became the operational principle in the formal constitutional negotiations soon after. 'From the very beginning', says Waldmeir, the ANC and the NP had ensured that 'the cards were stacked against' the smaller parties and groups. Before the Convention for a Democratic South Africa (Codesa) had even begun, the two major parties had concluded a deal, 'a formula for how Codesa's nineteen parties would take decisions'. Sufficient consensus represented agreement among all those who needed to agree, preeminently Cyril Ramaphosa for the ANC and Roelf Meyer for the NP. In Ramaphosa's own words, 'it mean[t] that, if we and the [NP] agree, everyone else can get stuffed'. Waldmeir further reported that the ANC's chief negotiator was 'clearly elated' at how the NP and the ANC could 'carve up power without worrying too much about anyone else's claim to a share of it'.[68] Not only Inkatha and extremist right-wing groups were excluded;[69] when COSATU attempted to gain a place at the negotiating table the government rigidly resisted, and the ANC and perhaps COSATU itself did not press the issue.[70]

From its beginning in 1984–85, the talks process had tended to confer recognition and importance on the ANC in exile and in prison, and to deny it in consequence to the popular internal forces represented by the UDF and COSATU. By 1988, decisively, according to Seekings, the initiative in opposition politics had 'for the first time…clearly shifted to the ANC', and talks became 'the exclusive preserve' of that party.[71] As negotiations were formalized and the acquisition of state power by the ANC moved closer, the subordination of organized participatory politics was deepened. The established nationalist leadership gained doubly from the negotiations process: 'as multiple lines of communication were opened between the government and the ANC', the UDF was transformed into 'a component of the ANC's strategy'.[72] The elitist approach to power had debilitating consequences: by late 1993 it had had, according to Raymond Suttner, former UDF regional executive member and an NEC member since 1991, 'a dissolving effect on mass organisations'. It was accompanied by 'a tendency for our constituency to become spectators'. If majority-rule elections were conducted in a similarly narrow electoralist manner, he warned, 'the dissolution could be deepened'.[73]

Although the Founding Elections in 1994 saw a turnout of about 85 per cent of the eligible electorate, the outcome here, too, was highly elitist. During the polling the lawyers in the Independent Electoral Commission (IEC) charged with the vital task of investigating irregularities and intimidation, had actually done little or nothing, being 'simply too frightened of offending the major parties'.[74] Around 3–5 May, as the counting process faced collapse – due to mismanagement, accident, fraud, corruption and computer sabotage – the leaders of the ANC, NP and the Inkatha Freedom Party (IFP) intervened to produce results acceptable to themselves. The chairman of the IEC, Judge Johann Kriegler, described the manipulations that took place: 'Let's not get overly squeamish about it ... [The parties] are in a power game with each other, and if they want to settle on the basis that they withdraw objections there's nothing wrong with it'. With the technical assistance of auditors and accountants, votes were *'awarded'* – Kriegler's word, my emphasis – by and among the three party chiefs.[75] The final results were mathematically perfect,[76] and a Government of National Unity came into being. The Democratic Party, one of the minor parties denied a role in the award-giving process, contended that their analysis of the results suggested that some 1.46 million votes were fraudulent.[77]

Mangosuthu Buthelezi and the IFP

The relationship between the ANC elite and Chief Buthelezi, and the immunity accorded to him, has the significance that is attached to the untouchability of Madikizela-Mandela. Buthelezi arose within the Bantustan system, he acquired political and military power, and he developed and used these in close cooperation with Pretoria against students and workers in general, and against the UDF and later the ANC in particular. In October 1979 he held a meeting in London with the ANC in exile at which he made clear his opposition to protest politics, economic sanctions and the external armed struggle. By the beginning of the 1980s he had direct control over the government of KwaZulu and of the Inkatha Freedom Party, and they functioned interchangeably as a virtual one-party state; by 1981 he also directly controlled the KwaZulu Police. As in other such systems, the autocratic Chief, the party and the government were in fact a unity.

From as early as 1982, Inkatha propounded the importance of paramilitary training, and soon after 'violence became institutionalised in KwaZulu', according to the TRC. A training camp was established that year near Ulundi, and Inkatha began to use force and violence against community organizers, students and trade unionists. Clashes between Inkatha and the UDF came to the fore in 1984, and many incidents of killing are documented. Inkatha's so-called 'A-Team', set up with assistance of the South African Police was, for example, responsible for at least 10 killings in Chesterville near Durban in 1983–84; and on 1 August 1985, Victoria Mxenge, a UDF executive member, was murdered in her home in Umlazi – at her subsequent memorial service, Inkatha mobs randomly slaughtered another 14 people. Buthelezi's speeches to Inkatha in the early 1980s were militaristic and aggressive. For instance:

> I believe we must prepare ourselves not only to defend property and life but to go beyond that and prepare ourselves to hit back with devastating force at those who destroy our property and kill us.[78]

In the latter 1980s, Buthelezi initiated military collusion with Pretoria's security forces. Inkatha's 'aggression', in the words of the TRC report, was 'directed at those who were advocating alternative structures and thus threatening its power base'. Pretoria promoted the covert alliance. As South Africa supported UNITA in Angola and Renamo in Mozambique as aspects of its strategy of total war, so from 1985 military assistance was directed internally to Buthelezi and Inkatha. In late 1985, Buthelezi asked Military Intelligence to provide him with the military capacity to confront the UDF, and 'Operation Marion' – Marion as in marionette – resulted. 200 Inkatha members were trained in great secrecy on the Caprivi Strip; the operation involved only the highest echelons of the State Security Council, on one side, and Buthelezi and his personal assistant, Zakhele (MZ) Khumalo, on the other. The 200 men were controlled and later commanded by Daluxolo Wordsworth Luthuli, who was 'unequivocal' in his testimony that the training was aimed 'at equipping Inkatha supporters to kill members of the UDF [and] ANC'. They knew, he said, that they were being trained as a hit squad. They continued to receive support and regular pay from the South African military until 1989, when most were absorbed into the KwaZulu Police; 'here many of them continued their hit squad operations'.[79]

In the early 1990s the IFP engaged with the ANC and UDF in a war for political supremacy in KwaZulu, in Natal and in other regions, particularly the Transvaal. The TRC found that IFP members were responsible, together with members of the state's security forces, for committing gross violations of human rights in incidents like the

Seven-Day War at Edendale, near Pietermaritzburg, in March 1990, where over 100 people were killed and some 3000 homes burnt down. Inkatha members were conscripted into armed units and their activities became 'widespread' in KwaZulu-Natal (KZ-N) during the 1990s. These operations stemmed from the Caprivi training. The Commission also heard evidence of the involvement of IFP supporters in the train violence around Johannesburg between 1990 and 1993, in which approximately 570 people died – knifed, shot or thrown from trains carrying commuters in and out of Johannesburg.

The IFP 'engaged in a campaign to disrupt the electoral process' in the run up to May 1994 in KZ-N. During this period '[it] received arms and ammunition from right-wing organisations [and] sections of the security forces', and the campaign 'continued until 29 April, just six days before the elections'. The TRC is explicit about the scale and significance of this terrorism and disruption. Overall, the IFP was found to be 'the foremost perpetrator of gross human rights violations' in KZ-N during the early 1990s. 'Approximately 9,000 gross human rights violations' were carried out by Inkatha there from 1990 to May 1994.[80] It was, moreover, 'the primary non-state perpetrator' of gross human rights violations in South Africa, 'responsible for approximately 33 per cent of all the violations reported to the Commission'.[81]

Nelson Mandela had kept in touch with Buthelezi from prison, writing, we are told, respectful letters to him, and on his release the Chief was one of the first people he phoned.[82] Mandela seems to have been influenced by his belief in the importance of cooperation among elites, and by his capacity for deciding alone. He felt that there was an intangible understanding between two men of royal blood, and he was sure that 'he could bring Buthelezi around'.[83] The way forward, as Waldmeir describes Mandela's thinking, was 'to give [Buthelezi] the love and approval he craved from the world – and especially from Mandela himself'. Within days of his release, Mandela proposed that the two men should meet. This was 'vehemently opposed' by the NEC, but it was supported, then or a little later, by Jacob Zuma who also felt that 'It was important for Buthelezi to feel welcomed, embraced, and part of the process'.[84]

Regardless of the carnage for which Buthelezi was primarily responsible, and for his long collaborationist record with the apartheid enemy, drawing Buthelezi into the political process is essentially what Mandela did, largely on his own volition, though with Mbeki's assistance. Much was ignored and conceded by him in achieving this. In March 1994 the Bantustan governments of Bophuthatswana and Ciskei were toppled by popular pressure, and Judge Richard Goldstone announced that he had uncovered a network of criminal activity linking the South African and KwaZulu Police and Inkatha. Joe Slovo believed that the time had come to overturn Buthelezi's murderous regime too; he said: 'Two down, one to go'. 'Many of his colleagues', Waldmeir states, 'still regret that this was not done'.[85] In early 1994, Thabo Mbeki as ANC deputy-president 'had a lot to do with bringing Buthelezi back', there were meetings in Durban between the two in which Cyril Ramaphosa did not participate. The outcomes 'sometimes surprised Ramaphosa', because concessions were made that were not part of the negotiations path.[86] Ultimately Buthelezi was hurriedly drawn into the elections which he had been doing his worst to disrupt until the previous day.

Inkatha thereafter was awarded 10 per cent of the national vote and acquired three seats in Cabinet. Chief Buthelezi was made Minister of Home Affairs, and his incorporation into the mainstream, essentially elitist political process has continued. President Mandela personally boosted the elevation of the Chief, naming him as joint peace advocate, with himself, to strife-torn Africa in March 1997. This bizarre step was taken just days after Inkatha had staged a march in Johannesburg in which three people were killed and more injured, and which commemorated his party's first march on the city three years previously when 50 people died in the Gauteng area. Mandela's courtship of Buthelezi is in sharp contrast with his ruptured relationship with F.W. De Klerk. While the NP leader was far more important to South Africa in the relatively smooth transition to liberal democracy, he quickly went from being a 'man of integrity', in Mandela's eyes, to being portrayed publicly as without integrity and a liar. De Klerk was, in Thatcherite understanding, a man with whom the ANC negotiators could and did do business, and he 'successfully delivered his constituency' to the ANC and the transition.[87] De Klerk feels today that he made enemies as a result among the white community, but that what he did was right in order to prevent further conflict and deaths.[88] Yet Mandela chose to depict him, not Chief Buthelezi, as a man contemptuous of black lives.

The position accorded to Buthelezi, and to Madikizela-Mandela, is distinctive and significant. Then Deputy-President Thabo Mbeki presented a lengthy document to the TRC in May 1997 which described crimes committed by the ANC during the liberation struggle. But it skirted parts of the recent past which continue to influence politics,[89] ignoring the actions of Madikizela-Mandela in Soweto, and avoiding consideration of Buthelezi and Inkatha; despite the great weight of evidence to the contrary,[90] the IFP's gross violations of human rights were said to be have been largely the work of outsiders.[91] The message to Chief Buthelezi was clear: injustice could be ignored, and the ANC and IFP could 'solidify common ground'.[92]

Various steps were mooted as to how this might be achieved. Existing amnesty laws might be changed, and Buthelezi could be offered a position in government 'befitting his stature as a leader'. But when these proposals were being made in mid-1997 they had not been canvassed, Chothia reported, in the NEC, COSATU and the SACP. The latter's national leadership was known in fact to have rejected the plan to elevate Buthelezi, and to have described the whole idea as 'mystifying'; COSATU's executive in KZ-N was believed to have opposed this too; their provincial secretary, Paulos Ngcobo, observed that 'if you give Buthelezi a finger he wants your hand'. But the proposals were nonetheless backed by Mandela, Mbeki and Jacob Zuma.[93] Zuma was then the ANC's provincial and national chairman, and chief negotiator with the IFP. His position was consistently that of the elite and quintessentially supportive of close collaboration between elites. The party had always maintained, he declared in mid-June 1997, that certain issues could only be resolved in talks involving national leaders.[94]

The ANC protected with secrecy and obscurity other, not unimportant, figures. Peter Mokaba, as boss of the Youth League, 'perhaps did more than any other individual to crown Thabo Mbeki as Crown Prince',[95] compensating for his lack of rank-and-file support in the early 1990s with the delivery of the League's then large constituency. Mokaba was also Madikizela-Mandela's 'long-time ally' from her Mandela United days.[96] But according to Gavin Evans, journalist and former ANC activist, Mokaba was also 'working with the [apartheid] system'. Indeed, 'everyone knew what he had done but no action was taken – instead there was a cover-up'.[97] The ANC's second submission to the TRC contained a list of names of former government spies, but as a confidential appendix. When Commissioner Wynand Malan asked why the party opposed naming these people, Minister Mac Maharaj replied: 'Government is a high office. People need to trust the Government.'[98]

Nurturing silence

Significant repercussions follow when a ruling elite seeks to obscure or deny vital truths. The 'Wall of Silence' which the SWAPO leadership in Namibia endeavours to maintain around the brutalities it practised on its members in the liberation war,[99] led on, according to Leys and Saul, to a kind of 'popular disempowerment' in politics.[100] Both justice and democracy suffer when a governing elite sets out to falsify big political issues. Mystification of the crimes committed by Madikizela-Mandela against defenceless boys and young women, and the killing of many thousands of people directed by Buthelezi over some ten years, leads to the distortion of public debate and the enfeebling of the people. The losers in such circumstances are not, as Friedman observed, those who have the resources to discover the truth and the capacity to express their views; the 'real losers' within the elite-contrived obscurity and silence are 'the poor and the voiceless'.[101]

The popular politics of the 1970s and 1980s have been obscured too. The widespread rank-and-file disgruntlement which accompanied the disbandment of the UDF in 1991 may have lingered on in members of the 'class of 1976' as anger. Anger particularly over the distortion of the origins and meaning of the protests and their consequences. Majakathata Mokoena led a group of students from Orlando High School then, and says that 'the most significant fact' about the events was that 'the children successfully resurrected the ANC', an organization that was 'for all intents and purposes dead'. Young people left the country in droves 'to replenish the largely dried-up membership' of the ANC in exile as MK soldiers. This fact, he notes, is 'ignored by many commentators'.[102]

Murphy Morobe was a student in Soweto and a prominent member of the South African Students' Movement before he later became a spokesperson for the UDF, and his experience, too, was of the spontaneity of what became the 1976 uprising. 'Our original plan', he recalls:

> was just to go to Orlando West, pledge our solidarity and sing *Nkosi Sikelele i'Afrika*. Then we thought we would have made our point [against the education authorities] and we would go back home. No one envisaged a process that would go beyond June 16th.

After the police started shooting, 'the only thing on our minds was to disperse everyone as soon as possible...but it was difficult...where must we go?...We were entirely out of our depth in terms of what to do.' Enraged young protesters set fire to state institutions and government-owned beer-halls and liquor stores. Despite over 500 being killed by the police on 16–17 June, violent protest spread to other townships in Gauteng by the end of the week. Struggle broke out in and around Cape Town in August, and thousands of black and

Coloured students marched in unison behind such placards as 'Freedom from oppression for our black brothers'.[103]

An Action Committee, according to Bonner and Segal, had helped to organize the initial march, but as turmoil continued in Soweto it condemned both police brutality and the burning of schools. It was instrumental in the formation of the Soweto Students Representative Council (SSRC) at the beginning of August to control and coordinate community action. Its immediate call was for the release of all school-children from detention; it organized a march on security police headquarters in John Vorster Square on 4 August, and it asked workers and parents to stay at home for three days in solidarity with these demands. About two-thirds of the black labour force heeded the call at the height of the three-day period. Many commentators began to refer to the SSRC 'as a shadow government in Soweto'. It 'denied having any official links with the ANC', and the uprising, Bonner and Segal note, 'had taken the ANC by surprise'.[104]

Emboldened perhaps by its initial success, the SSRC called a further three-day stay-away in late August from which considerable violence and a death toll of over 35 resulted in running battles between Zulu hostel dwellers and township residents. The call for a third such action, 13–15 September, saw the detention of some 300 people on a single day, and represented the climax of the uprising. Though the SSRC's young leadership was inexperienced and inconsistent, the movement had 'far-reaching consequences'. The 'most obvious' was the change in relationships between students and their parents. 'The struggle is ours', stated Khotsi Seatlholo, chairperson of the SSRC, '[t]he ball of liberation is in our hands'.[105]

Twenty four years later, this group of protestors, says Mokoena, 'instills subdued fear, or overt suspicion, among the leaders of the old political parties'. No political party in 2000, he further stressed, 'can effectively claim June 16 as its own defining moment in history'. The claim still stays with the 'so-called children of Soweto',[106] enwrapped in that 'culture of silence' that, Mamphela Ramphele said, threatens the gains made by South Africa's 'infant democracy'.[107]

5
Universalizing an Incomplete Predominance

The political strength of the ANC is readily apparent. It got 62.03 per cent of the vote in the 1994 elections and 66.35 per cent in 1999, and it was the majority party in seven of the country's nine provinces, 1994–99. The Democratic Party obtained only 1.7 per cent of votes in 1994, and 9.56 per cent in 1999 when it became the official opposition; the NP, renamed the New National Party, won only 6.87 per cent in the second election, when the IFP got 8.58 per cent.[1] Constitutional agreements had established an electoral system of proportional representation (PR), using party lists and without constituencies, a combination which effectively centralized the ANC's predominance in the hands of the party leadership. Voters elected parties, not individual representatives. Only members of a political party could seek election, and parliamentary office was not won or acquired through interaction between a candidate and a distinct community of voters, but in allocation by party chiefs relative to an individual's position on the list – hence to their standing with those chiefs – and the total votes cast for the party.

The liberal or representative form of democracy is based upon periodic voting in open, competitive elections, and great importance is placed on the direct link between the voter and his or her parliamentary representative. If the citizen is to have influence over government it largely occurs, within the liberal model, through this linkage. If accountability is to be achieved, it is the executive answering to representatives in parliament in the voter's name. The combination of party list with no constituency or territorial representation severs this connection, and is particularly destructive of citizenship.

This might well have been anticipated. Members of the National Assembly in Namibia are constitutionally deemed to be 'the servants of the people', but in 1990 the country acquired an electoral system very similar to that which South Africa subsequently adopted; in 1994 the ruling party, SWAPO, got 72.7 per cent of votes and it was apparent that 'members [we]re in effect representatives not of voters but of the party machine', dependent on its goodwill for their parliamentary position.[2] One-party predominance and the electoral system had effectively overridden the constitutional provisions for popular sovereignty inside four years. Further, alternative electoral systems exist: PR is combined with constituencies in Germany and New Zealand under the 'additional member system', and the plurality or first-past-the-post system can be made more proportional, with constituencies also in place, through the preferential vote system found in Australia.

The party leadership's power in South Africa is still further reinforced by an anti-defection clause, which provides that parliamentarians who resign or are expelled from their parties lose their seats, and the absence of any provision for by-elections. MPs come and go on the decision of party leaders and their own volition, on the latter usually for personal advancement without reference to the voters. More than a quarter of National Assembly members elected in 1994, 122 of the original 400, left parliament before the expiry of its first term. Parliament's ability to hold the executive to account is probably best exercised through scrutiny of persons and programmes within its committee system, but the turnover among portfolio committee chairpersons, a vital parliamentary office, was almost 50 per cent; by 1999 only 14 out of 27 remained.[3] Just half-way through the first parliament, some 70 MPs and Senators had gone, and the editor of the *Sunday Times* felt then that this constituted a 'huge betrayal of voters', who had every right to expect that the chosen people – however chosen – would serve a full term. When Saki Macozoma resigned as ANC MP and chair of the communications committee his salary entitlements totalled some R246 000, but as managing director of the parastatal Transnet he subsequently obtained at least R920 000.[4] Other hard-working effective MPs such as Carl Niehaus and Raymond Suttner were 'redeployed' by the ANC into diplomacy; both chaired important committees and their departure was at a cost to parliament's effectiveness.[5]

The ANC and the main opposition parties introduced artificial constituencies some three years into the life of the first parliament. The ANC characteristically assigned its MPs to so-called constituency offices not necessarily in the place where they came from or with which they identified. 'People's weekends' were established by the NEC in March 1997, where in a party spokesperson's words, 'members and supporters' were to be 'involve[d]' in things like 'the national budgeting process'.[6] 'Constituency weeks' are held by the major parties, where parliamentarians supposedly spend two weeks in their assigned wards. Their value to voters seemed at best decidedly mixed; some ANC parliamentarians reported 'enormous queues of people who need[ed] an MP to intercede for them' in struggles with the bureaucracy, and there were indications that those who did help were those who also worked hard in their parliamentary committees.[7] Each MP already received then R3000 a month to look after their 'constituents'.

All of the same features, the anti-defection clause, the principle that parties are elected not individuals, the exclusion of by-elections and of constituencies, were maintained into the second parliament in a deal brokered between the ANC and the NP.[8]

Deepening predominance

The notion of 'redeployment' further extended the power of the ANC leadership, and was adopted as part of a new Code of Conduct in November 1994. Relevant clauses stated that, 'All elected representatives … shall accept allocation by the organisation to specific constituencies or areas or organisational functions', and that 'Members of the assemblies shall be subject to recall from these structures for violation of the ANC constitution.'[9] These principles ignore the preferences and interests of voters. Patrick Terror Lekota was removed as Premier of the Free State in late 1996, 'redeployed', and replaced by an unelected parastatal bureaucrat – Ivy Matsepe-Casaburri, board chairperson of the South African Broadcasting Commission, supposedly an independent institution – without reference to the people of the Province. Premier Lekota had embarked on an anti-corruption drive, and there was evidence of his strong popularity both within the ANC membership and among voters there.[10] But President Mandela had apparently preferred party unity and central control over clean government and local preferences.[11]

Deployment and redeployment dovetailed with the existing ANC principle of consensus, given heightened importance in a democratic system of open electoral competition. It was the agreement among the top leadership, notably, 1996–99, Mandela, Thabo Mbeki and Jacob Zuma, identifying who would rise through fealty to the leadership, and who conversely would fall, before any elections did or did not take place. Bantu Holomisa was a young – 41 in 1996 – populist and maverick person from the East Transkei, who gave public testimony then to the questionably close financial links between the casino magnate

Sol Kerzner, the ANC and President Mandela himself.[12] For attempting to blow the whistle on apparent or actual corruption, he was precipitously sacked from the ANC and removed from parliament.[13] When he met the President, with whom he had an established father-and-son relationship, in Qunu privately in December, Mandela demanded an apology from him for, as it was put, dragging the ANC into the mud. Holomisa refused, saying it was ethically impossible.[14] This personal meeting convinced him 'that the ANC leadership [was] no longer interested in my services', and he abandoned his battle for reinstatement in the party.[15]

Independent action and criticism, as with Lekota and Holomisa, and independent political aspirations were equally offensive to consensus. The old distinctions between the exiles of the ANC and the internals of the UDF, MDM and the unions, partially smoothed over by the appointment of Ramaphosa as secretary-general in July 1991, deepened at this time.[16] Tokyo Sexwale, aged 43 in 1996, was a former MK member who spent 12 years on Robben Island as part of the 'Pretoria 12'. As Premier of Gauteng, he incurred the wrath of Deputy-President Mbeki through the latter half of that year. After his statement in December that he considered running for the state presidency in 1999 – necessarily directly challenging Mbeki – his departure from politics followed, through devious twists and turns.[17] Provincial premiers were voted for on party lists drawn up centrally, and decisions on placement and permanency were being reserved for ever fewer people.[18]

Mathews Phosa, former regional commander of the Political-Military Committee based in Maputo and, at 44, Premier of Mpumalanga, went much the same route as Sexwale. 'Behind the scenes moves led by [Mbeki]', according to Hadland and Rantao, were said to have persuaded Mandela that Phosa was too young to be deputy president of the ANC, as he had rashly indicated was his wish in the months preceding the party's December 1997 Mafikeng conference. Such an appointment, Mbeki argued, would be in violation of the long ANC tradition of succession, according to which Jacob Zuma was the next in line. He also felt that Phosa was unsuited to serve as his deputy. Mandela 'stepped in', and announced, 'without discussing it first with Phosa', that the Premier would step down.[19] He was left with few alternatives, and departed politics a little later.

Predominance and the opposition parties

The ANC has sought the further extension of its predominance. The elevation of Buthelezi was one ploy by which it reportedly sought to silence criticism through cooptation of organized opposition into the government.[20] The DP was offered a Cabinet post by Mandela in early 1997. Their leader, Tony Leon, said that on the terms of the proposal debate and discussion on key policy issues would have had to take place only in the Cabinet, away from public scrutiny. The DP would have been, he said, 'unable to play the role of a vigorous, probing and critical opposition'. The party declined the President's 'imaginative' offer with regret and gratitude.[21] Buthelezi 'is so important' to President Mbeki, according to his biographers, because 'it assures the two-thirds majority' in parliament which constitutional amendment demands. He was busy with the IFP leader, they said, in the same way that President Robert Mugabe coopted Joshua Nkomo in Zimbabwe,[22] creating a calcified one-party state.

The unacceptability of all opposition was vehemently and comprehensively expressed by President Mandela in a five-hour address to the ANC's 50th national conference in Mafikeng in December 1997. Those whom the ANC could not coopt would be frightened into submission. Almost any political party, civic group or institution which opposed or acted independently of the ANC was, by that fact alone, racist, committed to preserving the legacies of apartheid, and against social transformation. 'The role of the opposition parties' was entirely negative and reactionary, 'in their effort[s] to challenge and undermine our role as the political force chosen by the people to lead our country'. The experience of the three years since 1994 confirmed that the NP 'has not abandoned its strategic objective of the total destruction of our organisation and movement'. The DP, he obliquely acknowledged, has sought to present itself as 'the most effective parliamentary opposition', but this had no value in itself to the ANC; the DP had 'no policy differences with the NP', and was essentially an 'implacable enemy' of the ANC, capable only of 'villification of the ANC'. The latest grouping to join 'the miserable platoon of [our] opponents',[23] the United Democratic Movement of Bantu Holomisa and Roelf Meyer, also had, he said, the same single objective as the NP – the 'destruction of the ANC'.

Opposition to the ANC was weak and pitiful, and simultaneously comprehensive, determined and implacably destructive. The positions adopted by 'the mainly white parties' in parliament, the NP, DP and Freedom Front, showed that 'they and the media – which represents the same social base' – have strongly opposed the ending of racial disparities. The 'bulk of the media', he claimed, 'has set itself up as a force opposed to the ANC', and uses the democratic order to 'protect the legacy of racism'. Equally, he said, 'we have experienced serious resistance to the transformation of the public service'. Furthermore, 'many of our NGO's are not in fact NGO's'; they too worked to 'corrode the influence of the [liberation] movement', and some of them 'act[ed] as instruments of foreign governments and institutions'. There still further existed, he asserted, 'a network', supported by 'various elements of the former ruling group', which 'would launch or intensify a campaign of destabilisation', aimed among other things at 'the weakening of the ANC and its allies'; the 'use of crime to render the country ungovernable'; and the subversion of the economy.

Only two political parties were different in the President's view. The Freedom Front, for one, 'recognised the fact that it can only advance its cause by reaching agreement with the ANC'. It accepted its dependency. Inkatha, for the other, was serving with the ANC in the national and KZ-N provincial governments, and 'our two organizations are involved in a joint effort to consolidate peace' and 'encourage … tolerance'. We need to recall, he added, that 'many members of the IFP grew up in the ANC', and both 'share[d] the same constituency, especially the rural and urban poor'. No reference was made to Inkatha's bloody and collaborationist recent past, wherein so very many of that same constituency were the victims.[24]

The membership of the ANC, nonetheless, seemed ready to oppose, when and if they could, the domination asserted over them by the elite. Especially so with regard to the principles of democracy and non-racialism. Only two ballots actually took place at Mafikeng for six national leadership positions; in most cases elections were avoided by successful manoeuvres which secured the withdrawal of candidates, like Phosa or Sexwale, disapproved of by the leadership.[25] But in both cases where elections did occur, as Friedman noted, the presumed leadership favourite was beaten. Patrick (soon after Mosiuoa) Lekota won the national chairmanship in a landslide over the Minister of Sport, Steve Tshwete, who had been instrumental in his removal from the Free State premiership, and the SACP's Thenjiwe Mthintso defeated Mavivi Myakayaka-Manzini, 'who [wa]s close to' Thabo Mbeki, in the race to be deputy-secretary general. This extended the experience of the whole of 1997: 'every time the leadership backed a candidate in open elections, the other contender won'.

Elections to the NEC reflected a similar independence of view in the rank-and-file. The poll was topped not by a minister but by Cyril Ramaphosa, and number-three position was taken by Pallo Jordan, who is reportedly not liked by Mbeki. 'At least four' of the top ten positions were gained by people 'known to differ significantly with the new leadership'.[26] Additionally, Winnie Madikizela-Mandela dropped from fifth to fifteenth position, and Peter Mokaba, ally earlier of her and of Mbeki, fell from third to nineteenth. Stella Sigcau, Public Enterprises Minister, did not gain a seat among the 60 members. The NEC elections also reaffirmed non-racialism principles among the membership over the new Africanist tendencies near the top. As Dlamini noted, not only were seven Indians, five whites and five Coloureds included on the new executive, but only three blacks were voted into the top ten.[27]

His biographers report that Thabo Mbeki is 'paranoid about opposition, particularly internal opposition. Holomisa, [Mac] Maharaj, Ramaphosa, Sexwale – all of them left for one reason: either [Mbeki] couldn't tolerate them or they couldn't tolerate him.'[28] He has instead 'surrounded himself with "yes men"', with advisers whose chief quality, according to Friedman, is 'their inability, or unwillingness, to criticise'. But he remains, they say:

> closed and private, even to those he knows best and trusts most. He has simply always been that way, the product of ... an isolated youth and his submergence in adulthood in a movement that was forced to be clandestine and distant.[29]

His milieu, adds Trewhela, was at the top of a highly secretive apparatus, which 'constituted the whole of [his] political life' from his late teens onwards.[30]

Elite non-accountability: the crimes and impunity of Madikizela-Mandela

Antjie Krog noted the atmosphere of conspiracy and fear which surrounded the TRC's hearings into the Mandela United Football Club. Even before they opened a few weeks ahead of the Mafikeng conference, rumours circulated that she was intimidating witnesses. Her 'mere presence [wa]s intimidating ... from the start.' Outside the venue a group of followers from the ANC Women's League, chanted: 'Winnie didn't kill alone. Winnie had a mandate from us to kill'. The victims, even some of the Commissioners, found it difficult to look at her.[31] Another journalist likened her and this aura of threat to the Mafia boss, Al Capone. She too had surrounded herself with 'a motley group of poor, uprooted and brutalised young people', who exchanged love and absolute loyalty for care from an icon.[32]

Fear and intimidation was the group's mode of operation. One fol-lower, Gift Ntombeni, said that gang members had manned the gate of her house at all times, registering community complaints in a book. Club members 'would hunt that person down, and if [they] found them [they] would assault them'. Members 'would not ever dare' defy Madikizela-Mandela. 'If you did, you were branded an informer'.[33] Intimidation, criminality and depravity were all intermixed. Phumlile Dlamini, to quote from Krog's record, was three-months pregnant by one of Madikizela-Mandela's lovers – 'Winnie didn't like that. She hit me first. Then she told the Football Club: See what you can do with this one. Then they all assaulted me.' Xoliswa Falati, a close collabora-tor, said: 'I went to prison for her and she was so much ungrateful. She dehumanizes a person.' Asked why she protected Madikizela-Mandela and gave false evidence in the Supreme Court about the killing of Stompie, she said: 'That was our culture, to protect our leaders... I had seen how people were brutally beaten. She gives you orders, you don't have to reply.'[34]

Her house was known as 'Parliament', people were assaulted in the 'Fish Oil Room', and the shack at the back where abducted boys were kept was called 'Lusaka'. Certain places in the Mandela home were especially important. Bodies were often left lying near the jacuzzi, reports Krog, and Zinzi Mandela-Hlongwane's bedroom was used for 'pleasure' and for planning operations. Guns were stashed in her cup-board, and 'the team gather[ed] there socially'. Zinzi was not only beautiful, said a gang member, 'she [wa]s capable of anything'. Two of her four children were believed to have been fathered by Club mem-bers.[35] She was an active participant in gross human rights violations. According to Gift Ntombeni, Mandela-Hlongwane was the first to carve the initials 'ANC' and 'WM' into the chests and backs of victims, and she instituted the practice of burning victims' feet. Another witness, Lerothodi Ikaneng, said that he had observed the murder of Tholi Dlamini by Club member Sizwe Sithole, whom he described as being the father of one of Mandela-Hlongwane's children. Either the mother or the daughter ordered Dlamini's killing. 'Zinzi... has taken after her mother', said Ntombeni. 'They are capable of anything.'[36]

Close associations with the police were a part of those capabilities. Azhar Cachalia, prominent UDF member, noted on 27 November that Soweto people were aware that arms were present in Madikizela-Man-dela's house, that the Club was infiltrated by the police,[37] that shootouts sometimes flagrantly occurred, yet Madikizela-Mandela had neither been charged nor called for questioning. Sergeant Paul Erasmus, a security policeman, was often seen by Falati going into Madikizela-Mandela's room late at night.[38] She had a long-standing relationship, according to 'coach' Jerry Richardson, with this special branch officer, while Richardson himself was a police agent. Madikizela-Mandela had entertained Erasmus and, he said, other police officers, in her bedroom. These included H.T. Moodley, who was later the investigating officer into the murder of Dr Abu-Baker Asvat.[39]

Themba Mobotha was another with whom she was intimate. He was an Askari, or turned MK member, based at Vlakplaas, who later deserted in turn from the police, and transcripts of conversations indicated the intimacy of their relationship.[40] Security branch wire-taps were kept on her house, and transcripts showed, according to Captain Daniel Bosman officer in charge of the monitoring unit, that she was in Soweto, not Brandfort as she had claimed, over the crucial days the evening of Friday 29 December to Sunday 31 December 1988 when the four youths were abducted and Stompie Seipei disposed of. These wire-taps made nonsense of her alibi. Bosman informed the TRC that he had read the transcripts: 'From the Friday to the Sunday there were conversations on the telephone where she spoke.' He also confirmed that this information had been passed on to the Soweto murder and robbery squad, but it was withheld from her trial in the Supreme Court. He had been told, he declared, that the wire-tap evidence was 'too sensitive to be used'.[41]

Special Branch Sergeant Stefan (or Fanie) Pretorious was involved too, initially as the 'handler' of Jerry Richardson. Pretorious was shot dead when he, as Beresford reported, 'inexplicably ran into [Richardson's] house', in November 1988 when the place was surrounded by riot police.[42] The dead man's family said that he had been causing trouble in the police over their failure to act against Madikizela-Mandela, and they suspected that his killing was a set-up.[43] Mobotha was tortured by the police, and later handed back to the security branch; the Soweto branch commander Colonel Jan Potgieter then asked Eugene de Kock, Vlakplaas commander, to kill Mobotha.[44]

Further evidence exists of the complicity of state institutions in efforts to protect Madikizela-Mandela from justice. The elitism and inter-elitism that characterizes South African politics was at work. Sufficient evidence was in the hands of the state for nine years to charge Madikizela-Mandela with kidnapping Lolo Sono. The former driver, Michael Seakamela, made a statement about the disappearance of the badly beaten boy in 1988; he confirmed his statement to the police when the case was re-examined in 1995, and said that he was prepared to testify. But he went into hiding after the opening of the TRC hearings in November 1997 after allegedly being intimidated by Madikizela-Mandela. Seakamela's 1988 statement, contained in docket number 236/11/88 at Meadowlands police station, was then missing.[45]

When she was being charged with kidnapping Stompie Seipei in 1991, the then Attorney-General, Klaus von Lieres und Wilkau, according to both the *Mail and Guardian* and the *Boston Globe*, decided not to act on the Sono matter for political reasons. He told the *Boston Globe*: 'A second prosecution may have looked like deliberate harassment.' Von Lieres said to the *Mail and Guardian* that the matter was discussed in the normal course of events with the Minister of Justice, Kobie Coetsee, who had been so active in initiating talks with Nelson Mandela.[46] 'Politics may have played a role as far as the police were concerned', he went on, 'I did not think politicians were so keen to see a proper investigation.'[47]

Mail and Guardian investigators were told by the police that 'there was a sensitivity in the force to Madikizela-Mandela'. In about 1988 orders were issued to the security branch not to raid her home or question her without clearance from regional headquarters because of the likely reaction of the local and foreign media.[48]

Reactions to the crimes of Madikizela-Mandela from within the internal democratic movement of the 1980s, and from the ANC as it approached and gained state power, were totally different. Azhar Cachalia and Murphy Morobe addressed the TRC as members of the Soweto community and as leading figures in the UDF–MDM. Morobe had grown up near the Mandela house in Orlando West, he had passed it on the way to school and sometimes went in for tea. Cachalia came from a prominent anti-apartheid family;[49] he described cases of vicious assaults and mutilations practised on Soweto youths by Madikizela-Mandela's thugs, and added that some community members believed that 'Mrs Mandela was herself working with the police'.

Both were acutely aware – as many others were not – that it was chiefly weak and vulnerable boys and girls who were Madikizela-Mandela's victims. The UDF had campaigned consistently for the release of children in government detention, and against their abuse in townships. Immediate action had to be taken, said Cachalia, when a prominent leader of the movement was believed to be involved in violating children's rights.[50] The UDF considered, in early 1989, that the Crisis Committee established by Nelson Mandela had become ineffective 'in the face of Mrs Mandela's obstinacy'.[51] Stompie Seipei's body had been identified, confirming the movement's worst fears, and 'community anger was at boiling point', Cachalia said.[52] 'As national leadership of the UDF we knew we had to 'do something bold and imaginative. We decided to publicly distance ourselves from Mrs Mandela's actions.'[53]

The statement which they made on 16 February 1989 came at some cost to themselves. It has had, Morobe informed the Commission:

> a profound effect on me as an individual, on my relationship with Mrs Madikizela-Mandela (though always coming to me in undercurrents), [and] with many others inside and outside the movement... [But] this was an issue of principle that my organisation had to confront.

Cachalia added: 'It was one of the most difficult decisions I have ever made... I have often had cause to reflect on [it]. I hope that if I am ever confronted with having to make a similar decision that I will have the moral courage to do it again.' A part of me, he said, now wants to forget the nightmare; 'but another part says we cannot go forward until there's some accountability'.[54] This was an issue not just of the past but of the present and the future in South Africa; anyone found guilty by the TRC of gross human rights violations, he recommended, should be debarred from holding public office thereafter.[55]

After February 1990, Meredith reports, Madikizela-Mandela 'swiftly took revenge' on the group who had publicly condemned her the year before. Several people received threatening telephone calls. 'Stay away from Mandela', she told Cachalia, 'If you don't, you'll see what will happen.'[56] She continued such threats. The night before he testified in late November 1997, it was whispered, says Green, that Cachalia was part of an 'Indian cabal' within the ANC working against the Africanists like Madikizela-Mandela.[57] She expressed intimidatory and racist remarks directly before the Commission on 4 December, describing the testimony of Murphy Morobe as somehow the work of 'a cabal', and she twice referred to him as 'Murphy Patel'.[58] Krog states that Cachalia's and Morobe's declarations were greeted with a standing ovation in the hall. But she was uncertain whether this was for their moral courage or in recognition of the price that they have paid for exercising it. Once they were prominent UDF leaders, she remarks, but now they are 'nothing more than the backroom boys for politicians who still remember'; Morobe as chairperson of the Finance and Fiscal Commission and Cachalia then as head of the Safety and Security Secretariat under Minister Sydney Mufamadi.[59]

The position adopted by Crisis Committee members, and people at the top of the ANC in 1988–89 and 1997 was less principled and responsible. Aubrey Mokoena, by 1997 an ANC MP and parliamentary committee chair, had been ready, in January 1989, to accept Madikizela-Mandela's lies and obstinancy over the condition of the four abducted youths, and he remained eager to protect her. He told the TRC that 'Mama' had been so overcome by the 'altruism' of a social worker that she mistakenly associated with thugs, and he cast doubt upon Bishop Peter Storey's account of the actual hostage-negotiation situation at the house. The Rev. Frank Chikane was in 1997 head of the Deputy-President's Office, and recalled that, when the Committee had sought the release of the boys, 'Mama's' reaction 'was like a person under siege', and she had accused them of 'talking like the system'. The Crisis Committee, as Madlala records it, was as uncomfortable about testifying against Madikizela-Mandela as they had been about confronting her in January 1989. Mokoena's posture before the TRC was summed up by a participating lawyer as 'evasive and obstructive'.[60]

Dr Nthato Motlana, another Committee member, was known as a long-time associate of the Mandelas, and he was a prominent black businessman by 1997. When the hearings were in progress he told a reporter that Madikizela-Mandela 'is a friend of mine. I support her … If she approached me as an individual I would be pleased to give her a donation' for her campaign for the ANC deputy-presidency.[61] Cyril Ramaphosa, former Crisis Committee member, repeatedly declined to offer his testimony to the TRC.[62] Before the hearings opened on 18 November, the Minister of Justice, Dullah Omar, voiced support for Madikizela-Mandela on the grounds, which she herself used, that the struggle exonerated everything: murder claims against her, he said, were not comparable to atrocities by the former NP government, and they had to be seen in the context of apartheid.[63]

The murder of Dr Abu-Baker Asvat on 27 January 1989 stood in significance with the fate of the abducted youths and the slaughtered Stompie. Testimony exists that shortly before Seipei's death, Asvat told Madikizela-Mandela: 'This boy is seriously ill. He could die at any moment … You must take him to hospital.'[64] Further testimony states that Asvat had vehemently refused to provide Madikizela-Mandela with a confirmation that Cebekhulu had been sodomized by Paul Verryn. By 1997, Zakhele Mbatha and Thulani Dlamini had been sentenced to 30 years jail for Asvat's murder which took place in his surgery without robbery occurring.[65] Both men told the TRC that they were promised R20 000 by Madikizela-Mandela for killing Asvat; Mbatha offered considerable detail about the arrangements, and said that Madikizela-Mandela had explained that a certain man was disturbing her political work, that she wanted the man removed, and would appreciate it if they helped her.[66]

Ebrahim Asvat, brother to the slain doctor, told the TRC that the written statement of the two killers implicating Madikizela-Mandela was never produced in court. The police had merely told the family, he said, that they 'did not want to pursue that line'.[67] Asvat also said that he had found Madikizela-Mandela's behaviour after the murder strange, because he would have expected her to have been 'more supportive [of] my sister-in-law'. He felt that the subsequent removal, or smuggling, of Cebekhulu to Zambia pointed to a cover-up, and the 'deafening silence from members of the Crisis Committee' had added to this impression. He asked Albertina Sisulu, nurse-receptionist in the surgery, to confirm that Madikizela-Mandela and Cebekhulu had visited Dr Asvat.[68]

In a BBC interview with Fred Bridgland, Albertina Sisula had confirmed, by reference to her handwriting on a patient's card, that Cebekhulu had visited Dr Asvat's surgery on 30 December 1988.[69] But she stunned the subsequent TRC hearing when she testified that the handwriting concerned was not hers.[70] She tearfully spoke of the last hours of the man known as the 'people's doctor', and she affirmed their special closeness: 'Dr Asvat took me to be his mother; the clinic was a clinic of a mother and a son'. She allowed that the Football Club was 'doing havoc' in Soweto, but she could not understand why Madikizela-Mandela would kill Dr Asvat: 'I wouldn't think [she] would kill Dr Asvat. They were friendly', Sisulu said. Questioned gently about the contradictions in her statements, she seemed reluctant even to speculate about Madikizela-Mandela's motives.[71]

For some four days, on Krog's summary, Madikizela-Mandela was able to watch 'powerful men' – and a woman of high status in the ANC – 'bend over backwards to avoid saying anything bad about her'; clearly, 'those who didn't have the courage to stand up to her in the past, still [didn't] have it today'. At the end, Archbishop Tutu went still further and added his own and the Commission's prestige to a gratuitous endorsement of her claims. It was as if Cachalia and Morobe, and the relatives of her numerous victims had not spoken.[72] 'Many, *many* love you. Many, *many* say you should have been where you ought to be. The First Lady of the country … I love you very deeply … You are a great person.'[73]

The Report of the TRC, released a year later, was nonetheless cooly explicit. It found that the Mandela Football Club was involved in criminal activities, including 'killing, torture, assaults and arson'; that 'those who opposed [Madikizela-Mandela and the Club], or dissented from them, were branded as informers, and killed'; that 'she is accountable, politically and morally, for the gross violations of human rights' which were committed, and that 'Mrs Madikizela-Mandela herself was responsible for committing such gross violations'.[74]

The Report firmly addressed the vital issue, pursued by Cachalia and Morobe, but ignored by the ANC leadership, of accountability. Where amnesty had not been sought – as with both Madikizela-Mandela and Buthelezi[75] – 'prosecution should be considered where evidence exists that an individual has committed a gross human rights violation'. The Commission would provide the appropriate authorities with information in its possession concerning serious allegations against individuals. But the TRC ruled out Cachalia's specific recommendation of disqualification from public office, or lustration. It did this despite the fact that the earlier Skweyiya Commission concluded that 'no person who is guilty of committing atrocities should ever again be allowed to assume a position of power'.[76] The TRC decided not to recommend lustration because 'It would be inappropriate in the South African context.' No clarification of this conclusion was offered.[77]

When the hearings had been completed in December 1997, the editor of *Business Day* wrote that the ANC and the country were left with a problem:

It is time to stop fearing her and to take her on head-on. The governing party must take its membership into its confidence, and explain in clear and unequivocal terms why Madikizela-Mandela is unfit for public office.[78]

This did not happen at Mafikeng that month, even during President Mandela's very long and wide-ranging speech. It had not happened in the preceding days even when she presented the leadership with an excuse, in their own terms, to act purposefully against her.[79] Accountability for the elite sits uncomfortably with the party's traditions and with the principle that big issues are best decided among the very few. Some of her views and attitudes, moreover – on the preeminence of the armed struggle, that rule by the liberation movement constitutes the sufficient basis for democracy, that all criticism of the movement is reactionary, her racism – are not entirely her own, as Dullah Omar, Jacob Zuma, Thabo Mbeki and even Nelson Mandela in his Mafikeng speech seemed to indicate.

Predominance and the Mbeki–Zuma presidency

Few go further than Jacob Zuma in elevating the importance of the ANC. The ANC is above the law, the democratic constitution and individual responsibility. As national chairman, he cautioned party leaders in government, in Durban in November 1996, not to regard the country's 1996 Constitution as 'more important' than the ANC. No political force, he declared, could destroy the ANC; but 'once you begin to feel you are above the ANC you are in trouble'.[80] He spent 10 years on Robben Island and another 15 in exile, where he rose to be chief of intelligence in the 1980s. As he explained to an interviewer, the struggle is all, the ANC everything, and as an individual he is nothing.[81] These are among the qualities which made him the preferred candidate for the deputy-presidency in both party and state, and which gained him the chairmanship of the ANC's deployment committee too.

Thabo Mbeki emphasized immediately his presidential preeminence in June 1999. Cabinet ministers were summoned one by one till the early hours of the morning immediately after his inauguration banquet. Derek Hanekom was told that he was axed as Minister of Agriculture and Land Affairs at 2.30 a.m., and Pallo Jordan heard that he was no longer a minister at 3.00.[82] Significant appointments, of Nkosazana Dlamini-Zuma to Foreign Affairs and Penuell Maduna to Justice, were greeted by the *Mail and Guardian* with bafflement and amazement. The President assumed direct authority over the appointment of ANC provincial premiers. At the press conference to announce the new Cabinet he offered no explanation for his choices, and his response to questions was described in *Business Day* as 'terse and dismissive'.[83] He was not accountable to parliament for these decisions. As President, he immediately ceased to be an MP, and it was only through the Minister in the Office of the President, his right-hand man Essop Pahad, that parliamentary questions might be asked.[84] No COSATU MP was included in his cabinet. 100 days later, and the emphasis on 'hierarchical submission' was what stood out in the Mbeki government.[85]

A little later, and Azhar Cachalia lost his position in the safety and security secretariat. Mbeki was believed to have been 'gunning for' Cachalia for some time, partly because he saw no rationale for a large civilian secretariat as overseer to the police, and because Cachalia's human rights background and views developed within the UDF were unsympathetic to Steve Tshwete, successor to Sydney Mufamadi as Minister of Safety and Security. The secretariat had acted as a watchdog body against possible subversive tendencies in the police, but by late

1999 – despite Mandela's dastardly 'network' of just 10 months previously – these were deemed less threatening. Tshwete had 'cut Cachalia out of the loop' since taking office. Mbeki, furthermore, had appointed the former Director-General of Foreign Affairs, Jackie Selebi, as the new police commissioner, and Selebi was known to be a 'long-time [ANC] servant'. Cachalia was still being jeopardized for his democratic morality, while the consolidation of presidential power was furthered.[86]

When Mbeki made his state-of-the-nation speech in February 2000, an exile's approach to power where decisions were made in small groups and commands issued was evident in government. Parliament and people were simply being commanded or exhorted to follow.[87] Important institutional changes underlay this approach. A new single entity, 'the presidency', had come into being, with a staff complement of 334 people. The brief of the deputy president was reduced and refocused – unlike the broad mandate which Mandela had accorded Mbeki, it was now to 'fulfil tasks delegated by the president' and act as leader of government business in parliament. A minister without portfolio had been created in the presidency, who reported to the President and controlled all government communications – the long-trusted Pahad. The contracts of directors-general were now made with the President, rather than with their own ministries as before. Other changes strengthened policy coordination and advisory services; but the overall themes of all of the restructuring, according to Jacobs and other analysts, was the 'lack of accountability to elected representatives and the centralisation of power in the hands of a few individuals'. Neither Minister Pahad nor the directors of a new policy coordination and advisory unit were accountable to the legislature. No portfolio committee could summon them to explain decisions. They are accountable only to Mbeki. A highly organized, even an 'imperial presidency', had been established.[88]

Universalizing predominance

At the Mafikeng conference in December 1997, the ANC adopted a resolution on cadre policy. It noted 'the need to deploy [ANC] cadres to various organs of state, including the public service and other centres of power in society'. It mandated the NEC to put in place a deployment strategy; to identify key power centres, and establish deployment committees at all governmental levels. These would appoint party members not only to the public service but to 'parastatals, structures of the movement, and the private sector', and they would ensure that cadres remained accountable to the ANC.[89]

Plans were developed in the second half of 1998 in a document called, in short form, the 'State and Social Transformation'; it was drawn up by a committee which included Joel Netshitenzhe, described as Mbeki's 'most trusted adviser' in exile and perhaps the 'most central of all' in the 'innermost circle' recently;[90] he was a NEC and NWC member, and since January 1998 head of the Government Communications and Information Service; the committee was overseen by Thabo Mbeki. Transformation entailed, according to this paper, extending the power of the liberation movement 'over all levers of power: the army, the police...intelligence structures, the judiciary...and agencies such as regulatory bodies, the public broadcaster, the central bank, and so on.'[91]

An ANC national deployment committee, headed by Zuma, was established in November 1998. The party's control was to be both widely extended and simultaneously centralized; cadres appointed would be accountable primarily to party structures rather than to the institutions to which they were deployed; 'parliamentary caucuses', for example, were to be placed under the 'supervision and direction' of the party leadership.[92] The distinction between government and party, and the separation of constitutional powers between executive, legislature and judiciary, would be undermined or ended.

Through 1998–99, ANC members assumed control, for example, over the military (Lt. Gen. Siphiwe Nyanda was a former MK chief-of-staff, elected to the NEC in 1991), the police (Selebi), the intelligence services, the Reserve Bank (Tito Mboweni, Minister of Labour, as governor, and Gill Marcus, a London exile and NEC member, as deputy governor), the centralized national prosecution service (Bulelani Ngcuka, an ANC MP), the Government Communications and Information Service (Yacoob Abba Omar became Netshitenzhe's deputy), and in the Revenue Service.[93] The country's drug-safety watchdog was purged when it insisted on proper tests for a fraudulent anti-AIDS drug, called Virodene, backed by Deputy President Mbeki and his long-time stalwart and then Health Minister Nkosazana Dlamini-Zuma.[94] Already predominant in parliament and the country, with a small and lambasted opposition, the ANC sought 'to interfere with everything'.[95] President Mbeki was both 'Africanising society and wresting control of institutions of power'.[96] By the beginning of the new century, ANC cadres were in position, according to Leon, in almost every government department and most parastatals and statutory bodies.[97] Control had been asserted over the public broadcaster, the independent South African Broadcasting Commission; it was by this time, according to Kirby, 'more obsequious a tool of government than ever it was under the Nats'.[98]

Real predominance

Effective and durable one-party predominance actually means much more than numbers, of parliamentary domination and the subordination of the opposition. The continuing dominance of one party under democratic electoral conditions derives, according to Pempel, from the skilful mobilization of leading social forces, and the distribution in turn of resources to them.[99] As seen in Sweden and Japan, this further requires the creation of an effective developmental programme subject to debate and revision in open electoral competition. Collaboration between the ruling elite, the bureaucracy and other forces is important, but it is a process based upon a coherent developmental programme, and its conversion over time into a close approximation to the country's national identity or distinctive ethos. The creation of this distinctive programme and its cohesion with the society is what true predominance requires.[100]

Mosca, from a different but not dissimilar angle, stressed that a 'political formula' was vital to a successful and enduring ruling elite in a polity based on law and open competition.[101] People wished to feel that they were governed in terms of principles, not simply the brute force of an Idi Amin or the opportunism and manipulation, say, of Clinton and his triangulation. The political formula could not be based on fraud or subterfuge; it had to mean something to many people to be capable of winning and retaining their support. A coherent and meaningful ideology would justify rule by the particular elite, and it would in turn unify both them and the society. It could only do this if it was open to debate and revision in the light of changing circumstances. Sweden saw a cohesion existing over four decades between three distinct elements – the social democratic party and government; the Swedish Model of socio-economic development based on collaboration between corporations, unions and an interventionist state; and the Swedish people broadly. The Swedish Model represented the body of ideas on which the country's political institutions rested, and it became well-nigh synonymous with the ruling party and the country.

Predominance without content

Despite the great widening of its power, and the centralization of that power in the dual presidency, the ANC appears to be a long way from the achievement of predominance in the Swedish sense. A number of issues, 1998–2000, attested to a high degree of subjectivism, incoherency and irrationality in the thought and actions of President Mbeki, the emperor of the ruling party and government.

Issue one: the TRC Report

The Truth and Reconciliation Commission had been established by the government of Nelson Mandela, but the ANC, led by Party President Thabo Mbeki, endeavoured to prevent the release of its final Report in late 1998. Archbishop Tutu declared that he was 'devastated' by the ANC's eleventh-hour move, which was 'desperately distressing'. It took the matter to court in Cape Town, and in an overnight hearing Judge Wilfred Thring ruled that the party had failed to establish that the TRC had not adequately considered the ANC's responses to its findings. Mandela embraced Tutu when he received the Report, 'with all its imperfections' he observed, a few hours later.[102]

The TRC Chairman called on churches and the media to keep watch on the ruling party. 'We so easily jettison the ideals we had when we were struggling. It is important that we retain the vigour of our civil society organs that were part of [that] struggle', he soon told the *Sunday Times*. 'We've got to retain the same capacity to smell out corruption [and] the abuse of power'. He went on:

> Sycophants are the worst possible thing to have around you when you are in power ... there is no way in which you can assume that yesterday's oppressed will not become tomorrow's oppressors ... we shouldn't be surprised if it happens here.

Anger came from Thabo Mbeki. His spokesman, Ronnie Mamoepa, stated: 'Mbeki said that no member of the ANC can ever concur with the scurrilous attempts to criminalise the liberation struggle by characterising [it] ... as gross human rights violations.' The state president's spokesman, Parks Mankahlana, said that Mandela had not been consulted on the court action. Another party representative, Thabo Masebe, dismissed the idea that Mandela and Mbeki had disagreed on the blocking move, adding lamely: 'Mandela was informed about the decision to go to court. He did not have to agree or disagree.'[103] The ANC issued a statement defending its decision to resort to the law while also claiming that the TRC's Report 'made findings which are blatantly contrary to fundamental principles of international law'.[104]

This was untrue. The TRC had not adopted the so-called moral equivalence position, and it accepted the distinction between actions taken to uphold an unjust system, and those used to bring such a system to an end. It accepted both the international declaration of apartheid as a crime against humanity, and the view that the ANC's armed struggle represented a 'just war'. But it 'added the critical rider', Cherry explains, that 'a just war' could not and did not render all acts committed in pursuit of that cause as 'just'. And it followed that all civilians or non-combatants who were killed, tortured, abducted or suffered severe ill-treatment within the context of the political conflict were the victims of gross human rights violations, and those responsible for committing such acts were the perpetrators of such gross violations.[105]

In trying to prevent the presentation of the facts about MK's 'errors' or 'aberrations' – as the ANC styled it – Mbeki, according to Trewhela, was suppressing gross human rights violations in which he was himself complicit; through his high positions in the command structures that 'had at least endorsed and at worst directed these abuses'.[106] More generally, the ANC was again trying to prevent the dissemination of the truth about the struggle in the 1980s, including effectively the systematic crimes of Buthelezi, and Madikizela-Mandela's sustained abuses. It further threatened the knowledge in the hands of the people, and it facilitated the continuance of deceit within the elite.

The lies continue with scarcely diminishing momentum. Themba Khoza was the leading IFP warlord in the Gauteng area 1990–94 and, on the findings of the Goldstone Commission and evidence presented to the TRC, an agent of Pretoria's security apparatus. He was directly linked to the Boipatong massacre of June 1992, and bore heavy responsibility for the deaths of perhaps 14000 to 20000 people in the Gauteng township violence of the early 1990s; he could be placed, says Powell, 'among the top ten mass murderers in South Africa's history'. But when the then Inkatha MP died, aged 41, in May 2000, the ANC expressed its 'sense of grief', and commended his important role as a peacemaker.[107] The only thing for which Khoza had been successfully charged over 10 years was his absence from the National Assembly in 1999.[108]

Issue two: ethics in government

According to an ANC elections advertisement in 1999, people of high ethics and integrity were needed if the society was to achieve a better life for all, and on 25 June that year, in his inaugural address to parliament, President Mbeki 'reiterate[d]' his government's commitment to 'honest, transparent and accountable government' and our determination 'to act against anybody who transgresses these norms'. Just a few days later, the newly-installed premier of Mpumalanga province,

Ndaweni Mahlangu, stated at a news conference that it was usual and acceptable for politicians to lie: Lying 'is nothing new. It wasn't the end of Bill Clinton's life and I personally don't find it to be a very bad thing.'[109] He was one of three premiers 'hand-picked' by Mbeki, supposedly to clean up the country's 'corruption kingdom' (Mamparalanga),[110] and replace the ousted Mathews Phosa. A former magistrate and MP in the KwaNdebele administration, he was generally considered to be an unknown in leadership terms, essentially a 'lackey of the system'.[111]

South Africa's Public Protector, Selby Baqwa, described Mahlangu's statement as 'abominable, outrageous and unacceptable', and many others said much the same, but the ANC in Northern, KZ-N and in Mpumalanga provinces defended him.[112] Because his egregious remarks had been made in a prominent public situation, it was imperative, said Nyatsumba, that the issue be dealt with publicly by Mbeki. The President had both the opportunity and the need to show that he meant business on corruption and accountability, but spokesperson Mamoepa merely announced that President Mbeki regarded the matter as a party-political one which had to be dealt with by the ANC.[113] The President who had appointed him in the first place took no responsibility for doing so.[114] Mbeki had asserted control over ANC provincial governments;[115] he exercised his powers to choose a person with low or no ethics and integrity; and he failed to 'act against him' when the need arose.

Issue three: HIV-AIDS

The ANC government's readiness to 'interfere in everything', combined with President Mbeki's subjectivism and imprudence, are expressed conspicuously in the critical issue of HIV-AIDS. South Africa, next to Botswana, has the highest incidence of 15–24-year-olds with HIV-AIDS.[116] The infection was claiming, at the end of the 1990s, around 1700 people a day. Those most at risk, according to Epstein, 'are poor black people, particularly those who have been socially displaced', such as migrant workers, truck drivers, sex workers, miners from rural areas and their wives, girlfriends and children at home.[117] Developing countries like Thailand, Uganda and Botswana were responding to the threat by establishing programmes where HIV-positive pregnant women would be offered an anti-retroviral drug, AZT, nevirapine, or their generic equivalents. In 1998, a number of maternity wards in public hospitals in South Africa were planning pilot projects on the feasibility of providing AZT to every HIV-positive mother-to-be.

'Almost immediately' Dlamini-Zuma suspended public funds for these projects, because, she said, even short courses of AZT 'were too costly'. When Glaxo Wellcome offered the drug at a discount to the Health Ministry for use in public maternity wards, the offer was turned down.[118]

As President, Mbeki frequently mentioned the disease in his speeches and showed his concern, it was said, by wearing an AIDS ribbon. But he soon began to raise doubts in public about the connection between the HIV condition and the deadly disease, and associated his own thinking with the small minority of scientists in the field who denied the existence of the linkage. In an early address to parliament he affirmed that AZT was not only too expensive but also suggested that it might be toxic.[119] His telephone conversation with a prominent American AIDS dissident was described by Dr John Moore of the Aaron Diamond AIDS Research Centre in New York as 'giv[ing] lifeblood to a dead cause'; 'it's tantamount to Holocaust denial because the implications are so serious'. Lynn Morris, head of the AIDS unit at South Africa's National Institute for Virology, said that 'there is no debate amongst scientists that HIV causes AIDS ... this debate is being generated by people on the fringe'.[120]

The ANC government had then only recently abandoned the fraudulent AIDS cure Virodene,[121] when Thabo Mbeki appointed a presidential AIDS advisory panel. Leading dissidents were included among its 33 members, but experts from developing countries that had succeeded in curbing AIDS, such as Uganda and Senegal, *The Economist* noted, were not. A planned two-month's discussion exercise would cost more than R2 million in travel expenses.[122]

Dr Ruth Nduati, a scientist at the University of Nairobi, identified the likely consequences of the President's actions. 'Encouragement of dissident views by leaders of Mbeki's calibre has the potential of creating doubt and undoing strategies to prevent the spread of the disease', she said. 'Leaders should be careful about who they stand up for and support. People on our continent are more likely to believe Mbeki than all our top scientists'.[123]

President Mbeki responded to such cautionary comment with distortion, hostility and non-accountability. Spokesman and head of communications in the presidency, Parks Mankahlana, wrote a lengthy article in which he portrayed the reactions to the President's views as constituting 'scorn and ridicule', and 'abuse' of the government's efforts.[124] Scientists who threatened to boycott an international AIDS conference in South Africa because of their concern about Mbeki's immoderation, were described soon after by Mankahlana as 'utterly stupid', and they were, he said, 'welcome to stay away'. The President's office, he stated, 'did not owe any explanations' to anyone, and it had 'no intention' of clarifying Mbeki's stance on AIDS.[125]

Throwing reason to the winds, President Mbeki took the further step of writing personally in early April to President Clinton, his letter copied to Prime Minister Tony Blair and other world leaders. The letter described those who criticized his stance on AIDS as part of a 'campaign of intellectual intimidation and terrorism…born by a degree of fanaticism, which is truly frightening'. Mbeki declared that the West could not dictate Africa's response to AIDS. Those who denied differing views over the causes of AIDS were compared by him to 'the racist apartheid tyranny'.

The letter was said to have stunned the American government and, after a copy was leaked to the *Washington Post*, to have caused outrage among AIDS activists and researchers there and at home.[126] Clinton was reported to have replied through his Ambassador to the United Nations, Richard Holbrooke, who informed his South African counterpart, Dumisani Kumalo, that the American President wanted Mbeki to repudiate the statements he had made in his letter.[127] In London in May he expressed his singular attitude publicly again. Asked if the topic of HIV-AIDS had been raised in talks with Prime Minister Blair, he said, in Blair's silent presence: 'If it does come up, I am happy to educate the Prime Minister on these issues'.[128]

Mbeki's views brought no reaction, however, from within the ANC government. There was, noted Sipho Seepe, president of the Sebokeng campus of Vista University, 'a paralysing and deafening silence from ANC members, within and outside the government'. Are we experiencing a situation, he asked, 'where might determines right? Is there an unwritten rule that no member of the ANC can publicly differ with the president?' To state the obvious, he said, 'that one is a president does not endow one with infinite wisdom'. The country was wasting valuable time and resources in pandering to the President's misguided medical investigations, and there were worrying implications for the task of democratization in South Africa.[129]

President Mbeki seemed oblivious to the impact of his intemperate views and actions. His letter to Bill Clinton, as Barber described it, 'ha[d] raised serious questions about [his] judgement and temperament'.[130] His immediate responses to the perceived doubts were less than reassuring,[131] and he continued the same way. When some 5000 scientists and doctors published an affirmation that HIV was the cause of AIDS, and that the ideas of dissident scientists were to be condemned, the Mbeki government labelled the declaration as intolerant: 'We have never seen this kind of intolerance', said Mankahlana, 'and we don't want people bringing intolerance to South Africa'.[132]

Presenting the keynote address to the conference, High Court Judge Edwin Cameron, himself HIV-positive, accused the government of mismanaging the epidemic 'almost at every conceivable turn'. He described President Mbeki's 'flirtation' with those who, 'in the face of all reason and evidence', have sought to question the causes of AIDS as 'intractably puzzling'. It had created unbelief among scientists and consternation among AIDS workers.[133]

The obscurantism nonetheless continued, stressing sometimes that a virus could not cause a syndrome, casting doubt upon the impact even the existence of AIDS, and suggesting weird origins for the disease in Africa.[134] Addressing the ANC parliamentary caucus on 28 September, the President's views were extreme. The emphasis placed on HIV-AIDS was the result of a conspiracy by American drug companies; he said, according to Barrell's reporting, that if one agreed that HIV caused AIDS, it followed that the condition had to be treated by drugs produced by the big companies. These firms therefore promoted the thesis that HIV caused AIDS. He and his government were the target of a hostile campaign by powerful forces which included, he claimed, the Central Intelligence Agency and the same pharmaceuticals. The propaganda being put out by the companies, and covertly by the CIA, were all linked, he said. Reports being spread that he was 'deranged' – his word – were part of the campaign against him and his government. And he accused the AIDS lobby group, the Treatment Action Campaign, of being a leading agent in this manoeuvre, of being funded by the drug companies and of having infiltrated the trade unions to call for treatment for HIV-positive people.[135]

The NEC, on 3 October, endorsed Mbeki's position and also declared that all the controversy over HIV-AIDS resulted from 'a massive propaganda onslaught against the ANC, its President, and its government'. It criticized COSATU and the SACP for taking different views in public.[136]

Issue four: Mugabe and Zimbabwe

Additional damaging irrationalities arose in May 2000 when President Mbeki announced a major initiative to assist in the redistribution of some 118 white-owned farms in Zimbabwe. Purchase-funds of around R100 million, he indicated, were to come from Saudi Arabia and a number of Scandinavian countries, without regard for the prior establishment of control mechanisms to ensure that the land was distributed fairly and openly to the landless,[137] or for any other complexities either.[138] Previous offers of assistance, for instance from Britain, had made the control over redistribution an essential precondition for the release of funds. During a visit to Denmark in early June, President Mbeki held meetings with businessmen with interests in South Africa, and with the leaders of Denmark, Norway, Sweden, Finland and Iceland. But he was said to have startled his hosts on one occasion when he accused Americans of being 'ignorant' about the different countries of Africa, and the English of being 'very arrogant' about South Africa's information technology industry.[139]

In a subsequent interview with the *Sunday Times*, Mbeki insisted that the governments of Norway, Sweden, Denmark and the United States had said that they were ready to assist in the redistribution of 118 Zimbabwean farms. Malala reported that he made this claim 'only hours after' the prime ministers of the three Nordic countries 'stated unequivocally' that they would not contribute to the scheme. Led by Finland's Paavo Lipponen, the Nordic premiers said they would fund such a programme only if Zimbabwe itself initiated and contributed to it. Lipponen said that 'they were a bit reserved. We would not like Zimbabwe to use [money intended for land reform] for military purposes. The Zimbabweans should first organise land reforms themselves...' Sweden's Goran Persson also indicated how detached from reality was Mbeki's proposals. Sweden had suspended development assistance to Zimbabwe two years earlier. 'I will wait for a formal request and I will consider it', he told the *Sunday Times*. 'Naturally it must come from Zimbabwe.'[140]

The Mbeki government expressed support for Mugabe as the Zimbabwean economy collapsed, the rule of law continued to be flouted by the state, and international aid was suspended. It was heedless of economic consequences. After an investment meeting of southern African leaders in Windhoek in October 2000, Deputy President Jacob Zuma said that Mugabe had convincingly explained his policies. 'The delegates were quite appreciative of what he said and he did come across very well...I think he gave quite a reasonable explanation'.[141] As Reserve Bank governor, Tito Mboweni, insisted that land reform would occur in South Africa in line with the constitution, the rand touched new record lows against the dollar.[142] Nelson Mandela was holding private talks with Morgan Tsvangirai in a bid to find, it was said, an 'honourable exit' for Mugabe. Differing with his successor on this issue, too, he had made it clear that he believed that President Mugabe should resign.[143]

President Mbeki has associated South Africa with the boundless destructiveness of a demagogue – thousands of ruling party militants were occupying some 1700 farms in late 2000, demanding that they be given the land, while Mugabe refused to abide by court rulings ordering police to remove the squatters.[144] He goes further and depicts his actions as liberationist in continental terms, and he proclaims and demands all African support for his actions. On an official visit to Nigeria in early November, he said that the land-acquisition programme was 'progressing well', in line with the wishes of the people. 'All we are doing is making Africa more African', he claimed. International condemnation of Zimbabwe was that of the imperialist powers, 'not a condemnation of Africa … our African brothers, and in fact the third world as a whole, support[s] us', he said. 'It is a matter on which Africans must stand together'.[145]

An apparent influence on President Mbeki's readiness to intervene personally into complex issues was the intellectual brilliance which Hadland and Rantao, for instance, attributed to him.[146] Interviewed by the *Sunday Times* in February 2000, he made seemingly oblique reference to Mamphela Ramphele's criticism, a few weeks earlier, about the silence of the intellectuals, in an otherwise loose and self-congratulatory statement:

> You've seen some of the comments over the last few months from some of the black academics, some of whom say essentially: 'Can the President please stop speaking, because the problem is that when he makes his major statements we get intimidated into silence because we don't know how to engage him intellectually' … they ask me: 'But when do you find time to read all these things that you quote?'[147]

Presidential preeminence and widening predominance afford ready platforms for the expression of Mbeki's self-conceived brilliance, encouraged further perhaps by contrast with the mediocrities with whom he has associated himself. But they negate any hope for coherent programme development in the ANC. The emphasis over a decade has been more on the abandonment of ideological guidelines than on the necessarily slow task of constructing viable new ones. The task in any case cannot be left to a very small and rather isolated elite, least of all to Mbeki, alone. The party might have all the numbers, but without coherency and no meaningful broad-based policy debate its predominance will remain an empty shell.

Reproduced with the permission by Jonathan Shapiro, the artist.

6
Predominance and the Empowerment Goose

The Freedom Charter was approved by some 3000 delegates at the Congress of the People at Kliptown, Soweto, in June 1955.[1] It had formed, says Marais, an 'ideological bedrock' for the ANC, its idealistic phraseology bearing a 'close resemblance' to the French Declaration of the Rights of Man or the Declaration of Independence of the future United States.[2] It promised the nationalization of mines, banks and monopoly industries, and the redistribution of land. It declared that South Africa 'belong[ed] to all who live in it, black and white', and proposed equal status for 'all national groups'. It affirmed the right of all citizens not only to vote but to hold public office and to enjoy equality before the law. Free compulsory education, minimum wages protection, free medical care, and welfare for the aged were promised: 'Rent and prices shall be lowered, food plentiful and no one shall go hungry', it proclaimed; 'slums shall be demolished and new suburbs built'.[3] This was a non-racial, social democratic programme, in some elements even a socialist one.[4]

But the Charter had been placed 'above debate and dispute' in a kind of 'sacred zone of popular consciousness' in the ANC. Discussion of ambiguities in its assumptions and promises were 'either actively suppressed or smoothed over with platitudes'.[5] In this unquestioned position it served symbolically to assert the preeminence of the ANC in the liberation movement: 1985, for instance, had been declared 'The Year of the Freedom Charter' campaign.[6] Yet it was an eminence based in good part on the ideas in this document. At the public rally in Cape Town celebrating the formation of the UDF in 1983, 'successive speeches' celebrated 'the Charterist tradition and drew on Charterist symbolism', although 'key speakers insisted, the UDF was not a Charterist front'.[7]

Waldmeir reports that in 1990 'a deep suspicion of capitalism…per-
vaded all ranks of the ANC', and 'the intention' then was that 'an ANC
state would control, if not own, much of the economy after liberation'.[8] The subsequent Minister of Labour and Governor of the Reserve
Bank, Tito Mboweni, said in 1992:

> The ANC believes that a strategy of 'growth through redistribution'
> will be the appropriate new path for the South African econ-
> omy…accumulation depends on the prior redistribution of
> resources. Major changes will have to take place in existing power
> relations as a necessary condition for this new growth path.

Nelson Mandela even appeared to echo the point in 1994: 'While the
democratic state will maintain and develop the market, we envisage
occasions when it will be necessary for it to intervene where growth
and development require such intervention.'[9]

The elite and big business

Yet large changes of programmatic outlook were simultaneously occurring, initiated and carried forward within the political and economic
elites. The Anglo American Corporation, says Waldmeir, had been the
first to 'break the taboo on talks with the ANC', in September 1985 in
Lusaka, striking, as she says, 'a clever blow for capitalism'. Oliver
Tambo had been hesitant, Thabo Mbeki relaxed and outgoing. The
ANC group 'stuck to the policies' of the Freedom Charter, but it was
'the cordiality of the meeting' which 'almost overwhelmed' the businessman Tony Bloom. The ANC already had a close relationship with
the Corporation's Zambian office, and used Anglo's Lusaka headquarters as a 'postbox for sensitive mail'. Thereafter Mbeki treated the home
of managing director, Vernon Webber, as 'an unofficial clubhouse for
entertaining visiting South Africans'. Gavin Relly, another corporate
chief, found 'immediate common ground' with Mbeki over mutual
pipe-smoking. The exiled leaders sought to convey the message of their
patriotism, humanity, and moderation, and Relly was convinced that
'they were just a bunch of homesick South Africans'.[10]

Contacts were maintained at various levels. Anglo director, Clem
Sunter, was summoned to Nelson Mandela's prison cell in the late
1980s, 'to give him a briefing on the politico-economic scenario' in the
country, and Mbeki celebrated the news of Mandela's imminent
release in early 1990 over champagne with top Afrikaner businessmen.

Mboweni, Waldmeir adds, was 'bombarded with invitations' to conferences and engagements with local and visiting businessmen, and ANC officials were sent to Washington for familiarization courses at the World Bank.[11]

Mandela, after February 1990, 'constantly sought' the views of international businessmen and bankers. He 'cultivated close relationships with top local businessmen': he spent holidays with the Clive Menell family, entertained at the Johannesburg home of the flamboyant insurance magnate Douw Steyn, dined regularly with Harry Oppenheimer and participated in the latter's Brenthurst Group which drew together top businessmen and opinion-makers. The 'turning point' in his thinking, she believes, was the 1992 World Economic Forum in Davos. Afterwards he said: 'We have observed the hostility and concern of businessmen toward [*sic*] nationalisation, and we can't ignore their perceptions ... we are well aware that if you cannot cooperate with business, you cannot succeed in generating growth.'[12]

A warm reciprocal relationship was underway. His biographer, Meredith, states that Mandela was 'attracted to people of wealth and fame'. While he enjoys contact with common people, 'the company to which he is most attracted is that of the rich and famous; status impresses him'. Millionaires were quite willing to offer their services. Among them, Sol Kerzner helped pay for Zinzi's extravagant wedding and provided a honeymoon suite at one of his Mauritian hotels. When Mandela approached 20 leading businessmen 'for at least one million rands each to help him with election expenses, all but one complied'.[13] Kerzner, we know, obliged with R2 million, and thanks to the revelations prompted by Holomisa, Mandela saw 'nothing unusual' in this gift, about which he informed no one.

Tony O'Reilly was another new friend. The rugby-playing entrepreneur had earlier been given a choice between running a multinational company – Heinz – and running a small European country – Ireland – and had chosen the former. He had concluded, according to O'Toole, that once Ireland opened itself up to multinationals, the prospect of national control over the economy became untenable. Both he and Robert Mugabe had been educated by Irish Jesuits, and after 1980 friendship was established between them.[14] Later 'he quickly established a friendship' with Mandela too. The future President spent Christmas 1993 in O'Reilly's holiday home in Nassau. He came to accept the limits of state control, and the Irish corporate chief acquired ownership of Independent Newspapers, South Africa's largest print-media group.[15] With 14 titles and four million readers, the group worked hard, says

Haffajee, 'to position its papers as establishment voices, closely allied to the new political power'. Its most senior appointments, 1995–98, 'include[d] editors drawn from the [ANC] tradition'. The new parliamentary editor, Zubeida Jaffer, for example, said that: 'I see our role as both the court jester and the *imbongi*' (or praise singer). O'Reilly, a billionaire in his own right and known for his free-spending lifestyle, was 'used to rubbing shoulders with power'.[16]

The gift-giving by businessmen to the ANC has gone on, though the predominant colour of the givers may have altered. The party treasurer-general, Arnold Stofile, told the Mafikeng conference in December 1997 that donations of R2 million to the ANC had become customary among black businessmen. In return, he declared, 'we opted for the role of facilitators for black business in the country'.[17]

Nelson Mandela was also attracted to prominent Third World dictators, as were some of them to him. He visited Jakarta in October 1990 where he received, along with a state banquet, the award of the Republic of Indonesia Star and a cheque for $10 million for the ANC. He made no reference then to the suppression of the East Timorese people, and he actually described discrimination against Aborigines in Australia, which he also visited, as an internal matter for that country.[18] Other interlinkages may or may not have involved Mandela personally. Umno, the predominant ruling party in Kuala Lumpur, began a 'courtship' of the ANC after 1990; suggestions exist that Malaysia provided R10 million in cash to the ANC before 1994, with a further R23 million being offered in kind – automobiles, travel expenses, services – sometimes to individual members they felt they could influence.[19] Links with Morocco and Libya were also close and lucrative. The former donated about R3 million to the ANC before 1994. President Mandela later said that Libya and Syria 'helped us to where we are today', and that friendship with them 'is the moral code that I respect above everything else'.[20]

President Thabo Mbeki has established a 'very good' friendship, according to his spokesman Parks Mankahlana, with the Saudi prince Bandar Ibn Sultan Ibn Abdul Aziz who is his country's Ambassador to the United States and the owner of a very large estate at Glympton in England. The President stayed there on two occasions in May and June 2000, and Bandar offered him the use of his private aircraft to fly to Washington.[21]

A comfortable lifestyle was quite quickly embraced by the ANC leadership. Winnie Madikizela-Mandela remained an ANC MP, NEC member and chieftainess of the Women's League when she was divorced in early 1996. On evidence presented then, her monthly expenses totalled some R107 000 – among other things, salaries for 'six staff and secretary' of R11 000; travelling R10 000; entertainment R12 000; and clothing and cosmetics R12 000. A residence at Orlando West was estimated to have cost about R1.2 million. Her official income was, however, only R16 000 a month. Documents indicated that Nelson Mandela had given her about R3 million since 1990.[22] She has continued to play a prominent leadership role in the party, and was, for example, very active publically in the 1999 elections.

When Nelson Mandela purchased a house for R4.5 million in the exclusive Cape Town suburb of Bishopscourt in 1999, this was his fourth such acquisition in six years. He had bought a house in Johannesburg, and built another in his home village of Qunu. After marrying Graca Machel, he acquired a seaside residence in Maputo. He bought the Bishopscourt property from the chairman of Old Mutual, Mike Levett, who was relocating to Britain.[23] Soon after President Mbeki's installation, an expenditure of R5 million was announced for renovations on his official residence in Pretoria. A week later, and R2.6 million was allocated to improve his official home in Rondebosch, Cape Town. The previous year he had spent R3 million to modernize Oliver Tambo House, which had been allocated to him as deputy leader.[24]

Deputy President Jacob Zuma's two wives were to be given new cars, a Mercedes and a Toyota 4×4, at a cost of R550 000 to the taxpayer, it was revealed in parliament in April 2000. Tony Leon noted that MPs' wives did not get cars, and wondered if taxpayers would foot the bill for automobiles for the spouses of the entire cabinet. Spokesman Parks Mankahlana declared, however, that it was 'unreasonable and unfair' to compare the status of the Deputy President with that of an ordinary MP.[25]

Other ANC politicians have emulated this behaviour. Tony Yengeni at the beginning of the 1990s had been part of the self-styled populist group with Madikizela-Mandela, Peter Mokaba, and Holomisa, but near the end of the decade he was one of 'the new generation' of ANC politicians who 'enjoys politics and the limelight it brings to them'. Rantao pictured his interests: 'White is his preferred colour and Mercedes Benz his favourite wheels. He enjoys good food and drinks. He and his wife Lumka live in a luxurious house in Milnerton, Cape Town.' Born into relative poverty in 1954 in the Cape, he had 'dumped the military greens [of an MK soldier] for designer clothes'.[26]

Chothia described him shortly after as a politician who had won the confidence of the party leadership. He had been made ANC Chief Whip, entrusted with the task of maintaining discipline and ensuring the achievement of the party programme in parliament. He thought that Tony Leon was the worst politician in the legislature, and he criticized the opposition because they offered 'no praise or acknowledgement of what we have achieved'. He said that he had been a strong supporter of the government's macroeconomic policies 'from the word go', and he appeared to have some of the qualities that are so noticeable in Jacob Zuma. 'I am a champion of the policies of my government. I must stand by them ... and make sure that they are implemented', he declared.[27]

Yengeni headed the South African parliamentary observers team to the Zimbabwean elections in June 2000, and when the Mbeki government announced that they had indeed been substantially free and fair, this was on the basis of Yengeni's observations.[28] He was a member of the SACP, but he believed that there was 'nothing wrong morally or politically for black people to become millionaires. When there are millionaires in other race groups, it's not a question. Suddenly, it's a question [when it comes to blacks].'[29]

Meredith believed that President Mandela 'was seen to be "soft" on greed, as lenient with his colleagues as he had been with Winnie, showing them the same kind of perverse loyalty.'[30] Provincial government ministers of both the ANC and the IFP have displayed what Lodge terms 'grandiose expectations of privilege and deference'. An Mpumalanga transport minister, Jackson Mthembu, for instance, spent R2.3 million on a fleet of BMW 528s for his colleagues, explaining the expenditure as follows: 'I am a leader in my community and therefore have a certain status – you can't be saying that I should drive a 1600 cc vehicle?'[31] Informed estimates of the cost of corruption nationally are large. The accountants Deloitte & Touche suggested in 1997 that public sector fraud and mismanagement could exceed R10 billion that year. Judge Willem Heath, head of the special investigative unit, said in 1998 that his team had recovered, since 1996, R10 billion of public money which he believed represented only 5 per cent of all lost or embezzled funds[32] – some R200 billion had gone, 1996–98. Of the many causes of corruption, Heath singled out two: the appointment of people to positions they know nothing about, and greed. Greed, he added, was fundamental.[33]

Empowering the arms trade

The opportunities have not decreased. In September 1999 a large arms procurement deal was announced with a range of foreign suppliers, worth around R30 billion, phased over some 8–12 years, and generating supposedly about R70 billion in inward investment, local procurement by foreign companies and tens if not hundreds of countertrade arrangements. Trade and Industry Minister, Alec Erwin, said the total contractual commitments amounted to R104 billion, but 'the actual economic benefit [would] amount to about R70 billion over a period of 11 years'. There would be 'defence-related offsets worth R14.5 billion'; counterpurchases valued at R31 billion; and foreign investment of R24 billion. At least 65 000 new jobs, many of them skilled and in manufacturing, would be created. At the same time, the Finance Minister, Trevor Manuel, declared that no negative affects on the budget deficit would result.[34] A veritable businessman's tooth fairy, Mulholland surmised.[35]

Joe Modise, as Defence Minister and former MK supremo, had overseen the initial phases of this rich and loose programme. Earlier, over three decades in exile he explained, he had made contact with influential people around the world: 'Add to that my experience as Minister of Defence, when I travelled … marketing Armscor products, and you will agree that I have built enormous contacts. Business depends a great deal on contacts'. Less than three months after vacating his ministerial post in mid-1999, he had taken the chair of two companies, Conlog and Labat Africa, the latter a black empowerment group largely owned, it was said, by former liberation struggle cadres who shared his ideals.[36]

The structure of the weapons procurement programme required foreign suppliers to form partnerships with local companies. By around May 2000 two with close links to the head of the Defence Department's arms procurement committee, Shamin 'Chippy' Shaik, had been awarded 'the lion's share of local contracts'.[37] One, African Defence Systems (ADS), listed Shaik's brother Shabir as a director, while his wife Zarina was employed as a senior marketing executive. Retired Lieutenant-General Lambert Moloi was another director, whom Powell described as 'a close associate of [Joe] Modise'. Moloi's son-in-law, Tshepo Molai, was also a director of ADS. Both Moloi and Molai were directors, too, of the other successful company, Futuristic Business Solutions (FBS). ADS had already been paid R2.6 billion, it had given work on the arms package to FBS, and the latter had acquired a 20 per cent shareholding in ADS. Powell stated that 'FBS stood in line to secure around 70 separate contracts … many of which had been facilitated by ADS as officially designated integrator of various projects'. FBS simply functioned as 'a logistics co-ordinator', and 'lack[ed] any actual infrastructure or manufacturing capacity'.[38]

Several bidders for contracts had confirmed to Powell that Chippy Shaik had personally communicated to them that they would have to make arrangements with ADS and/or FBS if their bids were to succeed. Deals which were then proposed by both ADS and FBS included the payment by the bidding company of 'administration fees' to the value of hundreds of thousands of dollars. A North American aeronautics company seeking to supply helicopters to the South African airforce baulked at the suggestion that it make a prior arrangement with FBS, because the latter clearly lacked the capacity to deliver the services it would have been contracted to supply, and because fees in excess of $125 000 a month were demanded. In the event, the American manufacturer was overlooked in favour of an Italian company, Agusta, offering a unit price more than R3 million above the American helicopter, which was generally considered to be a far superior machine. The role played by both ADS and FBS had also come into question in the purchase of four Corvettes from a consortium which included the German manufacturer Thyssen and the French company Thomson CSE.[39] Three submarines were to be purchased, contingent upon the German consortium meeting offset guarantees to construct a stainless steel factory at the proposed deep-water harbour of Coega in the Eastern Cape.

By June 2000 there were indications, according to the *Mail and Guardian*, that 'officially sanctioned corruption' was occurring in the procurement programme. 'Senior government members' were manoeuvering to sideline officials in Trade and Industry who continued to insist that original guarantees were met. Stories were being told of 'ministers accepting gigantic bribes' and of officials 'holding shares in companies contracted to supply components'.[40]

An additional procurement programme, this time for the army, was announced around the same time. The initial focus here was on the development, over five to ten years, of a complex Ground Based Air Defence System, and the refurbishment and extension of the army's armoured-vehicle and tank capabilities. Expenditure in excess of R10 billion was anticipated. One of the features of this deal was that much of the material would be sourced from former South African Armscor or Denel subsidiaries recently sold off to foreign companies at very low prices. The big British manufacturer Vickers had, for instance, bought a controlling interest in the former Denel subsidiary Reumech, which made components involved in the deal. The new Vickers OMC, as the old Reumech was now called, stood to make 'billions of rand' from the weapons deals, but it had been sold by Denel as part of a privatization process for about R85 million.[41]

Helmoed-Romer Heitman (or Helmut-Rohmer Heitmann), *Jane's Defence Weekly* correspondent, also found the selling-price for Reumech very low, 'particularly if you consider that what was being sold was factories, tooling', as well as 'the rights to manufacture a variety of defence platforms', and that Vickers OMC also gets 'the maintenance contracts on various armoured vehicles thrown in'. That was not all. The former Reumech manufactured the carrier for South Africa's successful G6 self-propelled artillery, and negotiations were continuing for the possible sale of 100 G6s to Saudi Arabia; if this sale went through, it would earn Vickers OMC several times its purchase price.[42] As Joe Modise had earlier observed: 'Privatisation is the way to go the world over, and companies like Labat Africa should be the engines of the … process in this country.'[43]

The *Mail and Guardian* declared that it was 'baffled' that South African companies were 'being sold to foreign interests at a fraction of their real value'. The government seemed to have 'no interest in getting to the bottom of the affair'.[44] As Heitman noted, foreign ownership of strategic resources was also being facilitated; strategic in terms of both the country's industrial and its military capacities. Various aspects of the programmes faced difficulties – the stainless steel factory at Coega,[45] and the offsets promised by Britain and Sweden for the purchase of Hawk and Griffen aircraft; only one-quarter of a promised R55 billion had been realized, according to Powell.[46]

But the whole programme was inherently questionable. The practice of demanding investment offsets against foreign trade was being 'discredited internationally', said Powell. The European Union, the United States and Canada had recently agreed to a ban on investment offsets in relation to trade among themselves. Offsets had shown themselves to be 'little more than a recipe for corruption'.[47] The international arms trade was, moreover, intimately associated with corruption. There was the notorious case of the Bofors gun scandal in India in the late 1980s, when the Swedish arms maker had deposited some $40 million into various Swiss bank accounts in furtherance of the deal.[48] The traded equipment carried both very high and flexible prices, and the realized price was dependent upon the identity of the buyer and the seller. Middlemen, skilled and experienced negotiators, figure prominently in the cobbling together of deals.

The arms trade in South Africa had its own distinctive practice of secrecy and skullduggery. Denel was the biggest exporter of finished products in South Africa in the mid-1990s, selling, for example, R1 billion worth of arms in 1996. But its managing director, Johan Alberts, was forced to resign the following year when an audit revealed 'irregular payout of funds' to top managers; about R25 million had been placed in a profit-share scheme in 1995, and R5.6 million was shared out among 30 managers, including Alberts, in October 1996.[49]

The commission of inquiry headed by Judge Edwin Cameron had, at the end of 1994, revealed how Armscor had purchased arms from China, Portugal and Eastern Europe for onward shipment to Savimbi's Unita, with secrecy characterizing every stage of the arrangements. Judge Cameron had insisted on the publication of the relevant Armscor documents, over and against the determination of the Ministry of Foreign Affairs and the defence forces that the affair should remain secret.[50] The Cameron Commission recommended that parliamentary oversight of the arms trade was essential, but the Cabinet ruled in March 1996 against such public scrutiny and openness.[51] As Mulholland observed three years later, rumours of vast kickbacks to officials and politicians then was 'par for the course in the arms industry'.[52] Just more so, perhaps, with the latest procurement programme.

Reproduced with the permission of Jonathan Shapiro, the artist.

Getting rich quick

Cyril Ramaphosa embraced capitalism with gusto. By 1997 his personal wealth in one company alone, New Africa Investments Limited (Nail), was R33.7 million. He was an executive director, along with Madikizela-Mandela's friend Nthato Motlana, Dikgang Moseneke and Jonty Sandler, and the four enjoyed between themselves a combined salary of R2.4 million a month.[53] After taking the helm of Johnnies Industrial Corporation (Johnnic) earlier in the year, he had referred to the transformation of the corporate boardrooms as a 'new site of struggle'.[54] But harmony of interest, not conflict, seemed mostly involved; it was a matter of taking the opportunities that were opening up. Anglo American's Michael Spicer welcomed Ramaphosa to Johnnic with the words, 'I think we can call you chairman Cyril now rather than comrade Cyril'.[55] By early 1998 his personal wealth was put at about R80 million.[56] He had changed his understanding of the process in which he was so successfully involved, saying more accurately that the term 'black economic empowerment' confused people, and it should be dropped in favour of 'the development of black business'.

Not all businessmen approved of the new depiction.[57] Dr Motlana insisted that it was not wrong for a black man to be rich, and he and two other successful men, Enos Mabuza and Don Ncube, held 25 directorships between them in March 1997.[58] Motlana's had been a 'long walk to riches'. He opened the first black-owned private hospital, in Soweto, in the mid-1970s, and became, as noted, a prominent community leader there. He listed Nail on the stock exchange in 1994, and saw its shares rise in price from R20 then to R80 in 1996. It acquired 50 500 black shareholders, and it collaborated with the trade unions in acquiring control of Johnnic. But he insisted 'openly and without equivocation' that 'anybody who goes into business does it to make money for himself'.[59] The Rand Club in Johannesburg was an old bastion of white privilege, but in March 1997 Motlana and Ramaphosa accepted its invitation to become members. Ramaphosa declared: 'I am excited that we are starting the process of breaking down barriers. It is like turning history on its head.'[60]

Mzi Khumalo trained as an MK cadre, was jailed on Robben Island from 1978–90, and was briefly treasurer of the ANC in Natal after his release. He bought control of JCI, one of the world's leading gold producers, from Anglo American. Personal accumulation was his explicit goal. As company chairman he showed no compunction in firing almost 4000 miners at the Randfontein Estates mine, and he had no truck with notions of entitlement and empowerment. As he told the London *Financial Times*: 'I have spoken to the unions at JCI and made it clear. We are here to run a business. I'm not for any of this brotherhood stuff.'[61]

It soon emerged that he was not for sound corporate management either. JCI was administered with a mixture of 'lies, abuse of authority' and blatant violation of procedures, for which Khumalo, said Singh and Jones, was 'chiefly responsible'. He acted entirely alone, for instance, in committing JCI to buy a 20 per cent stake, for R252 million, in Southern Mining Corporation, a company in which he was both an investor and director and whose main assets consisted of exploration licences; he did not disclose his material interests until after the deal was concluded. When he resigned from JCI at the end of 1997, the company he directed had lost its own major assets and its share prices had dropped by more than half.[62]

However, he seemed to remain a prominent member of The Network (or Africanbond), which was an association of black business executives, politicians and professionals. It had existed since around 1996, but 'it came out of the closet' in July 1998, observed Haffajee, to celebrate the appointment of Tito Mboweni to head the Reserve Bank. Among the politicians present on the auspicious occasion were Thabo Mbeki and Ministers Steve Tshwete and Zola Skweyiya, and among top black businessmen were Khumalo, Eric Molobi the chair of Kagiso Trust Investments, and Seshi Chonco the chief executive of Denzel. Transnet's chief executive, Saki Macozoma, described The Network as 'a loose ˙grouping' with invitations going out by fax from his office, Chonco's, or that of the casino chief Reuel Khoza. A recipient, Haffajee revealed:

> ha[d] to be black in the broader sense. You're on the A-list if you're an investment banker, financier, accountant or other executive. Lawyers and doctors score well. So do academics or 'key opinion makers'. Membership is guaranteed if you head a parastatal.

The Network, he added, was 'intricately tied to political power'.[63]

But the black professionals at Mboweni's party clearly saw themselves, Leshilo reported, as under ill-defined threat from what they termed the opponents of transformation. Saki Macozoma declared darkly that parliamentary debates were being used to cast doubt on the credibility of black leaders, and other speakers attacked the media for supposedly waging a campaign to vilify blacks in high positions. Mbeki said that a recently published report alleging that the wife of Jackie Selebi – then director-general of foreign affairs – had been found driving a stolen car, was further proof of the existence of this campaign. But another member of the group accorded partial recognition to a substantive problem attached to the black elite themselves and the power and enrichment they were pursuing: 'The Network was formed to bring together black people to define [and implement] black economic empowerment', because 'the term has been prostituted'.[64]

Below these captains of finance and politics, there was a younger black middle class confidently determined to do well for themselves. Black yuppies of the business world in Johannesburg, around 1998, were already enjoying 'their new-found success'. Jacob Molefe, for one, hailed from a family of five in Dobsonville, Soweto, but was a senior portfolio manager in a property services company in Rosebank. His work experience, he said, 'has empowered me to do things that I want to do'. He had a luxury car, and he lived in a comfortable Randburgh townhouse. What he called his confidence and interpersonal skills, he had acquired from dealing with his white counterparts, and it had made it easy for him to adapt to suburban life. 'I went into this area', he said, 'because I deserve to be there'. Another was Itumeleng Kekana, 30, an entrepreneur from the township of Atteridgeville in Pretoria. He was a partner in an information technology company, and was also involved in a R23 million franchise hotel opening in Roodepoort later that year. He said that today's challenge for black graduates was to conquer fear: 'You must take your chances, especially during the current dispensation, as anything is possible.'[65]

At the end of the 1990s, black business operated, for the first time in the country's history, 'under a very sympathetic government'. Many policies such as those on procurement, tendering priorities and small business development, assisted this. Parastatals had employed black chief executives and black joint ventures had taken over private companies.[66] 1998 had seen 130 'black empowerment' deals worth some R21 billion ($3.8 billion), but the emphasis to-date had been on the acquisition of existing companies, not on the creation of new ones. With around one-third of the workforce out of work, no new jobs, at best, had been created.[67] Many, perhaps most of the black upwardly mobile professionals – early products of the empowerment programmes – may not have been overly worried by these limitations.

The opportunities were ripe. 'The first statement of expression' that one had arrived in the new black middle class, was the expensive car and home, the preferred overseas destinations, the credit cards and, according to Joe Mwase deputy president of the Black Management Forum, the people with whom one chooses to be seen. This latter factor was of particular importance. 'In the new South Africa the rising economic elite want to be seen to be in touch with the ruling elite – senior government officials. From there', he said, 'you move up fairly quickly'.[68]

There was general agreement among the black elite and the yuppies below them about the opportunities now opened. Mashudu Ramano, chairman of the National Empowerment Corporation and a director of many companies, had exulted in April 1997: 'Now is the time. If ever there was a chance, we have it now'. But like many members of The Network, he remained reluctant to fully describe the process in which he was involved. Much which could not be hidden might be admitted; but a great deal should remain under wraps and desirably obscured. Ramano's associates were the 'patriotic bourgeoisie', whom he asserted 'have the interests of the country at heart and are not motivated by self-interest alone'. The proclaimed goal of 'black empowerment' remained, and the 'prostitution' of the practice, by the likes of Khumalo, was ignored.[69] The opponents of elite transformation, as The Network portrayed it, were the probable cause of malpractice. The black elite should be judged by the values of the white elite – anything other would be unfair to them. It was inevitable that some blacks would become super rich, said Ramano, and 'there [was] nothing to be ashamed of' in that.[70] The joblessness and poverty of the black masses and the issue of fairness to them went unmentioned.

Reality denied this determined obfuscation. Ramaphosa resigned from the board of Nail in February 1999, supposedly in order to deepen and broaden his business interests.[71] Two months later, Nail's board asked its shareholders to approve the transfer of bank options – in the African Merchant Bank (AMB), a Nail subsidiary – worth more than R130 million to the four executive directors, Motlana, Dikgang Moseneke, Zwelakhe Sisulu and Jonty Sandler. The UDM leaders, Bantu Holomisa and Roelf Meyer, immediately expressed disgust at such 'short-sighted avarice, occurr[ing] in the name of black empowerment'.[72] At the general meeting of shareholders next day, sources within Nail, according to Vermeulen, revealed that 'massive restraint of trade payments' were made to the same four directors after the company's September 1998 year-end.

Chairing the meeting, Motlana refused to answer tabled questions on the matter, and further refused to allow debate. He also disallowed debate on questions about the erosion of share values by some R5 billion, which some shareholders interpreted as indicating the market's lack of confidence in Nail's management. This was reinforced by the revelation that Nail's legal advisers, Edward Nathan Friedland, had declined to assist in the documentation of the AMB options transfer. Shareholders accused Motlana of running an 'autocratic' meeting, and fund managers and other investors present expressed their disgust. When someone referred the chair to a statement in Nail's 1998 annual report which committed the company to 'openness, integrity and accountability', Motlana closed the meeting.[73]

Majakathata Mokwena, described as a prominent Soweto businessman, had been bluntly ordered to 'sit down' by Motlana at the meeting. Interviewed next day, he accused the Nail directors of 'want[ing] to take black people's money … [they] did not pay a cent for the shares they were going to get'. Mxolisi Mabutho, president of the SA Shopkeepers' Association, said that 'Black empowerment as Nail sees it has become a situation where wealth circulates only among a few'. Other community businessmen declared their disillusionment with empowerment as espoused by Nail, while Bheki Sibeko, an Orange Farm brickmaker, asked 'where are the jobs that black empowerment should have created?' The dream that Nail would become 'the golden goose of black empowerment', reported Mathiane, 'had been deflated for many'.[74]

Motlana, founder and chairman of Nail, and Sandler, executive director, resigned from the company and all its subsidiaries in early April after accepting a buy-out price of 'about R100 million'. It was understood, said Parker, that 'the pair's initial asking price for their combined stake was closer to R250 million'. The remaining directors, Moseneke and Sisulu, were said to have pledged to return their options and restraint payments, and to clean up the company.[75] This would not be easy. It was soon revealed that Motlana and Sandler would actually walk away from Nail with 'about R400 million between them' – R100 million from the sale of their shareholdings, 'plus about R300 million in other payments'.[76] Dr Motlana expressed neither shame nor remorse. He blamed supposed disturbances at the general meeting on a conspiracy by certain 'white individuals' in AMB who wanted to take over Nail, and declared: 'I have nothing to defend … If my departure will help save Nail and the image of all empowerment companies, then I am prepared … to carry the cross like Jesus Christ. Nail is a very successful group.'[77]

Nail's 'success' was in the enrichment of its directors and the marginalization and reduction of the shareholders' interests. The remuneration of the executive directors had risen from R7.3 million in 1997 to

R20.4 million two years later, and an incentive share scheme accorded to themselves had gone from 18 million shares to 164 million over a shorter period. Each of the four had received R25 million in the restraint-of-trade payments. However, the value of the low-voting 'N' shares in the company had dropped by nearly half since late 1998.[78] Goose was indeed for the very few.

The ANC and the promotion of black capitalism

During the second half of 1997, 'several ANC thinkers', as Friedman noted, had expressed interest in the formation of a black bourgeoisie; since 1990, he suggested, the ANC had been more influenced by international capital than by its domestic counterpart.[79] President Mandela, in July 1998, attacked what he termed the political left for criticizing the black business elite for allegedly enriching themselves instead of empowering the entire black population. History showed, he insisted, that most major companies had to grow first, and they did not start by creating large numbers of jobs.[80] He returned to this theme at the ANC's national general council in Port Elizabeth in July 2000. People had to understand that the new black business elite were still paying-off loans they acquired in establishing their businesses; profitability had prime importance for them. Black business people, he noted, had donated R1.5 million to launch a fund for veterans of the struggle against apartheid, and this, he declared, 'exposes those who are criticising black business' for being 'interested in personal enrichment'.[81]

But it was in November 1999 that President Mbeki gave explicit endorsement to the formation of a black capitalist class. Speaking at a conference of the Black Management Forum in Johannesburg, he stressed that South Africa was both a capitalist and a racist society. The goal of deracialization must therefore be addressed within the context of capitalist property relations. To confront racism required the creation and strengthening of a black capitalist class. 'We must work to ensure that there emerges a black bourgeoisie whose presence within our economy and society will be part of the process of the deracialisation of the economy and society', he declared. He too urged 'very strongly' that blacks 'abandon their embarrassment at the emergence of successful and therefore prosperous black [property] owners' – blacks must 'think and act in a manner consistent with a realistic response to the real world'. He made no reference to such cases as JCI and Nail, and he denied that wealth and income disparities among blacks were widening. He strongly implied, in fact, that the very idea of deepening inequalities was another racist red-herring:

> Our lives are not made easier by those who – seeking to deny that poverty and wealth in our country continue to carry their racial hues – argue that wealth and income disparities among the black people themselves are as wide as disparities between black and white.[82]

Racism justified the formation of the black bourgeoisie, and anti-racism – rather than good economics – seemed to serve, in Mbeki's thinking, as a large part of its patriotic mission.[83]

The formation of a black bourgeoisie is being promoted in agriculture too. The sector embraces some 20 million rural people whose support contributed significantly to the ANC's much touted landside victory in 1999. New programmes were announced in February and April 2000 that have the aim of shifting land redistribution resources towards the promotion of black commercial farmers. The policy of the former Land Affairs Minister, Derek Hanekom, had been to focus attention upon the weak, while the market, through the lending institutions, catered for the relatively strong. He had offered a R16 000 land-acquisition grant, and had aimed at ensuring that scarce state resources reached the maximum number of those in need.

The new plan of Minister Thoko Didiza offers a sliding scale of grants up to R100 000 which would be used to leverage bank finance; the beneficiaries being those who already possessed the experience, enterprise and assets to farm commercially. Didiza's radical changes were introduced without consultation – not with civil society, parliament, the Land Bank, nor even with the commercial banks which had been assigned a vital role in the programme. As Hlatshwayo summed up the situation:

> In 1994 the ANC drafted policies through consultative processes with a wide range of democratic forces … Since June [1999] that consultation has given way to centralised directives promising to reverse many of the gains secured for the poor over the past decade.[84]

Entrenchment of the ruling elite

Before he was summarily dismissed in the early hours following Mbeki's inauguration, Derek Hanekom was known as a 'conscientious and hard-working minister who spent much of his time tramping rural SA'. He was followed by the contrived resignation of Helena Dolny as chief executive of the Land Bank – set in train merely by a private letter to President Mbeki from a former Bank official, Bonile Jack, who alleged among other things that Dolny was racist.[85] She was an experienced rural economist who worked at least a 12-hour office day, and who had redirected the Bank's lending activities towards the rural poor; not incidentally perhaps, she was Joe Slovo's former wife.[86] The moves appeared interconnected and significant. Forrest concluded that 'left-wing whites who champion the down-trodden masses' represented a particular irritant to black nationalists, and that Mbeki's 'overriding priority [was] building a black ruling elite'.[87] Dolny's own understanding was similar: 'There's a different style of leadership emerging under President Thabo Mbeki. [His] emphasis is on an African renaissance built on personal loyalty to him.'[88] Subjectivism and a spreading 'anti-intellectualism' might also be added to the equation of Mbeki's distinctive elitism.[89]

Goose for the few, racism for the many

For all President Mbeki's protestations to the contrary, inequalities among blacks have been deepening through the 1990s. This has come after a period of relative prosperity for black workers. Born of capitalist development and a crumbling of apartheid laws, average real black earnings in manufacturing, 1975–90, increased by almost 50 per cent; for whites, the figure was 1 per cent.[90] Since 1994, it is the black middle class that has expanded apace. The proportion of black managers in the national public service went from 6 per cent when the ANC gained power, to 38 per cent in 1997, while in provincial government the latter figure was 66 per cent. Those in the private sector also rose rapidly 1994–96, then stuck at perhaps 20 per cent, largely because of the shortage of skilled blacks – the scarcity of the educated increased the market price of the few who were well-educated. The industrial firm, Barlow, for example, reportedly offered newly-qualified black accountants about 20 per cent more money than their white colleagues, plus an 'entry-level BMW', pension and health benefits. Promotion prospects were described as excellent, but 'after a few months', according to chief executive Tony Barlow, 'they are mercilessly head-hunted'. Demand for black high-fliers was 'ravenous'.[91]

While the educated middle class was doing well in pay, perks and promotion, basic job opportunities had plummeted. Fewer people were employed in 1998 than in 1980, and more than half a million jobs were lost 1994–99; another 210000 were expected to disappear in 1999.[92]

According to research carried out by Wharton Economic Forecasting Associates (WEFA) Southern Africa, R59 billion was redistributed in South Africa between 1991 and 1996; R54 billion of this sum was generated by economic growth, and R5 billion resulted from a loss of income by 80 per cent of whites. The proceeds of redistribution were narrowly diffused. Whites with a lower level of skills were 'sidelined' and, according to Andrew Whiteford one of the authors of the WEFA report, 'the poor are even worse off' than before. The average income of black households at the bottom of the economic scale fell by 21 per cent, and the poorest of white households experienced a 16 per cent fall in income. The poorest 40 per cent of blacks received only 0.1 per cent, or R55 million, of the wealth redistributed, but the richest 10 per cent of blacks gained R24 billion.[93] The numbers of best-off blacks also dramatically increased. Black households in the top quintile of income earners more than doubled, from 9 per cent in 1991 to 22 per cent in 1996, while the number of whites in the same group fell from 83 per cent to 65 per cent. Black middle-class numbers also went up by almost 80 per cent, from some 220000 to nearly 400000 in the same five years. Richest blacks were the biggest winners in this redistribution, while the poor in general were the biggest losers.[94]

Changes in the Gini coefficient, measured by Statistics South Africa, also point to a dramatic worsening of inequality. On a scale where perfect equality would be zero and its opposite one, the coefficient had arisen from 0.73 in 1995 to 0.80 in 1998. The trend was upwards among whites, Coloureds and blacks, but most extensively so among the majority group – in the three years it had moved from 0.70 to 0.81 among blacks.[95]

A study of Soweto in 1997 by Alan Morris and other sociologists from the University of Witwatersrand, found 'striking' levels of poverty. Of some one million residents, almost 31 per cent were unemployed but looking for work, while 5.8 per cent were not even trying. Among those aged between 20 and 29 years, 43 per cent were jobless, and only 21 per cent held full-time employment. Those who did have incomes received, nevertheless, very little. About one in three Sowetan households had a total monthly income of less than R1000, and 16.4 per cent of them got by on less than R500 a month, the equivalent of the pension for an individual.[96]

Research released in 1999 by Terreblanche noted that unemployment affected about eight million workers or 'at least 40 per cent of the potential labour force'. The income of the poorest 60 per cent of the population, mainly black and about 25 million people, declined from some 14 per cent in 1991 to about 11 per cent near the end of the decade. The top 20 per cent of income earners received then 72 per cent of total income. This group totalled between four and six million people, more than half of whom were black. This high-earning, big-spending black elite had emerged 'rather quickly', though its origins went back more than 10 years. The ANC's affirmative-action programmes created jobs for the upper echelon of black 'insiders', but had 'little effect' on black 'outsiders' in the lowest 60 per cent. Affirmative action was therefore 'an important reason for the growing inequality in black circles'.[97]

'The really poor', most of whom are black, lose in at least two ways, it is suggested, from policies of positive discrimination:

> They receive worse public services. Black-owned firms can charge more than white ones and still win government contracts. This helps black entrepreneurs, but means that the government builds fewer houses and lays fewer water pipes... [and] race laws hinder growth and aggravate unemployment.[98]

The ANC has not delivered to the people even what was allocated to them. On one summation:

> The party came to power in 1994 with a Reconstruction and Delivery Programme (RDP). Less than two years later, the RDP office, which had already been allocated R15 billion, was closed down and the unspent funds were absorbed by departments involved in developmental initiatives. [But] the Housing Department was in disarray and low-income housing initiatives died on the ground. Education, which gets about 46 per cent of the total Budget, continues to turn out thousands of matric failures each year. Welfare was not able to spend more than one per cent of the R204 million allocated for poverty relief in the 1998/99 financial year. Health failed to spend 40 per cent of the R109.7 million allocated to the HIV-AIDS directorate and the [Action Programme] in 1999/2000.[99]

The Ministry of Social Welfare left huge amounts of money unspent, not for reasons of generalized incompetence, but because delivery was hampered, notes Dolny, by the turnover of five permanent secretaries in five years. The attrition rate among experienced public servants in the departments of Agriculture and Land Affairs was also high.

President Mbeki's 'personal style', one of 'working with his chosen few', has 'influenced the way ministers run their portfolios'.[100]

According to Greig, reviewing the WEFA research and findings by the South African Institute of Race Relations, 'riches and poverty alike are fast becoming colour-blind' in the country. Under ANC government, 'it's now easier to get rich than to stop being poor'.[101]

The empowerment of the armaments industry, with its anticipated spending of some R70 billion, 1999–2010 – on Erwin's figures – promises still deepening divisions between the wealthy elite and the impoverished mass.

The naked emperor: empowerment and racism

In acquiring state power the ANC has moved, as Terreblanche has it, 'from a position left of centre to a position right of centre'. The Freedom Charter had underlain the former position, and the internal action of the 1970s and 1980s in the UDF and in COSATU expressed a popular social democratic and self-determining practice. Mandela's watershed speech in Mafikeng in 1997 not only denounced all opposition but the media in general, and even the organs of civil society. The ANC exemplified the armed struggle, and struggle continued against independent critical tendencies, large and small, real and imagined. But assertions, even by someone of Nelson Mandela's stature, did not constitute substantive justifications for rule, especially when the political and economic realities made plain that the poor majority were being forgotten. By 1999, when Thabo Mbeki inherited ultimate political power, the ANC chiefly represented, as Terreblanche noted, a 'strange contradiction'. The alliance partners, COSATU and the SACP, were 'still left-wing',[102] and the mass membership of the ANC remained non-racial and anti-elitist. The ANC government's identity was unclear, and its ideological representation was absent.

Mbeki's black capitalism speech of November 1999 expressed the notion that continuing racism justified continuing struggle. But the reality of the struggle, its constituent elements, stages, their very differing aims, remained unexamined, with prominent UDF leaders repeatedly harassed and vital truths about groups and individuals suppressed and distorted. Effective predominance was not to be built on obscurity and non-delivery. If Mbeki's position had any content, it was in the questionable proposition that the ANC's rule was justified through its fight against racism, interlinked closely with its promotion of black capitalism.

The President's thinking struck a responsive chord among the black bourgeoisie. 'Procuring empowerment' was a goal which, in Christine Qunta's thinking, contained a tightly race-based logic which almost overrode economics. The 'target group', she insisted, must be clearly defined in terms of those who suffered unfair discrimination historically. 'Of necessity [it] would relate to race, gender and disability, with race being the major factor'. But within the category of beneficiaries 'there should be a hierarchy... African women and men cannot be dealt with in the same manner as white women, although white women would enjoy preference over white males'. A 'point system' would be essential. Monitoring and evaluation were important, but state tender boards would be 'phased out' because 'they have created many more problems than solutions'. A holistic empowerment programme required that black business and government act as partners. The government must see empowerment as part of its programme to 'normalise this society' and stimulate the economy for the benefit of all. Government should recognize, she said, that 'patriotic black business may just be its most enduring ally' in pulling the economy out of its morass.[103] A possibly worrying assessment of the ANC's long-term support.

'Affirmative procurement' policies already existed under which 'previously disadvantaged individuals' (PDIs) were granted preferences in bidding for government contracts – their bids might be 10 per cent higher in price, for example, and criteria for capability and expertise might be lowered for PDIs. Government departments and parastatals between them were putting out tenders worth around R50 billion a year at the end of the 1990s.[104] But when a new Preferential Procurement Policy bill was before parliamentary committee in January 2000, the reaction of the Black Management Forum, the Black Business Council and the Black Information Forum was highly critical. Christine Qunta, on behalf of the Forum, claimed that the legislation would entrench the position of white men in the economy. The Bill proposed a points system for adjudicating tenders, but allocating only 10 of them for empowering the previously disadvantaged was, she said, 'laughable'. Black professionals, she added, felt 'ambushed and betrayed' by the proposals.[105]

The ANC's empowerment strategies had led to company failures, malpractice, and distortions. The collapse of NAIL and JCI was followed by that of other black empowerment businesses, such as Pepsi, African Bank, Community Bank and New Sorghum Breweries. How affirmative procurement might work in actuality was suggested by the company, Maru a Pula, run by a prominent black businessman, Gaby Magomola. When it won 'a major contract' from the Independent Electoral Commission for polling-station banners – when its bid was 'considerably higher' than some of its competitors – it immediately subcontracted the work to four of its losing competitors and 'pocketed the money simply for lending its name to the operation'. In effect, the PDI/10 per cent rule constituted a special levy on all taxpayers, 'with the proceeds handed to black businessmen who are on good terms with the government'.[106] Yet evidence suggested that 'whatever the government does' for the patriotic bourgeoisie, 'it is never enough for its clients'.[107]

When former Supreme Court judge, Rex van Schalkwyk, suggested that certain affirmative and empowerment legislation was threatening to the economy, and that the Employment Equity Act reintroduced the apartheid principles of job reservation, the head of the Black Management Forum, Bheki Sibiya, stormed out of the meeting of the Institute of Directors accusing van Schalkwyk of racism.[108]

Through early 2000 President Mbeki, according to Chothia, was increasingly focusing on racism in order to shore-up his credibility among blacks. Addressing a COSATU audience in February, he said that the ANC's success against apartheid had led many to reach 'the premature conclusion that racism is dead'. He made reference to a letter written by an unnamed company engineer in which various racist remarks were expressed,[109] and declared that this 'brings us face-to-face with the brutality of the racism that will continue to exist … unless all of us engage this monster'. The Human Rights Commission (HRC) would shortly convene a national congress against racism, which would speed up the eradication of racism at home and even show 'our commitment to the struggle for a nonracial world'.[110]

The HRC's hearings stemmed in large part from the notion of 'subliminal racism'. The Black Lawyers' Association and the Association of Black Accountants, racially exclusive societies, had filed a complaint with the Commission accusing the *Mail and Guardian* and the *Sunday Times* of this supposed offence.[111] The HRC decided in response to inquire into racist thinking and inclinations across the entire media.[112] Making a submission on behalf of the ANC to the HRC hearings, on 5 April 2000, Jeff Radebe, the Minister of Public Enterprises, said: 'Our struggle to create a non-racial society must … recognise the fact that the offensive against racism addresses the issue of power relations in our society'. Although the ANC government had initially emphasized national reconciliation, this was not enough, and it had 'led to the white media trying to set the agenda for Mandela'. Editorials in the *Sunday Times* and *Mail and Guardian* were identified as having pitted Mandela against his successor, exalted Mandela as a 'saint' and denigrated Mbeki.[113] 'There was a perception created of a Mbeki who ferrets behind closed doors and sticks his finger in every pie', a picture of 'Mbeki seeking to usurp all powers'. Five years after our liberation, the submission went on, 'white South African society continues to believe in a particular stereotype of the African'. 'The white media' consistently paints a picture of blacks as 'immoral, amoral, savage, violent...incapable of refinement through education, and driven by hereditary, dark, satanic impulses'.[114]

The ANC's submission further stated that an article denigrating Mbeki had been written by the editor of the *Mail and Guardian*, Phillip van Niekerk, but it had appeared in the paper under the name of a black woman journalist, Lizeka Mda.[115]

The editor, management and staff of the newspaper immediately issued a statement which called on the ANC and Radebe to withdraw their allegations, and to issue an unconditional retraction and full apology. Lizeka Mda, then executive editor on *The Star*, explained that her article in question had referred to Mbeki's apparent interference in the award of television licences which, she believed, made a mockery of the country's democratic institutions. She stated:

> I cannot imagine a worse insult to my professional integrity. But...coming from the ANC, which has sidelined every member who has dared not to toe the line, the idea of a black woman who can think for herself may be a novel one.

She described Radebe as 'yet to convince that he is anything more than a lackey of the executive'. It gave her 'a sinking feeling' that Mbeki 'wrote, or gave his express approval to, that nonsensical document that was presented to the HRC'.[116]

Secretary-general Kgalema Motlanthe affirmed that the ANC stood by its submission 'in its entirety'. Mda's lawyers served papers on the ANC for defamation, and van Niekerk was acting similarly, adding: 'Radebe read out the statement under oath before a commission set up under the constitution. He must take responsibility'. Mda said she would have been satisfied with a retraction and apology. 'They obviously think I'm just going to roll over. I have no intention of doing so'.[117]

The ANC's submission to the HRC came five months after President Mbeki's statement of support for black capitalists and about coincident with his persistent obfuscations on AIDS and his essentially supportive interventions into the state-contrived turmoil in Zimbabwe. But the statement of 5 April had perhaps the same significance as Mandela's Mafikeng speech and the ANC's declaration of support for the patriotic bourgeoisie. The ideas of the Freedom Charter and the aspirations of the UDF were now buried if not yet dead. The Freedom Charter's principle of non-racialism had begun to go with the return of the exiles in 1990; unlike the UDF, says Max du Preez, the exiles only knew a handful of white comrades.[118] 1994 saw 'a further step back', camouflaged for a time by the reconciliatory style – his Rainbow Nation – of Nelson Mandela; but the coming to power of Thabo Mbeki 'finally sealed the fate of non-racialism'. But even with the President's pervasive emphasis on race and white racism, 'the death of non-racialism was never really debated on a national level', du Preez observed.[119]

What had been lost had not been replaced by other values that might have meaning and relevance to the majority of the people, winning their acceptance through debate, criticism and revision. The sharp intolerance of debate and criticism is instead a hallmark of the Mbeki presidency.[120] Ideas on which real predominance might have been fashioned – of justice, equality and an active democracy – have been abandoned by the elite isolated in its chosen preeminence. Instead, 'a mean, insecure and fevered spirit [was] abroad in the ANC'. The anti-white racism which reached a then peak of expression on 5 April, served very few:

a group of men and women at the top of the ANC who fear that their huge gamble on economic policy will fail; people who sense that now is the moment to stress a blood bond in order to hold together a party which might otherwise blow apart ...[121]

Racism offers very poor cake for the bulk of South Africans, and contrasts glaringly with the goose which the minority enjoys.[122] Promotion of the black bourgeoisie, racism and elitism is an inter-related programmatic syndrome. Its selfishness is hard to disguise, and it offers no basis for sustained socio-economic advance.

Enduring alliances: elitism, racism and the people

Despite the fog of racism and empowerment, there are indications that not all of the people are entirely fooled. Opinion surveys had shown an approval rating for President Mandela in May–June 1995 of 76 per cent of South Africans, and in April 1999, just before his retirement, 85 per cent of people approved of his performance according to polling then by Markinor. But a wide-ranging survey by the Institute for Democracy in South Africa (Idasa), indicated that President Mbeki had the support of 71 per cent of people in May 2000; 66 per cent believed that he was discharging his duties satisfactorily in June–July; and his approval rating slumped to just 50.2 per cent of the populace on the data released in early October. This was a drop of 21 percentage points or of 30 per cent in under four months, and it was disapproval that attached to President Mbeki himself.

The ruling party, Idasa noted, had experienced no comparable fall-off in support. The independent press, despite the frequent attacks upon it from the ruling elite and the patriotic bourgeoisie, enjoyed a higher approval rating than the President; 58.4 per cent of South Africans trusted the press, as against 41.3 per cent who trusted Mbeki. This was also true among blacks – Just over 60.3 per cent of black South Africans trusted the newspapers, while 47.9 per cent put their faith in Thabo Mbeki. The issues of greatest concern to the people, in Idasa's survey, were the economy – only 10 per cent thought the government was doing 'fairly' or 'very well' on job creation – and crime, where the government's attempts to curb lawlessness were approved by 18 per cent of South Africans.[123]

The standing of the northerly demagogue before his people was far worse. Survey results released about the same time in Harare by the Helen Suzman Foundation indicated that only 14 per cent of Zimbabweans wanted President Mugabe to remain in office; more than half the respondents believed he should be put on trial for the crimes alleged against him, even if he resigned.[124]

Sowetans, interviewed ahead of local government polls in early November, expressed a general disgruntlement with the ANC. Ephraim Khuzwayo, who worked in a bottle store for R100 a week, said: 'I cannot think of any party to support. I have been let down by the ANC'. A taxi owner-driver, Vusi Manana, who lived in Meadowlands, said that there had been no delivery of services by councillors to-date: 'The water and electricity gets cut, there are no proper streets, no sewerage. What do we have to vote for?' Two women who lived on the edge of Orlando township said they had voted ANC in the past, but also claimed that the party had let them down: 'Why should we support the ANC? Let those who have benefited from them vote for them', the women declared. A group of pensioners and unemployed men on Xorile Street in Orlando West – once known as the turf of gun-carrying

ANC youth – were said to be unmoved by criticism that by voting for the new Democratic Alliance of Tony Leon they might be bringing back a white government:[125]

> What has a black government done for us? Our electricity and water is cut, pensioners have to queue for long hours to get their pensions. Who cares for us and our children who died to get the ANC into power?

one said. Another added: 'During the apartheid government, life was difficult, but I always had money in my back pocket.'[126]

Part IV
From Ancient to Future Worlds

7
Participatory Democracy: The Reality and the Continuing Aspiration – Athens, Britain and South Africa

As Rueschemeyer, Stephens and Stephens observe at the start of their important book, democracy, by any definition, was 'extremely rare in agrarian societies'. They note in passing the exceptionality of democratic Athens, but they repeat anachronistic criticisms of its democracy and fail to appreciate that its historical rarity enhances rather than decreases its importance[1] – as with the popular movement in South Africa in the present liberal capitalist period.

Originating in an insurrectionary movement by the lower classes in Athens at the end of the sixth century BC, a popular and participatory democracy was brought into being which existed for almost two centuries, 508 to 322 BC, and which has seen no equals since, even in modern times. Democracy here represented 'political power wielded actively and collectively by the demos', that is, 'all residents of the state who [we]re culturally defined as potential citizens', regardless of their class or status.[2] Women, resident foreigners and slaves were not citizens; women were excluded well-nigh universally from citizenship until the twentieth century,[3] and black Americans, for example, did not begin to acquire civil rights until the 1960s. Such exclusions were arguably of lesser significance than the issue of the inclusions in Athenian citizenship in class and status terms. Athens was slave-owning and imperialistic, and it 'upheld a stern ethical code predicated on duty to self and community',[4] but the issue is not whether it was attractive in twenty-first-century eyes or always just, but the reality and the significance of its participatory democracy.

The early elite theorists successfully propagated the view, at the height of the great democratization movement around the First World

War, that real democracy is always and everywhere an impossibility. Michels recognized importantly that organization was 'the weapon of the weak in their struggle with the strong', and that democracy was inconceivable without it. He noted that it brought 'other dangers', like non-accountability and leadership cults, 'in its train'; he assumed 'the perennial incompetence of the masses'; and he jumped to his dictum: 'It is organization which gives birth to the dominion of the elected over the electors ... of the delegates over the delegators. Who says organisation, says oligarchy.'[5] Weber asserted that the very idea of democratization was misleading; the demos could never rule, and the role of the people under universal suffrage was merely one of response to the initiatives of the leader, borne upon 'the law of the small number'.[6] The saliency of Athenian democracy, 'revolutionary in its energies, dynamic in its practices, and remarkably stable', is that it constitutes the substantive negation of this unproven elitist assumption.[7]

Elites of wealth and education existed in Athens, which was a class society. They were politically active and litiguous, and critical in speech and writing. But they were not, states Ober significantly, a politically dominant elite. Democracy had been brought into being through a largely 'leaderless' uprising, and the ordinary citizens established political, legal and ideological power thereafter. Their judges proscribed huge fines, banishment and death for those caught breaking the rules and, Ober observes, Athenian political life was 'hard, often unkind'.[8] But it was also voluntary, and the elite individual could choose to pay his taxes and liturgies like others did and keep out of politics. He was free to criticize democracy, as few did more severely in conversation and writing than Plato, but not to take his case into the public domain or encourage others to overthrow the system, as Socrates did.[9] The educated held undoubted advantages in public speaking, but Athenians, says Ober, believed in the wisdom of mass audiences; special education was not considered necessary for collective decision-making, since growing-up in the democratic polis was seen as an education in itself.[10]

Athenian political institutions expressed direct popular power. It was exercised by ordinary citizens in the Assembly, which routinely drew 6000 to 8000 participants. A meeting's agenda was drawn up by the Council of 500, whose members were selected by lottery and were forbidden to serve more than two annual terms – a large and rotating membership was not conducive to strong institutional identity and tendencies towards elite domination. Assembly meetings were presided over by a lotteried 'president-for-a-day' who announced the agenda items. Any citizen was free to speak, for as long as his fellows were willing to listen to him. A simple majority, usually by show of hands, decided the outcome. All important business, including foreign policy and taxation, was decided in this way. Attendance at Assembly meetings and most important official positions was remunerated on a daily basis, so that no citizen would be excluded on financial grounds.[11]

People's courts, meeting almost daily, heard both private and public suits. Litigants faced a jury of some 200 to 500 citizens chosen by random drawing. The jurors were also the judges, and after hearing both claimants they decided by majority vote in a secret ballot. Most official positions were, in fact, chosen by random lot, and all citizens aged above 30 were expected to staff an office. Only a few specialists, including military commanders and financial magistrates, were elected on renewable annual terms. Elections were seen by Athenian democrats as an aristocratic method, conferring, as in contemporary America, advantages upon the well-born, prominent and wealthy.[12] Executive and popular power in Athens were fused.

The conception of citizenship in Athens was actually profound. The democratic uprising had been preceded by prohibitions on debt-slavery and by legal reforms which, suggests Ober, made Athenians 'potentially responsible for one another's welfare'. Ordinary men began to see themselves not as clients of great families, but as citizens.[13] After 508 BC the citizen-juror tended to be deeply suspicious of the wealthy as a class. Democratic ideology and power 'encouraged voluntary redistribution of wealth and limited the political effects of wealth inequality'.[14] There was taxation and the large fines imposed in the courts. Meiksins Wood stresses the fact that, while Athens was a slave society, 'the majority of citizens were people who worked for a living'.[15] The status enjoyed by free labour in democratic Athens was, she says, without precedence, before or since. What was most distinctive about Athenian democracy was found in the 'union of labour and citizenship' and 'specifically in the *peasant-citizen*'. The polis was a form of political organization which 'united landlords and peasants into one civic and military community'.[16] This was no formal or passive unity, as has been seen. The democracy coexisted with slavery, but it also inhibited the concentration of property, and 'it limited the ways in which slavery could be utilised, especially in agriculture'. Peasant-citizens were able to use their political power in Athens to resist the exploitation and domination of the rich.[17]

The historic significance of Athens, for Meiksins Wood, is that it was an active, participatory and a majoritarian workers' democracy all at once. But the cultural status of labour changed most significantly, she believes, with the rise of capitalism. With John Locke's notions of 'improvement' and productivity, the virtues of labour no longer resided with the labourers themselves, but became the attributes of capitalists – who did not let resources lie idle but put them to work productively. The devaluation of labour and the empowerment of capitalists as true producers were also potent conceptualizations.[18] Locke not only fathered liberalism. He facilitated in addition the present arrangements wherein a formal democracy – citizens merely as masses periodically voting (or rather not voting in the United States and Botswana) for representatives/elites – leaves inequalities and class exploitation intact and free to deepen.

The Levellers' participatory impulse

The Levellers movement also denies the elitist presumptions of the incompetence and apathy of the masses, emerging in a transitional period when capitalism was first being emplaced, through revolutionary means. They arose out of the great clash between new parliamentary and rising capitalist forces, on the one hand, and old absolutist and feudal power, on the other. They represented chiefly a radical element within the New Model Army, an effective and popular revolutionary force.[19] They lasted no more than the last four years of the 1640s, but they spoke at their height, when parliamentary power was not fully consolidated, for many of the victorious soldiers, mustered thousands of signatories to petitions and prompted large demonstrations in London.[20] The leaders were men of some education and property, and their supporters were soldiers, small traders, artisans, apprentices and women.[21]

Women – Billingsgate fishwives, oyster- and kitchenstuff-women, and others – had first appeared demanding peace and clamoring for food in the early 1640s, according to Davies, and their action was significant because they came from 'the bottom of th[e] surging mass of near-destitution'. The Peace Women's assault, in their hundreds, sometimes thousands, derived its focus and attack, she says, 'from energies the Revolution liberated'.[22] The radicalizing process was strong and broad for some time. The waves of women who petitioned parliament in the later 1640s were led by 'gentlewomen' and women of 'middling' rank. 'The bonny Besses in the sea-green dresses' were prominent in the funeral of the executed Leveller Army leader, Robert Lockier, in April 1649 when 'staggering numbers shoaled through the city'. Women had also 'stood out vividly amongst the reputedly 10000 strong crowd' which had petitioned parliament the previous August to release John Lilburne or give him a fair trial, and thousands of them had demanded the release of other Leveller leaders, William Walwyn, Thomas Prince and Richard Overton.[23]

Women's concerns were with the conditions imposed by the times, the soaring cost of living and the scarcity of basic foods in London, high taxation, unemployment and arrest for debt. In the Levellers, Davies adds, women could see a group of people ready to speak to their needs and those of the community. Interests coincided. When Leveller printers were jailed, for instance, their wives continued to print and distribute.[24] Elizabeth Lilburne's struggles involved 'petitioning, marching, agitating, producing and dispersing subversive books', and bearing two children in prison – one in the Tower, christened 'Tower'.[25]

The Levellers demanded the right to vote, religious tolerance and the abolition of arbitrary power, whether located in the king, the Lords or, as they saw it fast becoming, in the House of Commons itself. Their underlying ideas were political equality and popular sovereignty. They expressed a radical Protestant belief in individual responsibility, believing it was imprudent and wicked to surrender control over one's fate to political leaders. True political authority derived only from the consent of the people,[26] and they endeavoured to draft and promulgate a basic constitution, the *Agreements of the People*.[27] The Levellers, Wootton emphasizes, never saw themselves as prospective rulers, but as spokesmen for a set of rules which should govern popular participation.[28] All power originated with the people, who entrusted their elected representatives with as much of it as they chose, for security, well-being and convenience. There should be a sovereign legislative body subject to recall by the electors and to frequent accountability, bound by fundamental laws which were unalterable by statute or enactment.[29]

Oliver Cromwell had led the army in a popular cause, but he and the other grandees were deeply opposed to popular sovereignty and equality. Calls for a widening of the franchise were not to be trusted. If the poor could outvote the rich, said General Henry Ireton, Cromwell's son-in-law and spokesman at Putney, 'why may not those men vote against all property?'[30] For the parliamentary leadership, people like Rainsborough, Lilburne and the others had gained quite enough already; they had seen the end of arbitrary rule by one man, and had won the right to be governed by constitutional parliamentary rule.[31]

Rainsborough had responded to Ireton at Putney by demanding to know 'what we have fought for', and this call echoed and re-echoed for some time, says Davies – democratic rights for all, without account of property. But the Leveller's claims on the franchise in 1647 extended at most to less than half the population of England – every male person, or possibly – there was ambiguity – every male householder. The 'poorest he' was not the 'poorest she', and Davies feels that the political rights of women, regardless of their status and property, actually fell in the process of the Revolution.[32]

These limitations continued everywhere for approximately another 350 years. Leveller ideas were nonetheless 'remarkable', says Aylmer, and so was the 'organization they formed'. They were 'the first democratic political movement in modern history'. Though defeated, the Cromwellian revolution was 'more thoroughgoing and more effective' because of their contribution. Nowhere else before the 1760s or 1789 was there 'the combination of radical journalism and pamphleteering, ideological zeal, political activism, and mass organization' that the Levellers developed within early capitalist development between 1646 and 1649.[33]

Parliament's victory saw tyranny replaced by oligarchy, buttressed by constitutionalism. Sovereignty lay not with the people but in elitist abstractions like 'the King in Parliament'. Liberalism entered political discourse not only as a restriction on state power, but also, says Meiksins Wood, as a *substitute* for democracy.[34] The framers of the United States constitution, she adds, subsequently worked in this tradition of oligarchic constitutionalism with a democratic facade.[35]

Equality and self-determination

Rousseau's thought was distinctive for its close concentration upon the meaning and significance of participation, and the importance of equality in a good democratic society. Participation and freedom are closely related. When Locke – following Hobbes – had defined freedom as being left alone (that is, negatively, the absence of constraint), Rousseau saw it totally differently as involving self-determination. We are free when we ourselves choose the principles which we follow in life – 'for the impulse of appetite alone is slavery, and obedience to a law which we prescribe to ourselves is freedom'.[36]

Extensive inequalities caused moral degradation and prevented a sense of common interest from developing in a society. Equality and democracy might grow together, however, through the active participation of the citizenry. Unlike Locke's emphasis on a citizen's merely tacit consent to government,[37] Rousseau proposed an active agreement frequently renewed. Participation would promote a sharing of values and experiences among the citizenry, and represent the basis for equality and democracy.[38] As in Athens, democracy meant for him not simply a form of government but a whole society founded on the principle of social equality.[39]

Active participation of all citizens was the basis of the good society; and the state or government was the agency for implementing the people's decisions (and might be variously organized). Popular decision-making would be binding on all citizens equally.[40] Social interaction would therefore be highly affirmative and interventionist, in sharp contrast again with Liberalism's quietist and negative freedom. As the Levellers had sensed in the 1640s, the freedom that mattered most to the poor in England was the freedom to escape from poverty: which could not be attained by them alone and unaided, since it necessarily involved challenging property-owners.[41]

Towards participatory democracy in South Africa

While Barrington Moore had famously declared 'no bourgeois, no democracy',[42] it is one of the great strengths of Rueschemeyer, Stephens and Stephens' work that they take a broad approach to democratization and reach contrary conclusions. It is an ongoing process involving chiefly, they suggest, increasing political equality – even better, perhaps, increasing equality, fullstop. Across the historical cases they examine, the urban working class was in these terms 'the most consistently pro-democratic force', the most frequent proponent, as they aptly phrase it, 'of the full extension of democratic rights'. Urban workers carried the process forward, because 'this promised to include the class in the polity where it could further pursue its interests', and because the working class, unlike other lower classes such as the poor peasantry, had 'the capacity to organize and express its interests'.

It was through this transformation of the class structure, the strengthening of working and lower middle classes in association with the expansion of production, urbanization and the growth of infrastructure, that capitalist development opened potentialities for democratization. Whether these could or would be seized, and the extent of the movement forward, remained of course highly problematic. The formation of new urban classes was also 'intimately related' to the growth and organizational density of civil society.[43]

South Africa testifies to the accuracy of this analysis, and the unique strength of the participatory democratic drive there over some three decades. Regardless of apartheid's intentions, capitalist development wrought great socio-economic change in the subordinate population from the 1970s, especially in urbanization, educational advance for blacks and the formation of an increasingly skilled black working class.

The black urban population steadily expanded from about 2.2 million in 1951 to 3.4 million in 1960, 4.4 million in 1970, and to 5.6 million by 1980.[44] Educational advance was very rapid. Between 1955 and 1970 the number of black pupils in secondary schools increased from 34 983 to 122 489, and in the subsequent five years it went up further to 318 568.[45] The expansion of secondary schooling in urban areas was notable and significant. In greater Soweto, for instance, there were eight secondary schools in 1972; 20 by 1976, with a three-fold increase in their student intake; and 55 by the end of 1984. Senior secondary education had by then been transformed from 'the prerogative of an elite' into a 'mass phenomenon', and an 'urban school-based culture and consciousness' emerged.[46]

A new activist political leadership was one of its products. Popo Molefe, for example, was born in 1952, grew up in western Soweto and, despite family poverty, achieved Standard 10 in 1976; Murphy Morobe was born a little later, but he was also in Standard 10 in 1976 at the well-known Morris Isaacson High School in Soweto. Molefe became general secretary of the UDF and Morobe its publicity secretary.[47]

Access to university education rapidly broadened. In 1960 there were fewer than 800 blacks at universities (excluding the distance-learning programmes offered by the University of South Africa, UNISA), but by 1983 there were about 20 000 at university, with another 12 700 enrolled at UNISA. Campus life provided the recruitment base for the Black Consciousness movement which disturbed Thabo Mbeki, and it was university graduates, notes Seekings, who took radical ideas into schools and townships, as teachers, doctors and, he adds, through drama groups.[48] Natal Medical School offered Mamphela Ramphele not only socially important knowledge and skills but, she recalls, 'an environment for the transformation of my life'; she became an activist in the South African Students' Organization, founded by Steve Biko in July 1969, and the 1970s were for her 'a time of immense personal growth'. She went ahead through various community activities, 'growing up the hard way'.[49]

The numbers of black workers employed in manufacturing went from 308 000 in 1960 to 781 000 in 1980.[50] In the country's industrial heartland of Gauteng, the workforce similarly arose from 160 000 to 375 000, and by the latter year around Johannesburg 'unskilled labour accounted for less than half' of all black employment there.[51] Wages in manufacturing went up steadily, too, through the 1960s, then increased sharply in the early 1970s. In the upshot, average wages in manufacturing doubled in value in real terms over the two decades. The formation of a 'fully urbanised, settled African working class' was occurring, most of whom enjoyed a rising standard of living, confined within inadequate and overcrowded living conditions,[52] and apartheid.

The trade union movement and the UDF

The political fruits of socio-economic development soon became evident. Over 100 000 black workers 'embarked on a series of spontaneous strikes' against deteriorating working conditions in the cities of Durban and Pinetown in January and February 1973. In doing this they began the transformation of the resistance movement, away from the exiled ANC's concentration on external assault on the apartheid state. More fundamentally, they also signaled the emergence of 'a democratic movement within the country, harnessed to independent working-class organisation'.[53]

As total non-agricultural employment rose from 4.7 million in 1980 to 5 million in 1985, trade union membership went from 808 000 to some 1.4 million workers, representing in the latter year a unionization density of 27.6 per cent. The 'most rapidly growing unions' through and beyond this period were those organizing mainly black workers, in particular those affiliated with COSATU, formed in 1985.[54] The union movement emphasized legal means of struggle with both capital and the state and, through their 'independent power base' they possessed the capacity both to mobilize and to restrain their members. They sought 'to win and expand legal space' in which to pursue 'a radical vision of a future society' by 'incrementalist' means. This strategy was 'in sharp contrast to the dominant approach in the national liberation movement'.[55] Its radicalism and its novelty were well-captured by Friedman. The struggle in the factories from the 1970s gave birth, he said, to a type of politics 'rarely seen among the powerless': a grassroots movement 'which stresse[d] the ability of ordinary men and women, rather than "great leaders", to act to change their world'.[56]

Two years earlier than COSATU's formation, the UDF was launched in Cape Town on 20 August 1983, with 10 000 people, representing a range of organizations, in attendance. It also represented a new democratization, as the developing social process as well as the merely formal goal of majoritarian parliamentary rule. The power of the UDF, Seekings makes clear, was based upon the settled black urban population, comprising 'both the urban industrial working classes and the aspirant black middle classes'. They were frustrated by the socio-economic restrictions of apartheid and their exclusion from citizenship. These new class formations provided the bases for the independent trade unions, the burgeoning civil society and for the UDF itself.[57] The three groupings became closely interrelated as the 1980s progressed.

Organization against elitism

The UDF operated more as 'a social movement' than as a political party.[58] It opened up, as little before had effectively done, popular challenge to apartheid; it aimed at being a nationwide movement 'to unite', as Popo Molefe said it, 'a broadest possible spectrum of people across class and colour lines ... to bring together a maximum number of the organisations of the people'.[59] And it also sought to encourage a sustainable forward movement in which, most profoundly, the people governed themselves.[60] Building upon the student and trade union action of the 1970s, these were radical new initiatives.

Seekings says misleadingly and without substantiation that the exiled ANC's role in 1983 was 'one of encouragement rather than direct instigation'; then adds Mac Maharaj's firm disclaimer, 'the UDF is not a creation of the [ANC]', and notes that Maharaj was taken by surprise by its emergence,[61] as so unpleasantly was Thabo Mbeki. Vladimir Shubin has none of Seekings' ambiguities. 'It should be underlined', he states, 'that the initiative for the creation of the UDF came from inside the country. One of my ANC friends told me soon after: "If some of our people say that the UDF was made by us, don't believe them"'.[62] The UDF represented, in fact, a huge break with the elitist practice of the exiled ANC. It was radical and novel in African and indeed broader historical terms.

All three of these tendencies were focused by the mid-1980s in the practice and goal of popular democracy. The second issue of the Front's theoretical journal *Isizwe*, March 1986, said: 'the building of people's power is something that is *already beginning to happen in the course of our struggle*. It is not for us to sit back and merely dream of the day when the people shall govern. It is our task to realise that goal now.' Organizations of popular power that were beginning to appear included street committees and people's courts, bodies concerned with self-government and dispute settlement. Together with trade union organized action in the workplace, these would, according to *Isizwe*, help to build a different kind of politics grounded in participation. The organs of people's

power, it was stressed, 'must be democratic and ... under political discipline'.[63] What was called civic struggles and the creation of people's
power went on together. As it was said at a UDF-convened conference
in Cape Town in April 1986: 'It is through civic struggles that we are
going to build structures that are deeply rooted in the community. Here
we are going to challenge the authority of the state and provide the alternatives.' Popular democracy represented self-determination. It involved
people taking political and administrative control over their own lives in
townships, schools and factories.[64]

As the historian of the UDF, acquainted with their path-breaking participatory practices, Seekings shows a readiness to elevate the role of the
exiled ANC close to the point of distortion. People's power, he claims,
'represented a marriage between the ANC's emphasis on armed insurrection and the organisational developments spreading across the country'.
He declares elliptically that the ANC in exile 'did not explicitly endorse'
the UDF's ideas of participatory power,[65] when the reality was, then and
later, that leaders like Mandela and Mbeki were deeply unsympathetic to
popular participation, and armed insurrection, endorsed by the latter
until the late 1980s, was their antithesis. He notes, accurately but con-
trariwise, that the talks process so prominently activated by Mandela
and Mbeki, had the effect of sidelining and eventually demobilizing the
UDF.[66] He knows, too, that the ANC elite's real concern was 'to control
state power from the top', and this was ultimately associated, as the
transition wore on, with what he terms the 'partial demobilisation of
protest inside the country'.[67] But he fails to allow that the ANC's position was opposed to popular participatory practice, and that their opposition to it, and to the UDF, intensified as the transition proceeded.

The UDF's conceptualization of democracy embraced, in 1987, an
awareness of the inadequacies of parliamentary representation. Locally-
based initiatives would establish the foundations for democracy, the
Front anticipated, before the transfer of political power to the majority.
The existing parliamentary institutions were insufficient, not only
because they excluded then the bulk of the people, but for the more
substantive reason that 'parliamentary-type representation in itself represents a very limited and narrow idea of democracy'.[68]

Early in that year Murphy Morobe, then the UDF's acting publicity
secretary, comprehensively described the participatory democracy
growing up in South Africa:

> We in the [UDF] are engaged in a national democratic struggle ... [It]
> involves all sectors of our people ... a democratic South Africa is one

of the aims or goals of our struggle ... [But] democracy is [also] the means by which we conduct the struggle. This refers to the democratic character of our existing mass-based organizations ... By developing active, mass-based democratic organizations and democratic practices within these organizations, we are laying the basis for a future democratic South Africa.

The creation of democratic *means* is for us as important as having democratic *goals* as our objective ... What is possible in the future depends on what we are able to create and sustain now. A democratic South Africa will not be fashioned only after transformation of political power to the majority has taken place.

A democratic solution in South Africa involves all South Africans, and in particular the working class, having control over all areas of daily existence – from national policy to housing, from schooling to working conditions, from transport to consumption of food ... When we say that the people shall govern, we mean at all levels and in all spheres, and we demand that there be real, effective control on a daily basis.

In other words, we are talking about direct as opposed to indirect political representation, mass participation rather than passive docility and ignorance, a momentum where ordinary people can do the job themselves.

'Rudimentary organs of *people's power*', he said, had begun to emerge in the form, for example, of street and defence committees and shop-steward structures in the workplace. He identified the 'basic principles of our organizational democracy' as (1) Elected Leadership, periodically reelected and recallable; (2) Collective Leadership; (3) Mandates and Accountability; (4) Reporting and Reporting Back; and (5) Criticism and Self-Criticism. These were, he stressed, 'fundamental weapon[s] of our struggle'.[69] Upheld by these potent principles, organizations would remain the weapon of the weak in their struggle with the strong, but not fall under elite or oligarchical domination. The people would have their organizations, but through these democratic devices they would control their leaders as well.

Seekings portrays these democratic principles as but a 'glorified understanding of both people's power in South Africa ... and the experience of socialist democratisation in Nicaragua and elsewhere'. He notes that the Front adhered to its model 'unevenly and intermittently', although 'generally through no choice of its own'.[70] By late 1987, most of the UDF leadership, as Marais describes it, were either in prison (70 per cent of detainees then were believed to be members of UDF affiliates), in hiding or dead; the Front was banned shortly after, but regrouped as the MDM later in 1988.[71] Heavy state repression ensured that from 1985 to 1989 much power shifted in practice within the UDF to key officials: Valli Moosa as acting general secretary, Morobe in charge of publicity, and Cachalia as treasurer. Decisions were 'rarely made' through the second-half of the 1980s 'on the basis of mandated positions, and the national leadership exercised consider-able latitude'.[72] Restrictions on the scope of decision-making were inevitable under Emergency conditions.

The Front nonetheless 'maintained an impressive level' in terms of its leaders reporting back to the membership and in the recognition of the importance of criticism and self-criticism of leadership. In public, Seekings notes, UDF leaders adopted a celebratory tone even during the worst of the state of emergency, but within the organization 'the UDF's own leaders were among the most focused of its critics'. It was Molefe, for instance, who reported to the 1985 national conference that the organization was 'trailing behind the masses'; Moosa, as acting secre-tary in Molefe's absence, who informed the 1987 national general council that the Front had been unable to maintain its regional struc-tures; and it was Molefe who declared to the national general council in 1991 that the Front was 'at its weakest in the entire history of its existence'.[73] It was in the same spirit and practice of the criticism of leaders, that they should be accountable to the people for their actions, that Morobe and Cachalia spoke out in public condemnation of Madikizela-Mandela in February 1989.

The reacquired strength of the ANC relative to the UDF came not only through the talks process and the celebrity of its leadership, but also in the area of financing. In exile the party was believed to have a budget of $50–100 million a year, and in South Africa in 1991 its administrative operational costs were around R4 million a month.[74] 'Generous funding from abroad' continued after its unbanning. Its election fund-raising target announced in 1993 was R168 million. These amounts, Seekings notes, 'dwarf[ed] the income of the UDF'. But the trade union movement, distinctively, 'commanded much more extensive resources'.[75]

That the unbanned ANC in 1990 'did not simply take over the UDF, use it as a convening structure, or even take over its offices', believes Seekings, 'indicated important differences between the organisa-tions'.[76] While these were, nonetheless, not publicly clarified by the ANC, strong indications were obliquely offered. Madikizela-Mandela attacked what she termed the 'cabal' in the UDF–MDM – believed to include in her thinking Moosa, Morobe, Cachalia and Ramaphosa – in 1990, 1991 and 1992, and she was especially vindictive towards Morobe and Cachalia.[77] Some UDF leaders were themselves critical of the denunciation of Madikizela-Mandela in February 1989, and at 'a head office [Front] meeting' in late January 1990 Morobe was rebuked for his role in this.[78] Aubrey Mokoena joined Madikizela-Mandela in attacking 'the cabal' that same year, describing it as 'a secret clique of activists', and condemning them for cherishing the ambition, as he more revealingly put it, 'that the UDF should exist as a parallel structure to the ANC'. The Front's very existence, the future ANC MP asserted in an open letter to the party, undermined the ANC and retarded the struggle, and it must therefore be dissolved.[79]

As the ANC reorganized and prepared itself and its leaders for the acquisition of power, its relationship with the UDF became both more problematic and acutely unequal. While Madikizela-Mandela was quickly rehabilitated within the ANC, the UDF's national leadership in 1990 was 'in constant flux'. Morobe went to study abroad in July, and Cachalia followed a little later.[80] Molefe was left as the only senior national leader continuing to perform UDF work full-time.[81]

Seekings attributes these differences to 'hostility' to the UDF leaders and structures from 'large sections of the Charterist movement'. He claims further that 'diverse groups' within the Charterist tradition 'saw the UDF as the vehicle of leaders whom they did not like and who, they were pretty sure, did not like them either'. He offers no explanation of the substance of this personalized hostility, nor of the extent and nature of its supposed reciprocation from within the UDF.[82] The estrangement of Mandela and Mbeki from participatory democratic practice was evident from the mid-1980s, as was the exiles' dislike for independent organizational initiatives; the overriding concern of the ANC leadership to gain state power was equally clear soon after. But the UDF's 'hostility' to all but non-democratic practice is much less evident. Madikizela-Mandela maintained a venomous personal dislike for Morobe and Cachalia,[83] and Mbeki seems motivated both by long-lasting friendships with a few and enmities towards others.

But the UDF's behaviour was different: its opposition, say, to the autocratic tendencies of Nelson Mandela, and the secrecy and aloofness of Mbeki, was far more on the substantive political grounds of accountability and openness than personal ones. The imputation of mutual hostility trivializes the principled distinctions between the elitism of the ANC and the active and open democratic aspirations of the

UDF. The latter opened the way to a truly new South Africa, while the former represented the nationalist party's 'reassert[ion of] its hegemony over the democratic movement',[84] and the stultification of the latter 1990s.

Seekings' frequent reference to the Charterist movement suggests that it still constitutes some meaningful entity associated closely with the ANC. He nowhere notes that this party, the implied carrier of the tradition, was extremely unlikely through the greater part of the 1990s to ground its position and policies on the egalitarian, non-racial and democratic values of the Freedom Charter. He harbours an associated belief in the supposed 'non-African' nature of the UDF, and offers the tendentious and question-begging conclusion that 'UDF leaders were certainly guilty of failing to promote African leadership as much as they might'. Popo Molefe observes, however, in a generous forward to the book, that

> layer after layer of activists rose to the challenge...even at times when almost every leader was either on trial or in detention. The success of the UDF was due in part to the nurturing of successive tiers of leadership.[85]

Options facing the UDF narrowed down to two between the end of 1990 and March 1991. One was to disband entirely as its continued existence was portrayed by some as likely to confuse the people, and that it detracted more substantively from the predominance of the ANC. The other was to transform itself into an overall coordinating front for civil society. The density and diversity of this sector then gave substance to this proposal; one estimate suggested that before the 1994 elections there were approximately 54000 non-governmental and community-based groups, and that civil society in South Africa was then 'probably at its peak'.[86] 'Molefe and other national leaders clearly favoured the second option', Seekings reports.[87] These did not include presumably the 'many senior UDF leaders' who were being 'pulled into top ANC positions' after February 1990; among them then, Archie Gumede, Lekota, Trevor Manuel and Cheryl Carolus.[88] More followed to the party of imminent government. Facing veiled but strong opposition from the ANC leadership, without the resources of the nationalist party, not least those of the patronage of office, the UDF was caused to collapse.

When Molefe addressed the National General Council in March 1991, the UDF, he acknowledged, had reached its nadir:

> Very few regional councils meet regularly. Most of the zonal structures have collapsed. There is nothing that provides for joint

strategising and joint decision-making. Leaders no longer operate on the basis of sufficient mandates, nor are they sufficiently accountable because meetings are irregular.

The remnants of its national leadership faced, in Seekings's phraseology, a 'burden of resentment and hostility', and the 'advocates of the transformation option floundered'.[89] Disbandment resulted, amidst widespread uncertainty, regret and disgruntlement, as Zohra Ebrahim and Marais noted.[90] The UDF had been the activist internal movement which conceived of democracy as a popular ongoing process, when the ANC leadership saw it as power for themselves plus electoralism. Seekings says that the UDF bequeathed to the nationalist party a robust culture of debate and self-criticism[91], but fails again to see that it is precisely this heritage which is so flagrantly ignored: the intolerance of debate, criticism and opposition, the equation of the one with the other, that characterized the ANC leadership at Mafikeng in 1997, which has escalated during the Mbeki presidency.[92]

COSATU and a highly-unionized society

COSATU and the trade union movement remained strong and possessed of an incrementalist strategy which, like the UDF's, avoided both the old fatalism and the 'futile quest for the revolutionary overthrow of the apartheid state'.[93] Through the 1980s, South Africa experienced what Macun terms 'an explosion in union growth', on route to its becoming 'a highly unionized society'.[94] By 1990, when total (non-agricultural) employment reached 5.3 million, trade union membership was 2 458 712, representing a union density of 46.3 per cent; in 1991 membership was 2 718 970, a union density of 52.3 per cent; in 1992 there were 2.9 million members, a density of 57.1 per cent; and in 1993 the density of union membership reached 59 per cent.[95]

The labour movement, according to Webster and Adler, 'played a crucial role both in the initiation of the transition and in the transition itself', as 'the best organized and the single most powerful constituency'. Strong unions were capable of 'reaching and enforcing agreements with capital and the state'.[96] Exerting countervailing power through negotiations represented 'gains for the powerless', say Friedman and Shaw, because it 'force[d] the powerful to share decisions they [we]re accustomed to take alone'.[97] Radical-reformist interaction with the state and business was not an area where the UDF principally operated, concentrating as it did on organizational development from the ground up. Corporate chiefs, they note, saw advantages in engaging with labour during the transition, while the unions aimed to force the government to share decisions – through, for instance, the establishment of a National Economic Forum – not only in labour's interests but 'those of the broader liberation movement'.[98] Democratization, as in Rueschemeyer and his colleagues' terms, was a broad process aimed at increasing equality.

Membership of COSATU-affiliated unions comprised 'over 40 per cent' of all union membership throughout the 1990s, and they were the fastest growing. In 1996 they comprised 20 affiliates with a membership of 1.74 million workers, or 58 per cent of the country's total union members.[99] COSATU's strength was in its location within the country's uniquely high levels of unionization in world terms. When union membership was in decline in most developed capitalist countries, 1985–95 – in Britain -27.7 per cent; United States -21.1 per cent; Germany -17.6 per cent; and Japan -16.7 per cent – South Africa experienced the world's largest increase, of 126.7 per cent, ahead of Spain with 92.3 per cent, Chile with 89.6 per cent, Thailand with 77 per cent, and 16 other countries where unionization also rose.[100] Union membership not only gave meaning to people's lives in South Africa in the 1970s and 1980s, it also paid-off for the average worker. Around the mid-1990s, on World Bank estimates, membership in a trade union increased a South African worker's wages by between 25 and 35 per cent, a much higher differential, they critically observed, than was found elsewhere.[101] Additionally, in the context of rising unemployment through the second half of the 1990s, union membership provided a worker with a better chance of holding on to a job.[102]

Webster and Adler stress that the unions played a central role in the transition to majority rule, loosely termed by them democracy. COSATU was not the target of the 'hostility' which the ANC leadership directed against the UDF after 1990. Not only that, but on Webster's and Adler's reckoning, the trade unions were in alliance with 'perhaps the most labour-friendly government ever to come to power in contemporary transitions to democracy'. Among the legislative and legal fruits were, they note, a 'union-friendly' Labour Relations Act and an entrenched Bill of Rights in the constitution, representing important protections for human rights.[103] Much has been achieved by organized labour in South Africa. 'By virtue of its independent power base labour is able to mobilize outside state structures', they note, 'yet through its alliance with the ANC it is able to influence state policy'. Support for labour was one early characteristic of ANC government.

But Webster and Adler go further and claim, following Jeremy Baskin, that 'a labour-repressive policy is neither possible nor likely to be contemplated by the current government'.[104] This again is only part of the broad equation. It might well be the case that, given union strength and other matters, actual repression is indeed unlikely. But the alternative, of the ANC more firmly embracing pro-capitalist policies, is not – under the rubrics of restructuring, adjustment and the promotion of black capitalism, such strategies were being implemented through the late 1990s with the rising unemployment and the deepening of inequalities that accompanies them.

Extending democratization in South Africa

Much more needs to be done by organized workers too. Webster and Adler observe that the labour movement, in 1994, 'partially achieved the longstanding goal of democracy',[105] but they do not consider just how partial or limited this majority-rule, electoral democracy actually is – its cohabitation in particular with inequalities of wealth and incomes, its demobilization of civil society, its promotion of elitism and non-accountability. COSATU retains a distinctive capacity to confront these continuing problems, and its roots in the new unionism of the 1970s and its cooperation with the UDF–MDM substantiates its commitment to democratization and equality.[106] It remains organizationally and financially independent of the ANC government, with the capability for the independent mobilization of its large membership.[107] It gets out the vote for the ANC at elections, and it can take strike action. These are significant strengths, not least in comparative domestic terms.

The ANC's predominance in parliament and government says little about party organization, membership numbers and elan. In Gauteng province, for example, party membership, according to Smith, was 120 000 in 1995, but was down to 65 000 by 1997 when the ANC nationally, she added, was in 'a disorganized morass'. The party's own estimates, as cited by Friedman, suggested that membership had fallen by two-thirds between the 1994 elections and 1997.[108] Thousands of the ANC's most effective organizers, Lodge observes, had found governmental and other employment which 'considerably distanced' them from their local communities.[109] Around 1997, on the summation of *The Economist*, 'the chaotic ANC party machine relie[d] on the slickly organised COSATU branches to get out the vote'.[110] Disempowerment of the party membership was what the ruling elite intended. Revisions to the ANC's constitution, signalled in 1997, extended the interval between its national conferences from three to five years, limiting further the leadership's accountability to its members and 'its more inchoate popular following'.[111]

The SACP expressed an orientation to the working class, but its experience, unlike the UDF and the unions, was in exile and clandestine politics in close association with the ANC. Internal democracy had only begun to improve in 1989, according to Shubin. A new central committee which 'included younger people' was elected in June, and out of some 50 participants seven came from inside South Africa. The growth of the Party inside the country in the previous six to nine months 'had been higher than in the previous twenty years'. About one-quarter of the membership was then in South Africa, of whom 60 per cent were workers.[112]

But by the end of the 1990s, it was believed to have lost as many as four out of five of the members it recruited after its unbanning at the beginning of the decade, according to a SACP discussion document. There were currently 13 803 paid-up members, and another 5000 to 7000 who had signed up and were expected to pay their dues, when there had been 80 000 paid-up members 'some years' earlier. The party had 30 'launched districts' and 355 branches on paper, but it frankly admitted that the numbers which actually functioned was unknown. An SACP 'party building commission', headed by general secretary, Blade Nzimande, had been 'relatively ineffective'. Moreover, 'very few' of the members of the party's central committee had taken an active interest in membership recruitment.[113] This was not altogether surprising, since the committee included such ministers as Geraldine Fraser-Moleketi, Public Services Minister, and Jeff Radebe, in charge of Public Enterprises, who were actively defining and implementing policies on downsizing and privatization to which the SACP was opposed; Radebe was merely a 'lackey of the executive', in Lizeka Mda's judgement, above. The incorporation of Party members into government threatened the identity and coherency of the SACP.[114]

The process reached a possible low point in August 2000 with the expulsion of the writer, Dale McKinley, from the party, charged with 'calling into question the credibility of the ANC and its leadership in a manner not befitting a member of the SACP'. The action related to his book, *The ANC and the Liberation Struggle*, published three years earlier, to wide press coverage then, and to articles expressing similar views. It was all 'closely related to the changed balance of power – one can clearly see the direction from which these [charges] have come', said an SACP member who did not wish to be named.[115]

COSATU's capacity for strike action was indicated in April 2000 when 'about 60 000 marchers…brought central Johannesburg to a standstill for five hours' in protest at job losses. It was said to be the biggest demonstration in the city since the 1994 elections. COSATU president, Willie Madisha, called on the private sector to end its 'investment strike' and create more employment. Further action was forecast. An opinion survey, by *The Sunday Independent* and the Plus 94 Harris Poll, indicated that 68 per cent of the paper's readers supported COSATU's action over jobs.[116] The SACP gave its endorsement, Blade Nzimande saying that 'the past ten years have been an appalling time for the workers of this land'. The post-1994 period, he also said, had marginalized workers 'from being beneficiaries of the achievements of the struggle'. But the action was not 'merely about working people. It was also about the struggle against poverty'. The problem was, he added, that 'local capital is not rushing to invest in this country'.[117]

Official policy was to make the country more investor-friendly by way of 'further adjustments', as Tito Mboweni, leading ANC member and Reserve Bank governor, declared in October 2000. These would bear heavily on jobs and workers. Privatization and labour reform – the latter understood as the weakening of the earlier job protections – needed to be pursued with greater urgency, and he warned government to give 'careful consideration' to factors that could improve business confidence.[118] In his 1997 budget speech, Finance Minister Trevor Manuel had challenged South Africans to call him a Thatcherite for the conservative policies he proposed;[119] workers were the intended targets of the adjustment programmes.[120] In 1998 a 'senior US official' had reacted to the high degree of unionization in South Africa by recommending that the ANC government give top priority to slowing the growth of union power and reducing labour costs. It was most important that South Africa passed legislation 'liberalising the way trade unions operate', he said.[121]

Strong as it was *vis-à-vis* the governing party, COSATU, nonetheless, faced organizational problems of its own, according to Webster and Adler. Organized labour 'lost significant layers of leadership' to government and the corporate sector through the 1990s, which 'seriously diminished' its pool of 'skilled and experienced senior leaders'. This had its consequences. There was 'a marked decline in the quality of service provided to members', and internal democracy suffered – the 'quality of mandates and report-backs' generally deteriorated. And there was 'a growing gap' between COSATU leadership and the base of the movement. Union power had historically derived 'from the close relationship between leaders, shop-stewards, and the rank-and-file', developing actively and cooperatively within self-determining struggles. But union chiefs were acquiring alternative relationships with the new political and economic elites.[122]

Organized labour remained the single most powerful democratic constituency, increasingly outstanding in a demobilizing political system. By early 2000, less than 10 per cent of South Africans remained active members of political parties, compared with 20 per cent in 1994; among blacks, the decline had gone further from an earlier 24 per cent down to 10 per cent. According to Johan Olivier, a researcher involved in the survey, the country was approaching what could be called normal levels of party activity.[123]

No other group possessed COSATU's capacity to address the growing social problems of jobs, poverty and inequality, and the latter two represented a broad challenge to the federation. For COSATU to seriously address these issues, said Friedman, 'it need[ed] to recognise that it cannot do this on its own'. It could play a role in an alliance for redistribution, but 'only as an equal partner of other interests'. Many of the poor are not organized at all, and they outnumbered unionists. Unless the unions found ways of helping the poor to organize, 'the battle against poverty will be fought by a minority and the voices of most of the poor will remain stilled'.[124] Confronting poverty compelled COSATU toward broad social struggle again.

The issue of democratization, inside COSATU and nationally, tended to do so too. The ANC successfully exerted its predominance over the UDF–MDM, and over the rest of a once burgeoning civil society, but only partially over organized labour. It was undermined historically and ideologically nonetheless. As Friedman and Shaw significantly state, 'the role of the union movement in th[e] transition has been undervalued or ignored'.[125] A particular interpretation of the struggle has been propagated which elevated the established ANC leadership – even incorporating such figures as Madikizela-Mandela and Buthelezi – and greatly diminished 'the Class of '76', the UDF, and the unions. Stifling the extensive democratization which they espoused too.

The strengthening of an elitist tradition has taken different forms and turns. Soon after he made his 'I am an African' speech in Cape Town in April 1998,[126] a large new project was activated to elevate Thabo Mbeki as a visionary of continental greatness. The African Renaissance Conference followed in Johannesburg in September, opened and presided over by the then Deputy-President, who 'inspired' the participants, from Africa, Europe and the United States, with 'the knowledge that an African renaissance was indeed within grasp'.[127] A committee was immediately set up both to advise the Deputy-President and, as Molebeledi reported, to 'pursue the African renaissance'.[128] A book, *African Renaissance*, edited by Malegapuru William Makgoba, and a dedicated Institute, soon followed. In a prologue, President Mbeki loftily declared that 'the new African world' would be 'one of democracy, peace and stability, sustainable development and a better life for the people'. It would come about only through protracted struggle but, 'yesterday is a foreign country – tomorrow belongs to us'.[129] A glittering launch took place at the Johannesburg Country Club in March 2000, attended by Jacob Zuma, Thami Mazwai, Makgoba, Essop Pahad and others; 8000 high schools would each receive a copy of the book.[130] The South African Chapter of the African Renaissance Institute was launched two weeks later.[131] Mbeki's initiative was grandiloquent and well-nigh impervious to the facts. Confronted by continuing barbarism from many quarters, he asserted in October 2000 that 'the renewal of the continent [had] started, however hesitantly'.[132]

The official reinterpretation of the popular movement goes on too. The Office of the Presidency had obtained funding worth some R6 million,[133] it was announced in August 2000, for a project to record the history of the anti-apartheid struggle. It aimed to

> document developments between 1964, when militant opposition to apartheid had been smashed, and the remarkable process of negotiations that began in secret in the late 1980s and culminated in the ANC's victory ... in 1994.

The South African Democracy Education Trust had been set up, and Essop Pahad would lead it on President Mbeki's behalf. Ben Magubane and Yvonne Muthien, 'considered in academic circles to be close to the [ANC]', would be prominent researchers.[134]

The threat to an activist and independent COSATU is not simply latent or ideological; Friedman and Shaw note, for instance, 'significant ANC resistance to union participation in decision making', in bodies like the National Economic Forum 'after the [1994] election'.[135] Home Affairs Minister Buthelezi takes his opposition to the unions at least as far as Treasury Secretary Rubin. He told a business luncheon in Durban in November 1998 that the economy was 'being hijacked by the influence, greed and unreasonable ambition of trade unions'. The government needed a showdown with the unions, and sooner rather than later; only an acceleration of wealth creation, he declared, would help the many people without formal housing and services like electricity.[136]

The ANC leadership's views were not totally dissimilar. President Mandela took the opportunity of his keynote address to COSATU's 6th national congress to accuse union leaders of being 'selfish' and 'sectoral', bent on protecting their interests at the expense of the nation's. At the SACP's 1998 congress, Mandela and Mbeki variously described Communist Party leaders as 'liars', 'revolutionary opportunists' and 'ultra-left[ists', who were adopting holier-than-thou attitudes.[137]

The pressures emanating from President Mbeki's universalizing tendencies are very active ones. Thabo Mbeki 'carefully co-opted' COSATU secretary general, Sam Shilowa, 'into his kitchen cabinet', say Fine and Grawitzky. But the move 'cost Shilowa credibility' in COSATU, and his successor Zwelinzima Vavi was being 'very careful to avoid a similar fate'. Mbeki's 'perceived candidate' for COSATU's president at elections in 1999, Vusi Nhlapo, 'lost out to Willie Madisha'. But some union activists were said to fear that President Mbeki 'wants to have a hand in choosing union leaders', just as he does with all senior appointments in central and provincial government.[138]

Both COSATU and the SACP complained in September 2000 that they were denied access to the government leadership, in particular to Mbeki. Tensions between the three formations had been growing. A COSATU discussion document said: 'Between 1996 and 1999... the government presented major proposals, especially on the economy, as *faits accomplis*, in some cases with no effective consultation'. Nzimande said in late August that the presidency was largely responsible for the lack of consultation, and relations were reported to be deteriorating between the so-called radical Vavi and President Mbeki.[139]

Confronting the issues of jobs, poverty and democracy would involve struggle, and thus, as it is pursued, the likely reintegration of COSATU's leadership with its mass membership as well as engagement with the wider community. Friedman said that the federation's influence would not remain limited to the workplace if it took up issues of wide social concern. Its president, Willie Madisha, firmly insisted in September that contrary to the incoherencies being continually expressed by President Mbeki, HIV causes AIDS, that government pronouncements were decidedly unhelpful, and that far more needed to be done to help the escalating numbers inflicted with the disease.[140] This was at a time when ANC leaders were twisting and turning to avoid disagreement with Mbeki, when, for instance, Education Minister Kader Asmal, once a man of some integrity, told reporters in Cape Town that 'he would not be pushed into a corner' on whether HIV caused AIDS, and that his personal views on this immense issue were irrelevant. As the government's communications chief, Joel Netshitenzhe, helpfully explained: 'Ministers generally formulated answers on the cause of AIDS based on President Thabo Mbeki's stance'.[141]

Madisha also unequivocally declared, at the same time, that the governments macro-economic policy had failed and had caused massive job losses. Proposed amendments to the labour laws appeared to reverse the ANC's commitment to a well-paid, highly skilled labour force, a position that went back to the Freedom Charter. Regarding proposals for liberalizing work on Sundays, he said, 'the apartheid Basic Conditions of Employment Act was better'.[142]

The Congress had earlier expressed opposition to the 'affirmative procurement' policies favoured by the ANC government and demanded by the patriotic bourgeoisie. Criteria other than the 'PDI/10 per cent rule' should be taken into account before a company was awarded a state contract. It should prove, for example, that it was up-to-date with its unemployment fund and worker compensation contributions, that it had complied with relevant bargaining council agreements, and that it was in good standing with the South African Revenue Service.[143] It backed up these criticisms by announcing 'worst employer' awards soon after, and presenting one of the first to the prominent empowerment and renaissance crusader, Thami Mazwai[144]; as boss of Mafube Publishing, Mazwai had done a 'sterling job' in breaking labour laws and bringing misery to South African workers, announced Willie Madisha.[145]

Jobs and workers' rights were also international issues, which COSATU recognized in April when it entered into an alliance with the Australian Council of Trade Unions (ACTU) – its first of this kind – to fight unemployment. The ACTU had a membership of two million drawn from the manufacturing, retail, building, stevedoring, teaching and other sectors. Madisha declared:

> We are committed to the global fight against globalisation, and the agreement will also have major spin-offs for [our] affiliates. The contacts will be between the federations, affiliates and locals. We are looking at other aspects ... This is a major breakthrough for COSATU, and it comes at a time when our members are facing retrenchments'.[146]

COSATU has much in its favour. It is embedded in a unionized working class, the country's largest popular constituency, and it has both an independent capacity and a need to work towards equality, justice and democratization.

The Unending Struggle

In terms of both the actuality of participatory democracy and the realistic possibility of its achievement, Athens and South Africa stand out. Participatory democracy endured for two centuries in Athens because of extensive institutional arrangements which empowered worker-citizens, and simultaneously restricted the political power of elites of wealth, status and education.

Controlling elites is at the heart of popular democracy – preventing them from utilizing their advantages, say, of money and knowledge to gain political dominance over other less well-endowed citizens; organizing the people for effective action; and preventing the development of large inequalities of wealth and incomes.

The Levellers were brave and inspirational in a 'world turned upside down', but their aspirations towards responsible and popular government had no real hope of success within the embryonic structures of early capitalism, against rising parliamentary elites buttressed by landowning power.

But controlling elites is also extremely hard to achieve within modern liberal capitalist polities. Defining democracy as rights exercised within the political sphere only, with a *laissez faire* state directed towards the protection of private property, allows full rein to elites of money and fame. The United States leads the way. Expenditure on the presidential and congressional elections in 2000 increased by nearly 50 per cent over 1996, to reach an estimated $3 billion. George W. Bush laid out around $100 million in his primary campaign – chiefly against John McCain who notably opposed the predominance of money in United States politics. Jon Corzine, for example, former head of Goldman Sachs, spent about $60 million of his $400 million fortune to get elected as senator from New Jersey. Money politics weakened the people, and gave unfair advantage to 'three groups of insiders': 'legacies', such as the sons and wives of presidents with names which were already famous; the mega-rich, who financed their own campaigns – the Democrats, for instance, recruited five multimillionaires to stand for expensive seats; and incumbents, who can sell or parlay 'the power of their office into political contributions'. In the House races, incumbents spent nine times as much as their challengers did. Politics operated within an 'iron triangle' of legislators, lobbyists and fundraisers. 'Money ha[d] a way of getting round the rules', which the Supreme Court facilitated by equating freedom of speech with freedom to spend unrestrainedly on getting elected.[1] Ordinary people are accorded no role here.

The model of unrestricted capitalism in the United States produces inequalities and injustices which liberal democracy, with its narrow and value-free concerns, is incapable of ameliorating. Limited liberal government means, as Lazare has said, limited democracy for the masses, and low participation in elections,[2] where their democracy is supposedly upheld. Botswana is the leading African variant of the liberal model, almost a mini-America. It is characterized by an American-style symbiosis between government and business, enduring inequalities, injustice for the San, and 'dull', non-participatory elections that President Mogae correctly perceives as integral features of its liberal democracy. The people of Botswana and of the United States appear almost equally powerless in relation to their ruling elites. All indicators suggest that democratic change in these polities would be at best both limited and very slow. Their peoples are subordinated, their dependency and alienation is entrenched, and they are without organizations.

South Africa is different because of structural-organizational factors, represented in good part in the recent past by the UDF, and in the present, too, by COSATU. The two arose within the concrete of advanced capitalist development, in production, infrastructure, urbanization, educational expansion and class formation, as an authoritarian racist system was beginning to fail. The unions and the UDF powerfully inspired self-determination among the people – the trade union strategy of radical reform, of building the future through steady, palpable improvements in the here and now, and a political practice designed to control elites and curb elitism – notably, the UDF's principles of 'organizational democracy': collective leadership periodically reelected and recallable; leadership governed by mandates, accountability and on reporting back to the membership; and the need for criticism and self-criticism of and by the leadership. These specific devices would facilitate the building of strong democratic organizations, and ensure that they remained free of elite domination. This was underlaid by the UDF's broad and active understanding of democracy, as a daily ongoing process in the community, school and workplace which preceded and was intended to go far beyond mere majoritarian parliamentary rule.

Representing a broad section of civil society and some two million people at its height, the UDF was disbanded in testament to its effectiveness, not by apartheid, but by the country's old nationalist elite – the exiled and imprisoned ANC leadership. This estranged and almost moribund group, reactivated through talks with the government through the mid-1980s, saw 'organizational democracy' as threatening to themselves, to their paramountcy, non-accountability and solitary decision-making. People overly venerated their returned leaders, as Bantu Holomisa observed, great hopes were placed in electoral democracy, and the demobilization of civil society was effected; the 'Aristocrats of the Revolution' – Mda's term – were enthroned.[3] By 2001, even electoral democracy is seriously constrained, by appointments centralized in one man and one-party predominance.

But a uniquely large unionized working class remains in the continent's most advanced capitalist economy, and COSATU is organized, active and independent. The inequalities which the patriotic bourgeoisie promotes, and the ANC government encourages, are increasingly manifest, and the popular capacities to challenge this elitist non-accountable and seemingly isolated alliance are present too. Nowhere else in Africa is there this capacity of resistance to elite autocracy. With the stultification of the ANC and the silence of the intellectuals, it is the richest resource of what could be a truly democratic South Africa.

Notes

Preface

1. Mauritius, where governments have changed as a result of elections, was independent in March 1968.
2. There were parallels with the democratization process based upon 'working-class self-help' in nineteenth-century England. Its characteristic was not individual effort but, as Hopkins stresses, 'co-operation' – people 'working together to safeguard employment, and to make provision for sickness and ill-health'. The friendly society movement greatly expanded, co-operatives did likewise, and the organization and action of trade unions led on to working-class representation in parliament. Eric Hopkins, *Working-Class Self-Help in Nineteenth-Century England: Responses to Industrialization*, London, UCL Press, 1995, p. 3.
3. 'Opposition to democracy is not as moribund as public rhetoric might lead us to suppose.' Anthony Arblaster, *Democracy*, Milton Keynes, Open University Press, 1987, p. 89.

1 Autocratic Elites and Enfeebled Masses: Africa, Botswana and South Africa

1. K. Good, 'Corruption and Mismanagement in Botswana: A Best-Case Example?' *The Journal of Modern African Studies* (Cambridge), 32(3), 1994. But in mid-2000 there were reports of driver licences and residence and work permits being obtained through corrupt means. Joseph Balise, in *The Midweek Sun* (Gaborone), 24 May, and Stryker Motlaloso, in *Mmegi* (Gaborone), 28 July 2000.
2. From 1966 to 1996 Botswana achieved the fastest growth of GDP per capita in the world. J. Clark Leith, *Botswana: A Case Study of Economic Policy Prudence and Growth*, Washington, DC, The World Bank Group, 31 August 1999, p. 1, and International Monetary Fund, *World Economic Outlook*, Washington, DC, May 1999, p. 146.
3. Leys uses Rosa Luxemburg's concept of capitalist barbarism, which referred to the destruction of culture, the dictatorship of militarism, dissolution into chaos and anarchy, and economic crises, and sees it gradually engulfing most of the sub-continent. Colin Leys, 'Confronting the African Tragedy', *New Left Review* (London), 204, March/April 1994, p. 34. What follows here is a consideration of representative and significant trends, not in any sense a complete audit of barbarism – Bokasa's Central African Empire, Idi Amin's Uganda, the warlords of Somalia, Mugabe's massacres in Matabeleland, and Dhlakama's Renamo in Mozambique, for instance, are not considered.
4. Mark Huband, *The Liberian Civil War*, London, Frank Cass, 1998, p. xvi.

5. According to Stephen Ellis 'the figure of 150,000 to 200,000 commonly used for war deaths over the whole 1989–1997 period are a very high estimate', and he suggests 'a total of some 60–80,000 deaths directly caused by the war' as 'no more than an order of magnitude'. Ellis, *The Mask of Anarchy*, London, Hurst & Company, 1999, p. 316.

6. Jean-Francois Bayart, Stephen Ellis and Beatrice Hibou, *The Criminalization of the State in Africa*, Oxford, James Currey, 1999, p. xv.

7. *Ibid.*, p. xv.

8. *Business Day* (Johannesburg), 8 January 1999.

9. *The Economist* (London), 9 January 1999. Roadblocks were mounted to prevent people from leaving, and whole streets of houses were set on fire, sometimes after locking the residents inside. Lansana Fofana, 'The Visitation', *BBC Focus on Africa* (London), 10(2), April–June 1999, pp. 28–9.

10. Bayart *et al.*, *op. cit.*, p. xv.

11. Fighting swayed backwards and forwards in the Congo in the late 1990s between 'Ninjas' and 'Cocoyes' militia forces, each led by a competing President, in which a victory was celebrated by the looting of the capital, and the country's main artery between Brazzaville and Pointe Noire remained disrupted for months. *The Economist*, 25 October 1997.

12. Jonathan Steele, 'A Catalogue of Hate and Murder', *Mail and Guardian* (Johannesburg), 23 December 1999.

13. The expenditure on armaments helped to maintain their lifestyles, of course. The report, 'A Crude Awakening', by the British pressure group Global Witness, discussed in *The Economist*, 15 January 2000.

14. Nicholas Shaxson, 'Endless War', *Business Day*, 10 March 1999.

15. Words of the report, cited by Abbey Makoe, in *The Star* (Johannesburg), 15 April 2000.

16. *The Economist*, 26 July 1997. Stephen Ellis added that Taylor gained a fortune from the timber, gold and other natural products of the regions which his forces controlled, as well as from his international criminal linkages (as Bayart noted), and used this to buy arms and thence to run a successful political organization. *Mail and Guardian*, 25 July 1997.

17. As quoted by Elizabeth Ohene, 'Chosen by God?', *BBC Focus on Africa*, 8(4), October–December 1997.

18. Huband, *op. cit.*, p. 219, and Chris McGreal, *The Guardian* (London), 13 August 1999. When Mary Harper visited President Taylor she reported that 'apart from being physically wrecked, Liberia is also a country living with fear... many people are worried that something terrible is still looming around the corner.' The 'man who makes sure' that 'fear and intimidation are always lurking nearby' was the Police Director, Charles Taylor's cousin. Harper, 'Think Big', *BBC Focus on Africa*, 10(2), April–June 1999.

19. The rebels could hardly have done better. They were given four ministerial posts, and Foday Sankoh was accorded the 'status' of vice-president, and control of the country's mineral-resources commission. *Business Day*, 9 July, and *The Economist*, 10 July 1999.

20. The United Nations, unusually, attached a disclaimer to this peace agreement, and there were indications that many ordinary people found it 'pure blackmail' and repugnant. Edward Conteh, a 52-year-old mechanic whose left arm was hacked off during the RUF assault on Freetown in January, said: 'I don't

want this type of amnesty. If we have to forgive, then we are ready. But they should not go scot-free. They should admit to their wrongdoings and say sorry.' E.E.C. Shears-Moses, President of the Sierra Leone Bar Association, said that 'the government had no right to mortgage the right of the individual to seek legal redress against the man who chopped off their arm or killed their child.' It laid the ground for future conflict, he added. As quoted by Chris McGreal, 'I Will Wait. Then I Will Kill Him', *The Guardian* (London), 6 August 1999. After eight years of civil war costing perhaps 100 000 deaths, the Algerian government offered an amnesty to rebels which specifically excluded 'blood crimes', rape or acts of terror in public places. Report by John Burns, *The Sunday Independent* (Johannesburg), 8 February 2000.

21. James Traub, 'The Worst Place on Earth', *The New York Review of Books*, XLVII (11), 29 June 2000, p. 62.

22. *The Economist*, 11 December 1999.

23. Quoted by McGreal, *The Guardian*, 13 August 1999.

24. The United States' presidential envoy, Rev. Jesse Jackson, had played a large role in gaining acceptance for the Lomé agreement, and he was quoted in early May as comparing Fodah Sankoh to Nelson Mandela. *The Economist*, 20 May 2000. Jackson was also rumoured to be close to Charles Taylor.

25. According to detailed evidence released by Stephen Pattison of the British foreign office, in *Business Day*, 2 August 2000.

26. 'Africa: the Heart of the Matter', *The Economist*, 13 May 2000.

27. *The Economist*, 15 January, and *Business Day*, 25 January 2000.

28. After ruling Gabon for 31 years, President Omar Bongo won another seven years in power in December 1998 after getting more than two-thirds of the vote in presidential elections. *The Economist*, 12 December 1998.

29. *The Economist*, 4 July 1998, p. 44.

30. Huband, *op. cit.*, p. 53, and *BBC Focus on Africa*, 10(1), January 1999. Huband notes that Compaore was also a 'significant element' in regional barbarism; he was linked through marriage to Charles Taylor and to Houphouet-Boigny of the Ivory Coast, and he and the Ivorian leader extended important assistance to Taylor. *Ibid.*, p. 105.

31. Bayart *et al.*, *op. cit.*, p. 5, and Editorial, *The Economist*, 3 January 1998.

32. Kaunda, Zambia's Founding Father, was accused of being a closet foreigner – thus ineligible for high public office – and of being a coup-plotter. President Konan Henri Bedie in the Ivory Coast similarly tried to ban his presidential rival, Alassane Ouattara, from competing in elections by declaring him a foreigner.

33. Per capita income fell from $330 in 1978 to $285 in 1996, corruption steeply worsened, and the country was reduced to what Ngugi wa Thiongo called 'ten millionaires and ten million poor'. Editorials, *The Economist*, 3 January 1998, and *Mail and Guardian*, 23 December 1999.

34. Robert Guest estimates that theft by Nigeria's military rulers totalled 'in the tens of billions of dollars'. General Abacha, it is said, transferred '$15 million or so to his Swiss bank account every day' in the 1990s. It continued till the very end of General Abubakar's transitional government, as the country's foreign reserves fell from $6.7 billion at the end of 1998 to $4 billion in March 1999. Robert Guest, 'A Survey of Nigeria', *The Economist*, 15 January, p. 6, and 'Face Value', *The Economist*, 5 February 2000.

35. Elizabeth Blunt, 'But Were They Clean?' *BBC Focus on Africa*, 10(2), April–June 1999.

36. Peter Cunliffe-Jones, *The Star*, 28 May 1999.

37. The term was used by Clinton during his visit to six African countries in March 1998, and it intentionally embraced the 'African Renaissance' notion used by Nelson Mandela and vigorously employed by his successor Thabo Mbeki. Ray Hartley, 'A New Wind for Bill Clinton', The *Sunday Times* (Johannesburg), 29 March 1998, and *The Economist*, 8 May 1999, p. 45.

38. Speaking minutes later, Kofi Annan, the Secretary-General of the United Nations, said: 'I find these thoughts truly demeaning, demeaning of the yearning for human dignity that resides in every African heart. So I say this to you, my brothers and sisters, that human rights are African rights.' Quoted in *Business Day*, 3 June 1997.

39. Africa's most democratically advanced constitution in the early 1990s, not least through the controls which were placed on presidential power; MPs were considered to be 'servants of the Namibian people', empowered to act as critics of the executive, but most have chosen to behave as loyal Swapo members instead. K. Good, 'Accountable to Themselves: Predominance in Southern Africa', *The Journal of Modern African Studies* (Cambridge), 35(4), 1997, pp. 556–63.

40. Cited by Mark Gevisser, 'Subtle Art of Being Gay the African Way', The *Sunday Independent*, 26 September 1999, and by Tabby Moyo, in *The Star*, 3 October 2000.

41. *Ibid.*

42. 'God created Adam and Eve', he declared. 'I did not see God creating man and man.' Quoted in *Business Day*, 29 September 1999. Yahya Jammeh, former coup leader and subsequent elected President in The Gambia, was equally confident of his understanding: 'I want to tell you', he told a visiting journalist, 'is that among my animals [in a zoo at State House] there are no lesbians, no gays or whatever. They do everything as nature ordered.' Veronique Edwards, 'Jammeh Speaks', *BBC Focus on Africa*, 10(4), October–December 1999.

43. Wairagala Wakabi, *The Star*, 10 January 2000.

44. Editorial, *Business Day*, 22 September, and *Business Day*, 5 October 1999.

45. Quoted by Wakabi, *op. cit.*

46. *Ibid.*, and Wakabi W Isabirye, *Sunday Times*, 21 November 1999.

47. *The Economist*, 17 June 2000.

48. One estimate put the direct costs at $500 million, equivalent to one-third of Zimbabwe's total budget for 1999. In early 2000 two key diamond concessions were handed over to a private Congolese–Zimbabwean joint venture between Comiex and Osleg. The main shareholders in Comiex were President Kabila and some of his ministers, while those in Osleg were the commander of the Zimbabwean forces in Congo, Vitalis Zvinavashe, the boss of the Minerals Marketing Corporation in Harare, Onesimo Moyo, another parastatal chief, Isaiah Ruzengwe, and the permanent head of the defence ministry, Job Whabira. 'The Mess One Man Makes', *The Economist*, 22 April, and *Business Day*, 5 May 2000. Osleg was in turn a major shareholder in Oryx, a Cayman Island-registered company with diamond concessions in Congo, which was reportedly controlled by Presidents Kabila and Mugabe. Ilja Graulich, in *Business Day*, 2 June 2000.

49. *The Star* and *Business Day*, 17 May 2000.
50. He added: 'in Africa today the terrible suffering [of the people] is not caused by external enemies, but from within.' Wole Soyinka, 'New Monsters Born in Africa', *Mail and Guardian*, 9 June 2000.
51. *The Economist*, 8 May 1999, p. 45.
52. *Ibid.*, p. 47.
53. Christopher Clapham, 'Africa Caught in a War of Wills', *Business Day*, 11 June 1998.
54. With a per capita income in 1997 of only $110, Ethiopia's economic strength was not to be exaggerated.
55. Clapham, *op. cit.*
56. 23 May 1998, p. 45.
57. *The Economist*, 17 April 1999, p. 56.
58. *Ibid.*
59. *The Economist*, 8 May 1999, p. 45.
60. Jonathan Steele, *op. cit.*
61. *The Economist*, 8 May 1999, p. 46.
62. *Botswana Daily News* (Gaborone), 24 April 1999. In July President Mkapa of Tanzania and President Chissano of Mozambique issued a joint denunciation of Africa's 'wasteful [and] shameful' wars. Quoted in *The Star*, 13 July 1999.
63. Estimate in *Business Day*, 25 January 2000. According to Peter Dickson, 75 000 civilians have been killed (further thousands mutilated), *Mail and Guardian*, 28 January 2000.
64. Its spending on armaments reached $467 million in 1999, when Eritrea's expenditure touched $236 million. *The Economist*, 20 May 2000.
65. Gerard Prunier, *The Rwanda Crisis: History of a Genocide*, London, Hurst, 1996, pp. 220–9. The killing was carried out largely by machete, at 'dazzling speed', and the Rwandan dead accumulated 'at nearly three times the rate of Jewish dead during the holocaust'. Philip Gourevitch, *We Wish To Inform You That Tomorrow We Will Be Killed With Our Families*, New York, Farrar, Strauss & Giroux, 1998, preface.
66. Leys had observed: 'it is getting hard to find African countries where the infrastructure is not deteriorating to the point of collapse, where corruption and extortion are not taken for granted, where violent city crime is not endemic, where malnutrition and rising morbidity rates are not widespread.' *Op. cit.*, p. 36.
67. Zainab Bangura, 'A Problem of Leadership', *BBC Focus on Africa*, 10(4), October–December 1999.
68. Quoted by Guest, *op. cit.*, p. 3.
69. Francis Nyamnjoh, 'The Politics of Development: Modernity, Power Elites and Popular Disillusionment in Africa', chapter in Jan Servaes and Rico Lie (eds), *Media and Politics in Transition*, Leuven, Acco, 1997, p. 201. A broad examination of the qualities of African leaders is made by Alec Russell, *Big Men, Little People: Encounters in Africa*, London, Pan Books, 2000.
70. Which might still occur when an organized opposition arises to channel wide discontent. The cartoonist Zapiro depicted the February 2000 referendum in Zimbabwe as follows: Circus master Mugabe, holding out a large ring, instructs small dog 'Zim' to 'Jump'; Zim jumps and bites Mugabe hard

on the buttocks. *Sunday Times*, 20 February 2000. In grossly unfair June elections, against violence and intimidation till the eve of the poll, 'Zim', in the form of the Movement for Democratic Change, reduced Mugabe's parliamentary majority of seats won to five.

71. Leys, *op. cit.*, p. 42.
72. Anonymous review of Bayart *et al.*, *op. cit.*, and Patrick Chabal and Jean-Pascal Daloz, *Africa Works: Disorder as Political Instrument*, in *The Economist*, 7 August 1999.
73. *Op. cit.*, p. 46.
74. Guest, *Op. cit.*, p. 3.
75. Michela Wrong, *In the Footsteps of Mr Kurtz*, London, Fourth Estate, 2000, pp. 207–9, and 253.
76. Black intellectuals refrained from speaking because of misplaced loyalty to the new regime, while white academics were silenced by their fear of being labelled racists. Speaking at a graduation ceremony, University of Cape Town, December 1999. Edited version of her address, *Mail and Guardian*, 10 December 1999.
77. From a report prepared by the First Merchant Bank in Harare, quoted by Michael Hartnack, 'Africa Too Tolerant of Bad Government', *Business Day*, 2 November 1999.
78. Quoted in *Business Day*, 30 March 1998.
79. Quoted in *The Star*, 15 October 1999.
80. Consider perhaps the closest political parallel case in Africa: 'usually seen as a peaceful, orderly country, a liberal democracy since its independence 40 years ago, with a fast growing economy presided over by a decent president… [It] has a tradition of tolerance and freedom of speech. Human rights have always been more or less respected… [Abdou] Diouf, aged 64, has been president for 19 years and was prime minister for ten years before that… Senegal is a democracy in theory only.' Electoral change only occurred in March 2000. 'Beneath the Calm', *The Economist*, 26 February 2000. The origins of Botswana's elite capitalist democracy are examined in Chapter 2 below.
81. T.J. Pempel (ed.), *Uncommon Democracies: The One-Party Dominant Regimes*, Ithaca, NY and London, Cornell University Press, 1990.
82. Among the few who perceived this as a disaster for democracy in Botswana was the editor of *The Botswana Gazette* (Gaborone), 27 October 1999. The Botswana National Front became the official Opposition with six seats, but these included its aged and egocentric leader, Kenneth Koma, some who were little more than his cronies, and another convicted of 177 counts of forgery in the 1980s. The editor had earlier observed that when Botswana has no credible opposition 'the country as a whole suffers'. K. Good, 'Enduring Elite Democracy in Botswana', *Democratization* (London), 6(1), Spring 1999, pp. 59–60; Bashi Letsididi, '"Honourable" Crooks vie for Parliament', *The Botswana Guardian*, 15 October 1999; and D. Thobela, 'Koma Must Quit Now', Letters, *Mmegi*, 18 February 2000.
83. Staffan Darnolf and John D. Holm, 'Democracy Without a Credible Opposition: The Case of Botswana', mimeo, 29 February 2000.
84. There is also a shadowy intelligence service located in both the BDF and in the police Special Branch, which reports to the Minister for Presidential

Affairs, and which appears to concentrate upon criminal surveillance. The creation of a formal National Intelligence Service, rumoured in February 2000, was officially described as 'rubbish'. *The Botswana Gazette*, 1 March, and *Mmegi Monitor*, 7 March 2000.

85. Titus Mbuya, 'Profile: President to Be', *Mmegi* (Gaborone), 14 November 1997.

86. Patrick Wadula, in *Business Day*, 1 December 1997. Kofi Annan also said soon after that 'Africa can no longer blame the white man', pointing to the 'colossal human tragedies' of the 30 wars or more fought on the continent since 1970. *Business Day*, 17 April 1998.

87. *The Botswana Gazette*, 17 June 1998.

88. His name, for instance, was conspicuously absent from the list of ministerial debtors in early 1994 – discussed below – and the anti-corruption demonstrators in Gaborone in February gave him alone their vocal support. K. Good, 'Corruption and Mismanagement', *op. cit.*, p. 514.

89. It was after he became President, beginning around July 1998, that his questionable association with Motswedi, a supposed citizen empowerment consortium whose other main shareholders were Chief Justice Julian Nganunu and a leading businessman, the Botswana Development Corporation, and Owens Corning Pipe Botswana, came to light. Information emerged in the private press that Motswedi, a group without assets or expertise, was a shareholder in Owens Corning, which had successfully tendered to supply pipes to the large North South Water Carrier project, but full and clear explanations were not forthcoming from the President. See, for example, *The Botswana Guardian*, 21 August, and 4 and 11 September 1998, and *Mmegi*, 24 July, and 14, 21 and 28 August 1998.

90. As quoted by Barry Baxter, *Mmegi*, 10 April 1998.

91. Mike Mothibi, 'Khama Shoots Up, Again', *Mmegi*, 10 April, and Baxter, *Mmegi*, 24 April 1998.

92. Following the resignation of the sitting BDP Member, a by-election was held in Serowe North, home of the Khama family. K. Good, 'Enduring Elite Democracy' *op. cit.*, p. 61. He dismissed the question that as MP, Minister and Vice-President he should step down as a Paramount Chief, with the words, 'I do not have any intention of relinquishing the chieftainship.' *Mmegi*, 24 April 1998.

93. He told Rebaone Odirile: 'My motivation [in relinquishing command of the BDF] is not politics, of being a politician, but management and administration... Politics does not attract me.' *The Botswana Guardian*, 17 April 1998. He added shortly after that he had not intended to leave the army at this time, but had 'allowed [him]self to be persuaded' by friends in the private sector. Neither had he wanted, he said, to be sidelined into a minor political post. Baxter, *Mmegi*, 24 April 1998.

94. He acted in terms of a new statutory instrument of 1998 which restricted the serving of liquor in restaurants in the evening to between 6 and 11p.m., which was 'believed to have been largely influenced by Ian Khama.' It had never been enforced before New Year's Eve. *The Midweek Sun* (Gaborone), 6 January 1999.

95. Pretoria and Gaborone gave no prior announcement of their incursion to the Lesotho people either, and in the immediate repercussions of shock and

anger in the country widespread destruction of urban property and considerable loss of life ensued. K. Good, 'Enduring Elite Democracy', *op. cit.*, pp. 54–5. That apartheid South Africa had made heavy military raids on Lesotho previously, compounded the shock in 1998.

96. The Vice-President was 'probably the only man in Botswana politics who can have his cake and eat it'. *The Midweek Sun*, 15 September 1999.

97. As quoted in *Mmegi*, 24 September 1999.

98. *The Botswana Guardian*, 17 April 1998.

99. Prof Malema noted that General Khama seemed 'bored' with his job. *Mmegi*, 3 December 1999.

100. Text of Mogae's speech, *The Midweek Sun*, 8 December 1999.

101. As quoted in *The Botswana Gazette*, 8 December 1999.

102. 'Comment', *ibid.*

103. Figures from Mpho Molomo, 'The Political Implications of the 4 October 1997 Referendum for Botswana', *Democratization*, 5(4), 1998, pp. 151–75.

104. Such abysmal participation was related to the fact that government-controlled print and radio media ran a largely 'No' campaign and certain ministers were particularly opposed to extending the vote to youths. *Midweek Sun* and *The Botswana Gazette*, 8 October 1997.

105. Personal communication, Independent Electoral Commission, Gaborone, 4 November 1998.

106. Out of an estimated eligible electorate of 800 000, valid votes were cast by 336 982.

107. Independent Electoral Commission, *Report to the Minister of Presidential Affairs and Public Administration on the General Election 1999*, Government Printer, Gaborone, p. 4.

108. Quoted in 'Botswana: Proud to be Dull', *BBC Focus on Africa*, 11(1), January–March 2000, p. 6.

109. For details of all three, and for the NDB, see K. Good, 'Corruption and Mismanagement in Botswana: A Best-Case Example?' *op. cit.*

110. Quoted in *ibid.*, p. 509.

111. A refrain supplemented by the Minister for Foreign Affairs, Dr Gaositwe Chiepe who accused the press of 'breeding...a culture of mistrust and abuse where you bundle everyone into one group without verifying the facts'. *Ibid.*, p. 513.

112. Speaking in an interview on 15 February 1994, quoted in *ibid.*, p. 515.

113. The period and process is examined, rather overoptimistically, in K. Good, 'Towards Popular Participation in Botswana', *The Journal of Modern African Studies*, 34(1), 1996.

114. Malema in *Mmegi*, 1 April 1999.

115. Wesbank is a division of First National Bank of Botswana. *The Botswana Gazette*, 26 April 1999. 'Staff Writer' also named De Beers as the source of the funds, *Mmegi*, 16 and 23 April 1999.

116. Joseph Malise in *Midweek Sun*, 26 April 1999.

117. The Minister summoned journalists to his office to tell them this. *The Guardian*, 4 June 1999.

118. As quoted by Dikarabo Ramadubu, *The Guardian*, 23 July 1999.

119. Dada himself had close business links with Minister Kedikilwe. The latter owned a farm in the Tuli Block, and had sold 60 per cent of the shares in

this property to Dada in 1995. Satar Dada soon after became landlord of a shopping complex in Serowe, and Kedikilwe intervened to ensure that a Spar supermarket, anchor tenant in Dada's centre, obtained an extended trading licence. In February 1996 Kedikilwe said: 'I only subsequently learnt that Mr Dada was a landlord of the premises ... If I had been aware I would probably have declared my interest.' But Dada said: 'I have known Mr Kedikilwe [since] long ago ... ', adding later 'we have been family friends for many, many years.' K. Good, *Realizing Democracy in Botswana, Namibia and South Africa*, Pretoria, Africa Institute, 1997, p. 130, and *The Botswana Guardian*, 2 October 1998. That newspaper soon after claimed that, when Kedikilwe came under pressure to pay his debts to the NDB in 1994, 'Dada came in and bought into Kedikilwe's [Tuli] farm'. Around 1998 Kedikilwe supported the creation of a Foreign Investment Fund specifically set up, it was said, to finance – to the extent of some P50 million – a company called Haltek, which was negotiating for the purchase of Algo Spinners from Dada. Kedikilwe said: 'that I'm close to Dada is irrelevant. I have supported ... facilities aimed at creating employment for Batswana.' The prevailing conjecture, according to *The Guardian*, was that 'Dada [was] cashing in on the social capital he has invested in Kedikilwe.' *The Botswana Guardian*, 11 September 1998.

120. The BDP's Ntuane asserted in May that non-disclosure of party funding was common elsewhere in the world, neglecting the fact that Belgium, Germany, France, Italy, Sweden and Spain, all require public disclosure, some of them for gifts as small as a few hundred dollars. Four ban foreign donations altogether. The downfall of Helmut Kohl as icon of Christian Democracy and unity in Europe was not because he pocketed donations to his governing party, but that he failed to disclose them. 'Is Europe Corrupt?' *The Economist*, 29 January 2000. Kohl's party was fined a swingeing $21 million for non-disclosure in February, and his successor as party leader resigned the next day. *Ibid.*, p. 31.

121. NDB employees were encouraged to act in February 1994 when it appeared that they and their jobs were to be made to pay the price for the Bank's collapse. An unsigned document listing indebted Ministers and MPs and the top 15 debtors was faxed to various recipients including the press. K. Good, 'Corruption and Mismanagement', *op. cit.*, pp. 510–11.

122. Mokone's solid and thoughtful response to his earlier, and much criticised, 'shrinking President' story. *The Guardian*, 21 January 2000. But Rampholo Molefhe, secretary-general of the Botswana Journalists Association, also accused Mokone of 'abuse' and of 'self-engrossment', in Talking Point, *Mmegi*, 4 February 2000.

123. Sixty seven thousand registered voters faced exclusion from the poll when the President issued a writ of elections before the Independent Electoral Commission had certified the roll, and the error was corrected through the declaration of a state of emergency – the country's first – to facilitate his re-call of parliament and the passing of amending legislation. The BCP's Michael Dingake accused Mogae of incompetence, and said an emergency should not be declared 'to rubber-stamp the negligen[ce] ... of the executive.' *Business Day*, 6 and 8 September 1999. President Mogae admitted his mistake, 'I take the blame', he told a press conference on 8 September, in

qualified form: ' ... maybe had they been more generous with information, drawn my attention to the consequences of the decision, then we would have acted otherwise.' Quoted by Dikarabo Ramadubu, *The Botswana Guardian*, 10 September 1999.

124. A device which might have contributed to an increase in accountability was a register of member's assets, proposed by the nominated MP, Joy Phumaphi, in parliament in February 1996, over the opposition inside the BDP caucus, it was said, of Kedikilwe, Kwelagobe and President Masire. Minister for Presidential Affairs Kedikilwe nevertheless informed parliament on 22 March that the register would be ready 'within one and a half months'. Phumaphi subsequently ascended into the ministry but inaction ensued on her register. In July 1999 a Bill to establish a register was again deferred to another day. K. Good, *Realizing Democracy in Botswana, Namibia and South Africa, op. cit.*, p. 133, and *Midweek Sun*, 14 July 1999.

125. Participation not only in the acquisition of the vote but also in the creation of an array of working-class self-help or civic groups – friendly societies, co-ops, trade unions – as industrialization progressed. John King, 'Socioeconomic Development and Corrupt Campaign Practices in England', chapter in Arnold Heidenheimer, *et al.* (eds), *Political Corruption: A Handbook*, New Brunswick and London, Transaction Publishers, 1993, and Eric Hopkins, *Working-Class Self-Help in Nineteenth Century England: Responses to Industrialization*, London, UCL Press, 1995.

126. Editorial, *The Economist*, 22 January 2000.

2 Routinized Injustice: The Situation of the San in Botswana

1. Eric. R. Wolf, *Europe and the People Without History*, Berkeley and Los Angeles, University of California Press, 1982.

2. Willemien le Roux, *Torn Apart*, Kuru Development Trust and WIMSA, November 1999, p. 83.

3. Le Roux notes that San is preferred as an inclusive group name for the people known as Bushmen and Basarwa by WIMSA (the Working Group on Indigenous Minorities in Southern Africa) and herself, until the time when a new representative name has been accepted by everyone. *Ibid.*, p. 2.

4. Ornulf Gulbrandsen, Marit Karlsen and Janne Lexow, *Botswana: Remote Area Development Programme, Report Submitted to the Royal Norwegian Ministry of Development Cooperation*, Bergen/Gaborone/Oslo, 1986, p. 184.

5. Robert Hitchcock, *Monitoring Research and Development in the Remote Areas of Botswana, Report to the Ministry of Local Government and Lands, Botswana, and the Ministry of Development Cooperation, Norway*, Bergen/Gaborone/ Oslo, 1988, pp. 4–73.

6. Central District, they estimated, accommodated then some 17 000 Remote people out of a total national population of perhaps some 60 000. Campbell, Main and Associates, *Western Sandveld Remote Area Dwellers*: Report Submitted to the Ministry of Local Government and Lands and Norwegian Agency for International Development Cooperation, Gaborone, 1991,

pp. 32 and 65. Which did not imply that linguistic differences among San were not important elsewhere.

7. *Ibid.*, pp. 16–17.

8. However, he had also said in 1988: 'I would estimate the total population of remote area dwellers to be approximately 180 000 people', adding that 'it is not possible to give an exact figure.' *Op. cit.*, pp. 3–35. Hitchcock, 'Indigenous People's Participation in Development and Empowerment, with Special Reference to the San', mimeo, n.d., p. 13.

9. Rein Dekker, 'A Demographic Estimate of the San People Residing in Ghanzi District of Botswana', mimeo, Kuru Development Trust, D'kar, n.d.

10. R. Hitchcock and John D. Holm, 'Bureaucratic Domination of Hunter-Gatherer Societies: A Study of the San in Botswana', *Development and Change* (London), 24, 1993, p. 328.

11. The country's population growth rate had dropped from 2.5 per cent in 1997 to 2.3 per cent in 1999, when the HIV prevalence rate among adult men was an estimated 27 per cent and among women 37 per cent. United Nations Development Programme and Botswana Institute for Development Policy Analysis, *Botswana Human Development Report 2000*, Gaborone, 20 October 2000, p. 3. A report compiled by the United Children's Fund pointed to a drop in life expectancy in Botswana from around 69 years to 41 between 2000 and 2005. *The Botswana Guardian*, 3 March 2000.

12. As for the San in Botswana, figures on Saami depend on definition, and tend to range between 35 000 and 50 000. Sidsel Saugestad, University of Tromso, personal communication, 16 June 1999. Aborigines in Australia represent less than 2 per cent of the national population.

13. To exclude such subjective interpretations as Elizabeth Marshall Thomas', 'the harmless people', and Laurens van der Post's famous depictions of a dying, mystical race. On the reality of the harmless notion, consider the stories that Breyten Breytenbach relates of San outlaws in the Boland during his youth, men like Koos Sas and Gert April (a.k.a. Gert Kaffer), who struck their victims with ferocity and brutality, ran 'fast and invisible like the wind', covering great distances, and struck again. Gert April was known as a deadly shot, who always warned the police about the location of his next attack. To the people 'they [we]re resistance fighters. How else can you die when there is no hope of redress?' *Dog Heart: A Travel Memoir*, Cape Town, Human and Rousseau, 1998, pp. 133–41.

14. Maoris in New Zealand, Aborigines in Australia and native peoples in North America have used their indigenous status to press successful claims for the ownership of land and other resources upon the legal and political institutions of their respective countries. Additionally, these and other movements, assisted by human rights organizations, have campaigned over recent decades for a wider recognition of the rights of indigenous people through institutions like the International Labour Office and the General Assembly of the United Nations. Sidsel Saugestad, 'Contested Images: Indigenous Peoples in Africa', *Indigenous Affairs* (Copenhagen), 2, 1999, p. 6.

15. J.D. Lewis-Williams, *Discovering Southern African Rock Art*, Cape Town and Johannesburg, David Philip, 1990, p. 18.

16. Suzanne Miers and Michael Crowder, 'The Politics of Slavery in Bechuanaland: Power Struggles and the Plight of the Basarwa in the Bamangwato

Reserve, 1926–1940', in S. Miers and Richard Roberts (eds), *The End of Slavery in Africa*, Madison, Wisconsin, University of Wisconsin Press, 1988, pp. 174–75.

17. Wylie describes this principle as 'the core concept' of the Tswana political system in the nineteenth century, and notes that the term *kgosi* meant both a chief and a rich man. Diana Wylie, *A Little God: The Twilight of Patriarchy in a Southern African Chiefdom*, Hanover, NH, and London, 1990, pp. 25 and 27.

18. Neil Parsons, 'The Economic History of Khama's Country in Botswana, 1844–1930', in Robin Palmer and Parsons (eds), *The Roots of Rural Poverty in Central and Southern Africa*, London, Heinemann, 1977, p. 119.

19. He testified: 'The Masarwa are slaves. They can be killed. It is no crime, they are like cattle … If they run away their masters can bring them back and do what they like in the way of punishment. They are never paid … ' Quoted in Miers and Crowder, *op. cit.*, p. 172.

20. *Ibid.*, p. 187.

21. *Ibid.*, p. 188.

22. *Ibid.*, pp. 191–2, and John Iliffe, *The African Poor: A History*, Cambridge, University of Cambridge Press, 1987, p. 146.

23. Miers and Browder, *op. cit.*, pp. 196 and 177.

24. *Ibid.*, p. 195.

25. G.B. Silberbauer and A.J. Kuper, 'Kalahari Masters and Bushman Serfs: Some Observations', *African Studies*, 24(4), 1966.

26. When Iliffe examined long-term structural poverty in Botswana he recognized the prominent position of the San, but also stressed the 'unusually large' size of the stratum in 19th century Botswana, 'the starkness of the dichotomy of rich and poor', and 'the extraordinary continuity' between the poor of independent Botswana and their predecessors. *Op. cit.*, pp. 78–81 and 236.

27. George B. Silberbauer, *Report to the Government of Bechuanaland on the Bushman Survey*, Gaborone, 1965, pp. 12 and 13.

28. These critical factors are further examined in K. Good, 'Interpreting the Exceptionality of Botswana', *The Journal of Modern African Studies* 30(1), 1992; 'At the Ends of the Ladder: Radical Inequalities in Botswana, *The Journal of Modern African Studies*, 31(2), 1993; and 'Enduring Elite Democracy', *Democratization*, 6(1), Spring 1999.

29. Considered below.

30. Victoria Quinn, Cohen, Mason, and Kgosidintsi, 'Crisis Proofing the Economy: The Response of Botswana to Economic Recession and Drought', in G.A. Cornia, R. Jolly and F. Stewart (eds), *Adjustment With a Human Face*, Vol. 2, OUP/UNICEF, 1988, pp. 3, 14 and 16.

31. *The Economist*, 13 January 1990, p. 79.

32. *Ibid.*

33. They said that it was 'difficult to understand the system used for issuing rations'. Campbell, Main and Associates, *Western Sandveld Remote Area Dwellers*, Gaborone, April 1991, p. 50.

34. *Ibid.*

35. Gulbrandsen, Karlsen and Lexow, *op. cit.*, p. 23.

36. Alice Mogwe, *Who Was (T)here First?* Gaborone, Botswana Christian Council Occasional Paper no. 10, March 1992, p. 38.

37. Robert K. Hitchcock and John D. Holm, 'Bureaucratic Domination of Hunter-Gatherer Societies: A Study of the San in Botswana', *Development and Change*, 24, 1993, p. 320.

38. By 17 per cent from 1979–81, in contrast with a drop of only 12.5 per cent in Ethiopia, and of 11 per cent in food output in Sudan, where severe famine occurred. *The Economist*, 13 January 1990.

39. Quinn *et al.*, *op. cit.*, pp. 17–18. LBRP is also known as Labour Based Drought Relief (LBDR).

40. In Inalegolo, five out of 367 people earned P52 a month when in LBRP; and in Groot Laagte, where the Settlement population had fallen following the suspension of drought relief benefits in mid-1990, 41 persons got P55 a month during part of the year from LBRP. *A Monitoring Programme for the Settlements at Thankane, Kokotsha, Inalegolo, Monong, Ngwatlhe and Groot Laagte*, Prepared by Economic Consultancies *et al.*, Ministry of Local Government and Lands, Gaborone, May 1991, pp. 9, 26, 53, 73, 93, 113, 121 and 138.

41. Corjan van der Jagt, *Kgalagadi District: Socio-Economic Baseline Survey*, Final Report, Ministry of Local Government, Lands and Housing, 1995, pp. 28–9 and 31.

42. *Ibid.*, pp. 29 and 32.

43. Quinn, *op. cit.*, p. 17.

44. Point made by Sidsel Saugestad with regard to the ostensible gap that exists between Botswana's democratic polity and the government's *de facto* policy towards the San. *The Inconvenient Indigenous*, University of Tromso, August 1998, p. 313.

45. Republic of Botswana, *Report of the Presidential Commission on the Review of the Incomes Policy*, Gaborone, 10 March 1990, pp. 39 and 44.

46. Republic of Botswana, *The Revised National Policy on Incomes, Employment, Prices and Profits*, Draft White Paper, n.d., p. 39.

47. *Ibid.*

48. Gary W. Childers, *Report of the Survey/Investigation of the Ghanzi Farm Basarwa Situation*, Republic of Botswana, Gaborone, September 1976, pp. 45, 47 and 84.

49. *Ibid.*, pp. 14 and 50.

50. 'It should be a crime', he said, 'for farmers to continue paying [San labourers] P2–P3 per month'. *Ibid.*, pp. 86 and 92.

51. Monageng Mogalakwe, *Inside Ghanzi Freehold Farms: A Look at the Conditions of Farm Workers*, Ministry of Local Government and Lands, Applied Research Unit, Gaborone, April 1986, pp. 22 and 25.

52. Gulbrandsen, *op. cit.*, p. 30.

53. They referred here to both Basarwa and other Remote people. *Ibid.*, p. 112.

54. Campbell, Main and Associates, *op. cit.*, pp. 44–5.

55. Another said: 'Although we may agree on the amount of our pay when we start work, we are never actually certain how much we will receive until we see the money'. *Ibid.*, pp. 45–6.

56. Economic Consultancies, *et. al.*, *A Monitoring Programme…*, pp. 27, 93 and 119.

57. H.K. Siphambe, 'Minimum Wages in Botswana: Should They Be Increased?' *Barclays Botswana Economic Review* 3(4), n.d., p. 6.

58. *The Star* (Johannesburg), 16 and 17 March 1999.
59. Wilmsen and Denbow, 'Paradigmatic History of San-Speaking Peoples and Current Attempts at Revision', *Current Anthropology*, 31(5), December 1990, pp. 495–6.
60. On the possible Khoisan origins of certain Setswana agricultural words, see Jeff Ramsay, 'Zoowholand?' *Mmegi* (Gaborone), 22 May 1992, p. 16.
61. Evidence in Robert Hitchcock, Childers and Gulbrandsen is noted below.
62. Miers and Crowder, *op. cit.*, p. 177.
63. Wilmsen and Vossen, 'Labour, Language and Power in the Construction of Ethnicity in Botswana', *Critique of Anthropology* (London), 10(1), 1984, p. 18.
64. Childers, *op. cit.*, pp. 5 and 14.
65. Further detailed in Good, 'Interpreting the Exceptionality of Botswana', *The Journal of Modern African Studies*, 30(1), 1992, pp. 83 and 91.
66. Hitchcock, *Monitoring Research and Development ….*, pp. 4–8 and 4–15.
67. *Ibid.*, pp. 2–17, 3–4, 3–9, and 4–68.
68. Gulbrandsen *et al.*, *op. cit.*, pp. 131, 134 and 153.
69. *Op. cit.*, p. 63.
70. *Ibid.*, pp. 16 and 57.
71. The San acquired citizenship in 1966 of course, but without the resources to exercise it effectively.
72. *Op. cit.*, p. 112.
73. 'For more than a hundred years', they add, '[Remote Dwellers] have belonged to a servant class at the bottom of the social hierarchy and … are conditioned to doing whatever they are told.' *Op. cit.*, pp. 58, 63 and 65.
74. 'Bureaucratic Domination of Hunter-Gatherer Societies', *op. cit.*, p. 313.
75. Childers, *op. cit.*, p. 50.
76. Hitchcock, *Monitoring Research and Development …* , p. 4–51.
77. 'The direct result' of Childers' original report. Childers, Joyce Stanley and Kathryn Rick, *Government or People's Community: A Study of Local Institutions in Ghanzi District*, Applied Research Unit, Ministry of Local Government and Lands, and Land Tenure Centre, University of Wisconsin-Madison, Gaborone and Madison, June 1982, p. 5.
78. *Ibid.*
79. *Ibid.*, p. 6.
80. *Ibid.*, pp. 10–11.
81. *Ibid.*, pp. 15–16.
82. *Ibid.*, p. 14.
83. *Ibid.*, pp. 14, 31 and 33–4.
84. H.G. Korfage, 'Paper on the Extension of the Remote Area Dweller Settlements Development Areas', a discussion paper for Ghanzi District Land Use Planning Unit, Ghanzi, June 1992, pp. 1, 4 and 10.
85. *Op. cit.*, p. 13.
86. Korfage, *op. cit.*, p. 2, and K. Good, 'At the Ends of the Ladder: Radical Inequalities in Botswana', *op. cit.*, pp. 211–16.
87. Chr. Michelsen Institute, Development Studies and Human Rights, *NORAD's Support of the Remote Area Development Programme (RADP) in Botswana*, The Royal Ministry of Foreign Affairs, Oslo, February 1996, p. 10.
88. *Op. cit.*, pp. 4–6.

89. 'The "Sacred Cow" Wins Against RADS', *The Botswana Guardian*, 21 August 1998.
90. The official view was that the receipients should prove that they would not eat the cows. Willemien le Roux, personal communication August 1999.
91. CMI, *op. cit.*, p. 13.
92. *Ibid.*, pp. 25–6.
93. Monitoring Programme, *op. cit.*, p. 117.
94. *Op. cit.*, p. 134.
95. Hitchcock, 'Settlements and Survival: What Future for the Remote Area Dwellers of Botswana', 13 October 1995, p. 2.
96. Interview with board members of the Kuru Development Trust and Rein Dekker, D'kar, 4 May 1999.
97. Interview, D'kar, 4 May 1999.
98. Interview with Roy Sesana, First People of the Kalahari, Ghanzi, 3 May 1999.
99. As reported by the CMI, *op. cit.*, p. 31. Korfage, in his paper of June 1992, refers to the securing of the farms for the three settlements as an accomplished fact, *op. cit.*, p. 8.
100. CMI, *op. cit.*, p. 31.
101. *Africa Confidential* (London), 32(9), 3 May 1991, pp. 5–6.
102. *Op. cit.*, p. 31.
103. Richard White, 'Is the Livestock Industry the Enemy of the Environment?' Symposium of the Kalahari Conservation Society, Gaborone, 13–14 November 1992, p. 15.
104. Bashi Letsididi, 'Small Farmers Take Dim View of Policies', *Mmegi*, 14 May 1999.
105. *The Botswana Guardian*, 23 April 1999. The system chosen by the Botswana government was the then untested intraruminal bolus, which involved inserting an electronic device into the stomach of the cattle. A computerized system of livestock identification and brand registration was being established. Sello Motseta, *Business Day*, 19 July and 17 October 2000.
106. Wendell Berry, *Another Turn of the Crank*, Washington, DC., Counterpoint, 1995, p. 8.
107. *The Citizen* (Johannesburg), 22 March 1999.
108. *Ibid.*, and *The Star*, 16 and 22 March 1999.
109. Richard Juergens, 'Deal Struck in the Shade of a Shop', *The Sunday Independent*, 20 December 1998.
110. 'A Sorry Tale', *The Economist*, 9 September 2000.
111. *Ibid.*, 27 March 1999.
112. See for example Pauline E. Peters, 'Struggles Over Water, Struggles Over Meaning: Cattle, Water and the State in Botswana', *Africa* (London), 54(3), 1984; Diana Wylie, *A Little God: The Twilight of Patriarchy in a Southern African Chiefdom*, Hanover, NH and London, 1990; and Hitchcock and Holm, 'Bureaucratic Domination of Hunter-Gatherer Societies'. The RADP is discussed below.
113. Kagiso Rapula, 'Basarwa Land Dispossession Continues', *Mmegi*, 27 October 1995, which reported on a seminar presented by Hitchcock at the University of Botswana.

114. 'Bureaucratic Domination...', *op. cit.*, p. 320.
115. Panos Oral Testimony Programme, 'A Project on the Social and Individual Impact of Resettlement', mimeo, September 1998, p. 3.
116. For an account of the conditions experienced by Palestinian refugees in the Gaza Strip, the West Bank and elsewhere see, David Grossman, *The Yellow Wind*, London, Picador, 1989.
117. Highland peasant-warriors were a barrier to the extension of sheep production in the early nineteenth century and were dispossessed of their homes and fields. In a characteristic depiction of the process: 'No compensation was given for the houses burnt, neither any help to build new ones... Some people were removed three or four times, always forced farther down until at last the sea-shore prevented them from being sent any farther unless [and until] they took ship for the Colonies...' John Prebble, *The Highland Clearances*, London, Penguin Books, 1969, p. 84 and *passim.*
118. *Op. cit.*, p. 56.
119. As quoted in Central Kalahari and Khutse Game Reserves. Second Draft Management Plan, Gaborone, Protected Areas Development Units, 7 May 1999, p. 16.
120. Hitchcock, *Monitoring Research and Development...*, and Emily Pedder, 'Report on the Central Kalahari Game Reserve', mimeo, p. 18.
121. As quoted in Ditshwanelo, *When Will This Moving Stop?* Report on a Fact-finding Mission of the [CKGR], Gaborone, 10–14 April 1996, p. 15.
122. Pedder, *op. cit.*, p. 19. The figure of 4000 residents is from Silberbauer.
123. The population data are from the government's Fact-Finding Mission Report of 1985, quoted in *ibid.*, p. 19.
124. *Ibid.*
125. Ditshwanelo, *op. cit.*, pp. 15–16. On ethnic differences in the Cape interior earlier, Breytenbach observes: 'Nobody can tell whether he is white or brown. When you are poor enough these distinctions fall away with time.' *Op. cit.*, p. 35.
126. Pedder, *op. cit.*, p. 19.
127. *Ibid.*, pp. 21–2.
128. *The Botswana Gazette* (Gaborone), 20 December 1995.
129. *The Botswana Daily News* (Gaborone), 15 February 1996.
130. Statement by John Hardbattle of the First People of the Kalahari, *The Botswana Gazette*, 17 April 1996.
131. John Hardbattle and Roy Sesana had set-up the First People of the Kalahari in Ghanzi in 1993, as an advocacy group for the San, and Hardbattle soon became an effective community spokesperson.
132. Quoted in Pedder, *op. cit.*, p. 23.
133. Ditshwanelo, *op. cit.*, pp. 12 and 14, and *Okavango Observer* (Maun), 28 March, and 17 June, and 1 August 1997.
134. Ditshwanelo, *op. cit.*, p. 13.
135. Mokone, 'Basarwa Lose Removal Battle', *The Botswana Gazette*, 29 October 1997.
136. Quoted in *Okavango Observer*, 5 April 1996.
137. *Daily News*, 19 and 26 June 1996.
138. As quoted in *The Star*, 19 June 1997.

139. Paul Weinberg and Tony Weaver, 'The Bittereinders of the Kalahari', *Mail and Guardian*, 2 July 1999.
140. Pedder, *op. cit.*, p. 25, Erni, 'Resettlement of Khwee Communities Continues', *International Working Group for Indigenous Affairs*, 3/4, 1997, and Ditshwanelo, *op. cit.*, p. 14.
141. He was an adviser to CKGR residents and to the First People of the Kalahari. He presented a statement which he had addressed to the then Vice-President designate, Lt. General Ian Khama, to a meeting of the University of Botswana's Basarwa Research Committee.
142. *Central Kalahari and Khutse Game Reserves. Second Draft Management Plan*, pp. 17 and 28.
143. *Ibid.*, p. 29.
144. *The Sunday Independent*, 31 August 1997.
145. Letters to the Editor, *ibid.*, 7 September 1997. Rather similarly, Minister Kgoroba was said to have told Xade residents earlier that the search for minerals in the CKGR had proved fruitless. Samora Gaborone, 'Resettling of the [CKGR] Basarwa: Who Gains or Loses in a State Sponsored Dispossession', Dept of Adult Education, University of Botswana, March 1997, p. 12.
146. As quoted by Suzanne Daley, 'No room in desert for "human dodos"', *The Guardian* (London), 16 July 1996.
147. Quoted in *The Star*, 19 June 1997.
148. *Second Draft Management Plan*, p. 18. Some 90 people had walked back to Mothomelo carrying their belongings on their backs. Interview with Jumanda Gakelebone, FPK, Ghanzi, 6 May 1999.
149. Weinberg and Weaver, *op. cit.*
150. Spencer Mogapi, in *The Botswana Gazette*, 5 July 2000.
151. Alpheons Moroke, 'Do You Trust This Government?', *The Midweek Sun*, 12 July 2000.
152. E.B. Egner and A.L. Klausen, *Poverty in Botswana*, National Institute of Development and Cultural Research, Gaborone, 1980, p. 27.
153. *Ibid.*, p. 27, and Gulbrandsen et al., *op. cit.*, pp. 25–6.
154. No San were given special game licences because, as the Assistant Game Warden in Mabutsane explained, it might encourage them to encroach on the ranchers' privileges. Gulbrandsen, *op. cit.*, pp. 147 and 153.
155. Monitoring Programme, *op. cit.*, pp. 143 and 152.
156. Alice Mogwe, *op. cit.*, pp. 11–14.
157. White, *op. cit.*
158. Hitchcock, 'Settlements and Survival: What Future for the Remote Area Dwellers of Botswana?' University of Nebraska, mimeo, 1995, pp. 3–4.
159. Chasca Twyman, 'Rethinking Community Resource Management: Managing Resources or Managing People in Western Botswana', *Third World Quarterly* (London), 19(4), 1998, p. 757.
160. *Ibid.*, p. 758.
161. Hitchcock, 'Indigenous Peoples' Participation, Development, and Empowerment, with Special Reference to the San', mimeo, n.d., p. 8.
162. Quoted by Ross Herbert, 'Dumped in a Bleak New Home', *The Sunday Independent*, 29 March 1998.
163. Reported by Rebaone Odirile, *Guardian*, 21 March 1997.

164. *Op. cit.* p. 761.
165. Van der Jagt, for example, reported that crafts in general constituted the largest income earner for the people in northern Kgalagadi Settlements, larger even than LBRP. *Op. cit.*, p. 29.
166. It was 'an important wild resource which women exploit extensively in the central and western Kalahari'. Hitchcock, 'Seeking Sustainable Strategies: The Politics of Resource Rights Among the Kalahari San', mimeo, p. 20.
167. *Ibid.*, pp. 20–1.
168. Marketing of Devil's Claw had been encouraged since the 1970s by the locally-based non-governmental group Thusano Lefatsheng, and a large international market was believed to exist. Lin Cassidy, personal communication Gaborone, July 1999.
169. Hitchcock, 'Indigenous Peoples' Participation...', p. 9.
170. *Ibid.*
171. Noted in the *Second Draft Management Plan*, p. 20.
172. Report by Ditso Anneleng, *The Botswana Gazette*, 28 April 1999.
173. *Business Day*, 26 August 1999, and Honourable B. Gaolathe, *Budget Speech 2000*, Gaborone, Government Printer, 7 February 2000, p. 7.
174. One of the largest, Chobe Holdings, held six game lodges in Botswana and was partly owned by a British Virgin Islands-registered firm. *Business Day*, 26 August 1999. The terms 'settler' and 'citizen' were as much indicative of intensified rivalry as of reality; some of the so-called settlers being citizens, and the 'citizens' being native-born Batswana.
175. Writing in *The Botswana Guardian*, 1 October 1999.
176. Mokone, *ibid.*
177. *Ibid.*
178. As quoted by Mesh Moeti, 'Where is the Beef?' *The Botswana Guardian*, 17 September 1999.
179. Mogae had once declared that 'all cattle farmers pay less tax than you and me...and I resent it', and as Finance Minister in 1995 he had reclassified the BMC so that it paid tax on turnover rather than on profits. Outsa Mokone, 'War Between Cattle and Game', *The Botswana Guardian*, 17 September 1999.
180. *Ibid.* Reference to Khama's 'financial interest in tourism' was repeated in *The Guardian*, 1 October 1999.
181. *Ibid.*
182. Ditso Anneleng, *The Botswana Gazette*, 5 May 1999.
183. Twyman's own emphasis, *op. cit.*, p. 753.
184. Maitseo Bolaane, 'Community Challenges of Wildlife Enterprise Development Strategies in Botswana', SADC Phase Two Special Studies, Gaborone, April 1999, p. 4.
185. *Ibid.*, pp. 5 and 6.
186. *Ibid.*, p. 14.
187. *Ibid.*, pp. 12 and 15.
188. Roberta Rivers, personal communication Gaborone, October 1999.
189. Bolaane, *op. cit.*, p. 15.
190. Caitlin Davies, 'Tempers Flare Over Concession Areas', *Mmegi*, 9 April 1999.
191. *Op. cit.*, p. 15.
192. The speaker was probably the chief of the returnees at Molapo, Seqo G//anako. Quoted in Weinberg and Weaver, *op. cit.*

193. Interview with Jumanda Gakelebone, Community Organizer, FPK, Ghanzi, 6 May 1999. One of the planned sites was Molapo. G//anako also said: 'I think [the government] will move in one day soon and order us out of here, they will come with guns and cars...' Quoted in Weinberg and Weaver, *op. cit.*
194. Telephone interview, Rivers and Ngakaeaja, 10 May 1999.
195. Little heed either, she adds, to the experience of other countries; in community-based wildlife management projects in southern Africa, such as CAMPFIRE in Zimbabwe and ADMADE in Zambia, governments, she says, failed to devolve adequate authority to residents. *Op. cit.*, pp. 747, 751 and 760.
196. Cornelis van der Post, personal communication August 1999.
197. Quoted in Twyman, *op. cit.*, p. 760.
198. *Ibid.*, p. 758.
199. John Iliffe, *The African Poor: A History*, Cambridge, Cambridge University Press, 1987, chs 4 and 5, and K. Good, 'The State and Extreme Poverty in Botswana: The San and Destitutes', *The Journal of Modern African Studies*, 37(2), June 1999.
200. Botswana Institute of Development Policy Analysis (BIDPA), *Study of Poverty and Poverty Alleviation in Botswana*, Working Paper, Phase One, Vol. 1, Gaborone, n.d., pp. 163 and 169.
201. BIDPA, *op. cit.*, p. 173.
202. *Ibid.*, pp. 174–5.
203. *Ibid.*, pp. 170, 172 and 175.
204. *Ibid.*, p. 164, and Mogwe, *op. cit.*, p. 38.
205. Draft White Paper, Recommendation 9.51, p. 36.
206. K. Good, 'The State and Extreme Poverty...'
207. Festus Mogae, *Budget Speech*, Government Printer, Gaborone, 12 February 1996, p. 8, and 10 February 1997, p. 18. In February 2000 the old-age pension and the destitutes allowance were both increased by 6 per cent, but the average inflation rate through 1999 was 7.2 per cent. Developmental expenditure on the military at the same time was set at P309 million. Gaolathe, *Budget Speech 2000*, pp. 8, 28 and 30.
208. *Botswana Gazette*, 1 April 1998.
209. Interview at D'kar, 4 May 1999.
210. Bester Gabotlale, 'Help Comes too late for Mmekhwe', *The Botswana Guardian*, 13 August 1999.
211. *A Poverty Datum Line for Botswana, November 1989*, quoted at length in K. Good, 'The State and Extreme Poverty...'
212. Constitution of Namibia 1990, referred to at length in K. Good, *Realizing Democracy in Botswana, Namibia and South Africa*, Africa Institute, Pretoria, 1997.
213. The concept was given an airing in the ruling party's manifesto for the October 1999 national elections in the following terms: The BDP will 'pursue the issue of the "living wage" further with a view to reaching consensus on the difference between a minimum income for survival and the minimum wage. We will work closely...to find ways to bridge the gap where it exists...in the interest of giving Batswana a living wage without jeopardizing employment creation.' Botswana Democratic Party, *1999 Manifesto, A Millennium for Opportunities*, Gaborone, March 1999, p. 10.

214. The original Bushman Development Officer, Elizabeth Wily was, according to Hitchcock, concerned that the Botswana government would oppose the programme as supposedly constituting 'separate development', and the then Vice-President Masire put forward the more generalizing concept of the RADP. *Monitoring Research and Development ...*, part 2, pp. 5–9. That the programme should in fact have been firmly founded upon positive discrimination, if the historic deprivation of the San was ever to be corrected, was apparently an indefensible proposition in government.
215. Christian Michelsen Institute, *op. cit.*, p. 74.
216. The next largest district was Kweneng with some P97 000. But the focus in expenditure was specifically towards Ghanzi; Kgalagadi, it might be noted, received only P5198. *Monitoring Research and Development*, part 2, pp. 9–10.
217. Hitchcock and Holm, 'Bureaucratic Domination of Hunter-Gatherer Societies', pp. 316 and 324.
218. *Op. cit.*, p. 75.
219. 'Bureaucratic Domination ...', p. 325.
220. *Op. cit.*, pp. 75, 77–78 and 80.
221. Quoted in *The Botswana Gazette*, 7 October 1992.
222. *Ibid.*, 27 January 1993.
223. Johan Helland, personal communication Gaborone, 17 March 1995.
224. Hitchcock, 'Settlements and Survival', p. 5.
225. Saugestad, *op. cit.*, p. 318.
226. 'Bureaucratic Domination ...', p. 325.
227. Interview, Ghanzi, 3 May 1999.
228. Interview, D'kar, 6 May 1999.
229. Willemien le Roux, *op. cit.*, chapter 6, theme 4.
230. *Ibid.*, pp. 84 and 91.
231. *Ibid.*, p. 95.
232. She was subsequently transferred, and the children coaxed back after reassurances were offered that the children's emotional needs would be cared for. *Ibid.*, Summary and p. 82, and Lorato Maleke, *Mmegi*, 5 March 1999. Neither account is precise on detail.
233. Botswelo Tlale, 'Indiscipline Rocks Primary School', *Botswana Daily News*, 12 November 1999.
234. Photos of the open graves appeared in the press. *Mmegi*, and *The Botswana Guardian*, 17 September, and *Midweek Sun*, 3 November 1999.
235. *Guardian*, 17 September 1999.
236. Discussed at length in K. Good, 'The State and Extreme Poverty ...'.
237. *Op. cit.*, p. 64.
238. As quoted by Keineetse Keineetse in *Mmegi*, 22 October 1993.
239. *The Inconvenient Indigenous*, *op. cit.*
240. Text of his speech, 'I Pledge to Help you Realise your Dreams',*The Botswana Gazette*, 8 April 1998. Much as a White Paper had said in 1972: a concern for equality 'must not lead us into assuming that the living standards of all the population can be raised by redistribution of the assets of the few people who are relatively well off.' Quoted in Liz Wily, *Land Allocation and Hunter-Gatherer Land Rights in Botswana*, London, Anti-Slavery Society, 1980, p. 107.
241. P.H.K. Kedikilwe, *Budget Speech*, Government Printer, Gaborone, 8 February 1999, p. 28.

3　The Liberal Capitalist Paradigm: Elitism and Injustice in the United States

1. 'Millions of poor and working-class Latinos and African Americans ... are being locked out of the great American middle class by falling wages and shrinking educational opportunity' Indicators suggest that by around 2050 a Latino underclass could total 25 to 30 million people. William Finnegan, *Cold New World: Growing-Up in a Harder Country*, London and Basingstoke, Picador, 1998, pp. xix and 232.
2. Christopher Hitchens, *No One Left to Lie To*, London and New York, Verso, 1999, pp. 65 and 68.
3. Noted by Jeff Madrick, 'In the Shadows of Prosperity', *The New York Review of Books*, 14 April 1997, p. 40.
4. Figures adjusted for inflation. John Gray, *False Dawn: The Delusion of Global Capitalism*, London, Granta, 1998, p. 114.
5. Andrew Hacker, *Money: Who Has How Much and Why*, New York, Scribner, 1997, p. 62.
6. *Ibid.*, p. 238, and Madrick, *op. cit.*, p. 41.
7. Gray, *op. cit.*, p. 114.
8. Simon Head, 'The New, Ruthless Economy', *The New York Review of Books*, 29 February 1996, p. 47.
9. Hacker, *op. cit.*, pp. 48–9.
10. *Ibid.*, p. 51.
11. *Ibid.*, pp. 60–1.
12. *Ibid.*, pp. 59–60.
13. Robert Kuttner, 'Never Mind the Sex', *Mail and Guardian* (Johannesburg), 22 January 1999.
14. Hacker, *op. cit.*, pp. 49 and 72.
15. *The Economist* (London), Editorial, 30 May 1998.
16. *Op. cit.*, p. 53 and chapters 4 and 5 (his analysis is reviewed in Madrick, *op. cit.*).
17. *The Economist*, 1 March 1997.
18. *Ibid.*, 11 September 1999, and Robert Kuttner, *ibid.*
19. *Ibid.*, 9 October 1999.
20. Hacker, *op. cit.*, p. 53.
21. Figures provided on the website www.paywatch.org and quoted in *The Economist*, 30 January 1999, p. 57.
22. 'Own correspondent' quoting the work of Michael Lind and others in *Business Day* (Johannesburg), 20 September 1995.
23. Finnegan, *op. cit.*, p. xvii.
24. *The Economist*, 28 August 1999.
25. Figures of the Department of Agriculture, in *Business Day*, 15 October 1999.
26. Hacker, *op. cit.*, p. 52.
27. A report by the Institute of Fiscal Studies, reviewed by Kamal Ahmed, in *The Guardian* (London), 28 July 1997.
28. *Business Day*, 20 September 1995.
29. *Op. cit.*, pp. 53–4.
30. *Ibid.*, p. 49.
31. He is quoting Felix Rothatyn, a senior investment banker. *Op. cit.*, p. 47.
32. Gray, *op. cit.*, pp. 93 and 115.

33. At Chrysler, General Motors, and Ford in the 1970s two-thirds of the hourly workforce were members of the United Auto Workers. In the mid-1990s, with outsourcing, only one-quarter of the components workforce were union members. This de-unionization 'had a devastating effect on the earnings of workers throughout the auto industry'. Head, *op. cit.*, p. 48.
34. Words of Bill Bamberger and Cathy Davidson, quoted in a review of their book, *Closing: The Life and Death of an American Factory*, Double Take/W.W.Norton, in *The Economist*, 13 June 1998.
35. Richard Sennett, *The Corrosion of Character: the Personal Consequences of Work in the New Capitalism*, New York, Norton, 1998, p. 49.
36. Louis Gerstner was recruited as CEO after he was told that he had a moral imperative to take the job for the good of the country, and he was offered a stock-option of 500 000 company shares; Gerstner felt he was worth a million, but accepted on the promise of future considerations. Wally Seccombe, 'Contradictions of Shareholder Capitalism: Downsizing Jobs, Enlisting Savings, Destabilizing Families', in Leo Panitch and Colin Leys (eds), *Socialist Register 1999*, Rendlesham, Suffolk, 1999, p. 83.
37. *Op. cit.*, pp. 122–6.
38. *Ibid.*, p. 49.
39. A report by the Institute for Policy Studies also noted that downsizing recently involved big companies such as AT&T, Kmart, BellSouth and Lockheed Martin, which were mostly profitable, *The Economist*, 27 April 1996, p. 56. Greed rather than rationality appeared the prime principle at work.
40. Meyer Friedman, quoting from *The New York Times Weekly*, 'Letters', *The New York Review of Books*, 8 October 1998.
41. Daniel Lazare, 'America the Undemocratic', *New Left Review* (London), 232, November/December 1998, p. 7.
42. Finnegan, *op. cit.*, pp. 345–6.
43. Abraham S. Eisenstadt, 'Political Corruption in American History', chapter in Arnold J. Heidenheimer *et al.* (eds), *Political Corruption: A Handbook*, New Brunswick and London, Transaction Publishers, 1993, p. 546.
44. David Beetham, *Max Weber and the Theory of Modern Politics*, Cambridge, Polity Press, 1985, p. 105.
45. J.A. Schumpeter, *Capitalism, Socialism and Democracy*, London, Unwin, 2nd edn 1947, p. 269.
46. Political democracy, said Weber, would not alter the dominance of 'small groups'; the essential role of the masses was to respond to the initiatives of the leaders. Beetham, *op. cit.*, pp. 105–6.
47. Anthony Arblaster, *The Rise and Decline of Western Liberalism*, Oxford, Blackwell, 1984, pp. 327–8.
48. French liberalism draws on a different tradition, not of complacent property ownership, but of a radical republican liberty, equality and fraternity. Arblaster, *op. cit.*, cs. 11–12.
49. Eisenstadt, *op. cit.*, p. 546.
50. Jacob van Klaveren, 'Corruption: The Special Case of the United States', chapter in Heidenheimer, *op. cit.*, p. 563.
51. *Ibid.*, p. 558.
52. John Carlin, 'From America', *The Sunday Independent* (Johannesburg), 17 May 1998.

53. Review of Vivien Stern's, *A Sin Against the Future: Imprisonment in the World*, in *The Economist*, 16 May 1998.
54. *The Economist*, 19 February 2000.
55. Scott Christianson, *With Liberty For Some: 500 Years of Imprisonment in America*, Boston, Northeastern University, 1998, pp. 275–5, and review, 'A Land of Bondage', *The Economist*, 13 February 1999.
56. Daniel Bergner, 'How We Punish the Wicked', *Talk* (New York), October 1999, pp. 89–96.
57. For example, in 1993 the male homicide rate was 12.4 per 100 000, compared with 1.5 for the European Union, and 0.9 for Japan; for rape, the figures were 1.5 in Japan, and 42.8 in the United States. Gray, *op. cit.*, pp. 116–18.
58. Carlin, *op. cit.*
59. Though executions per million people are far higher in small, authoritarian Singapore, the rate of execution there since 1994 was only one every nine days. *The Economist*, 3 April 1999, p. 53.
60. *The Economist*, 24 July 1999.
61. The others are Iran, Nigeria, Pakistan, Saudi Arabia and Yemen. Lazare, *op. cit.*, p. 6.
62. Carlin, *op. cit.*
63. Gray speaks too of the 'hollowing-out' of its social institutions, *op. cit.*, pp. 116 and 119.
64. *Ibid.*, pp. 89–90.
65. *Ibid.*, pp. 90, 92 and 94.
66. *Ibid.*, pp. 89 and 92.
67. Editorial, *The Economist*, 3 April 1999.
68. New York's highly publicized programme of 'zero tolerance policing' was accompanied by a big drop in the crime rate in the city, 1993–96, but Young notes that crime rates fell in 12 out of 17 advanced industrial countries at much the same time, as it also did in 17 of the 25 largest American cities, in some which had adopted less aggressive policing policies, in others which utilized community-oriented policing, and in still others where no change in policing methods occurred. Jock Young, *The Exclusive Society*, London, Sage, 1999, pp. 122–5.
69. 'The Sultans of SWAT', *The Economist*, 2 October 1999.
70. Hitchens, *op. cit.*, p. 69.
71. Ellis Cashmore, 'Young, Shafted and Black', *The Independent* (London), 6 August 1999.
72. *The Economist*, 2 October 1999.
73. *Ibid.* Many people and politicians in turn applaud such firmness.
74. Christianson, *op. cit.*, p. 281.
75. *The Economist*, 3 April 1999, p. 40.
76. Young, *op. cit.*, p. 87.
77. Everyone has a right to refuse a search unless the police have a warrant or have arrested them for an actual crime.
78. The hard-pressed lawyer will probably advise the poor black client to plead guilty in the expectation of a speedier trial and, just possibly, lighter sentence.
79. 'Bum Rush', review of David Cole, *No Equal Justice: Race and Class in the American Criminal Justice System*, in *The Economist*, 19 February 2000.

80. Their first book, *Re-engineering the Corporation*, 1993, sold nearly two million copies, and their ideas became 'familiar to most high corporate executives'. Head, *op. cit.*, pp. 49–50.
81. Finnegan, *op. cit.*, p. 66. His emphasis.
82. *Ibid.*, p. 231.
83. *Ibid.*, p. 321. Pearl's emphasis.
84. *Ibid.*, p. xvii.
85. *Ibid.*, pp. 346 and 348.
86. Przeworski, 'The Neo-Liberal Fallacy', chapter in Larry Diamond and Marc Plattner (eds), *Capitalism, Socialism and Democracy Revisited*, Baltimore and London, The Johns Hopkins University Press, 1993, p. 40.
87. 'Campaigning in Clinton Country', *The Economist*, 5 February 2000, p. 19.
88. Assessment and figures of James S. Fishkin, *The Voice of the People: Public Opinion and Democracy*, New Haven and London, Yale University Press, 1995, pp. 45–7.
89. This campaign spending amounted to an estimated $1 billion, but included only the money that was regulated by the Federal Election Commission. The unregulated money spent by interest groups and political parties in support of particular candidates may have totalled an additional $345 million. 'Did money talk? Is water wet?' *The Economist*, 7 November 1998.
90. Michael Lind, 'Why There Will be no Revolution in the US', *New Left Review*, 233, January/February 1999, p. 105.
91. Lars-Erik Nelson, 'Undemocratic Vistas', *The New York Review of Books*, 12 August 1999, pp. 9 and 10.
92. 'Washington, Babylon?' *The Economist*, 29 July 2000.
93. The supposedly competitive American two-party system amounts to a single corporate party with two right wings. Gore Vidal, interviewed by Tim Sebastian on 'Hard Talk', BBC World, 3 November 2000.
94. Hitchens, *op. cit.*, p. 22.
95. The coining of 'triangulation' is attributed to Clinton's advisor Dick Morris. *Ibid.*, p. 26, and Lars-Erik Nelson, 'Clinton and His Enemies', *The New York Review of Books*, 20 January 2000, p. 18.
96. As cited by Hitchens, *op. cit.*, pp. 29–30 and 64–7. The effects of the 1996 reforms were extensive, for they signalled to the well-off that for the poor and needy welfare was over, while those 'trimmed' from the welfare rolls 'disappear[ed] into a twilight zone of casual employment, uninsured illness, intermittent education for their children, and unsafe and temporary accommodation' – the ballooning underclass.
97. *Ibid.*, pp. 34–5.
98. Among other beneficiaries-benefactors were the Waltons of Wal-Mart ($216 000), David Geffen of Dreamworks ($389 000), and the Nortons of Norton Utilities ($350 750), *ibid.*, pp. 58–9.
99. Cited in *ibid.*, p. 61.
100. *Ibid.*, pp. 61–3.
101. Abbreviating Democratic Congressman, David Schippers' statement of 10 December 1998, 'There's no one left to lie to', cited in full in *ibid.*, p. 24.
102. Daughter Chelsea was publicly silent and perhaps traumatized, but Hilary Clinton indicated that she placed calculated careerism well above her

husband's immorality and abuse of office, when she described the published evidence of Flowers as 'trash for cash', compared stories of her husband's affairs to UFO sightings, and was one of the first to point divertingly towards a 'vast right-wing conspiracy'. 'Lexington', *The Economist*, 3 October 1998.

103. As 'Lexington' described it: 'tolerance especially of people's private sexual and social arrangements, combined with a wish not to seem to preach about what may be right or wrong.' Within the booming economy, society becomes just a 'feast of alternative lifestyles' wherein the non-responsible elite and the masses are believed to enjoy equal shares. 'The Price of Perjury', *The Economist*, 28 November 1998.

104. In early December 1998, for instance, his approval rating was just over 60 per cent, while 90 per cent of Americans opposed impeachment. *The Economist*, 5 December 1998.

105. Hitchens, *op. cit.*, pp. 87, and 107–13.

106. It was through the Jones case that 'his affair with Miss Lewinsky came to light, as well as his lies under oath to conceal it'. *The Economist*, 21 November 1998.

107. *The Economist*, 17 April 1999.

108. 'Clinton's private vileness meshed exactly with his brutal and opportunistic public style.' Hitchens, *op. cit.*, p. 87. A panel of American historians, in February 2000, ranked Clinton 41st among his presidential peers in terms of 'moral authority', below Richard Nixon. *Mail and Guardian*, 3 March 2000.

109. Gray, *op. cit.*, pp. 120 and 130. Fukuyama has purveyed the view, in an article entitled 'The End of History', then in a book re-affirming his thesis, that 'democratic capitalism' constitutes the 'final form of human government', and its global reach 'the triumph of the Western idea'.

110. *The Economist*, 10 February 1996.

111. He includes Italy, Japan and Israel too. Sennett, *op. cit.*, p. 53.

112. In path-breaking moves Germany had introduced health insurance in 1883 and a general pension scheme for age and invalidity in 1889. Donald Sassoon, *One Hundred Years of Socialism*, London, Fontana Press, 1996, p. 137.

113. *Ibid.*, pp. 42 and 44.

114. *Ibid.*, p. 123.

115. *Ibid.*, pp. 141 and 149.

116. *Ibid.*, p. 445.

117. He concluded that 'the only countries in the world in which almost no one is poor after taxes and transfers are those that pursue social democratic policies'. *Op. cit.*, pp. 48 and 53.

118. Gray, *op. cit.*, pp. 93–4. No date is given for von Pierer's statement.

119. Birgit Mahnkopf, 'Between the Devil and the Deep Blue Sea: the "German Model" Under the Pressure of Globalisation', in Panitch and Leys, *op. cit.*, 153–4.

120. Keynes showed that full employment is not the natural outcome of a market equilibrium. Gray, *op. cit.*, pp. 85–6 and 90.

121. In the recent recognition of the World Bank, *Taking Action to Reduce Poverty in Sub-Saharan Africa*, Washington, 1997, p. 8.

122. It produced constant crises with terrible political effects like global war, dictatorships and massive unemployment. Sassoon, *op. cit.*, p. 446.

123. *The Economist*, 2 May 1998.
124. 'One True Model?' *ibid.*, 8 April 2000, reporting on the recent research of Richard Freeman of the United States' National Bureau of Economic Research.
125. *Ibid.*
126. Sennett, *op. cit.*, pp. 22–5.
127. Senator John McCain, in his short run for the Republican presidential nomination in 2000, attacked 'lobbyists and big money', and sought to attract independent and Democratic voters to his side. He represented thereby a 'gigantic threat to the way the establishment does business'. He talked credibly of things like sacrifice and principle, and audiences, it was reported, were 'surprised, even shocked, by his candour'. *The Economist*, 5 and 19 February 2000.
128. Mahnkopf, *op. cit.*, p. 149.
129. Discussed in Chapter 7 below.

4 Elitism's place in the ANC

1. Dale T. McKinley, *The ANC and the Liberation Struggle: A Critical Political Biography*, London and Chicago, Pluto Press, 1997, p. 8.
2. *Ibid.*, p. 18. Seekings believes that the ANC became for the first time a 'mass-based movement' in the 1950s, but this was entirely suppressed shortly after. Jeremy Seekings, *The UDF: A History of the United Democratic Front in South Africa, 1983–1991*, Cape Town, David Philip, 2000, pp. 4–5 and 8. The Defiance Campaign represented an attempt to mobilize newly-settled urban communities in 1952, but it was brought to an end by the Criminal Law Amendment Act of the following year. Philip Bonner and Lauren Segal, *Soweto: A History*, Cape Town, Maskew Miller Longman, 1998, pp. 49 and 51.
3. Glenn Frankel, *Rivonia's Children*, London, Weidenfeld & Nicolson, 1999, p. 57.
4. *Ibid.*, pp. 100–1.
5. *Op. cit.*, p. 56.
6. 'Factions were formed and factions within factions'. Adrian Hadland and Jovial Rantao, *The Life and Times of Thabo Mbeki*, Johannesburg, Zebra Press, 1999, pp. 30–3.
7. McKinley, *op. cit.*, p. 51.
8. *Ibid.*
9. Cited, without date, in Vladimir Shubin, *ANC: A View From Moscow*, Bellville, Mayibuye Books UWC, 1999, p. 312.
10. Paul Trewhela refers to a 'mutiny of about 90 per cent of the ANC's trained troops' in Angola. Letter to the Editors, *The New York Review of Books*, XLVII(16), 19 October 2000.
11. Testimony of Diliza Mtembu before the Truth and Reconciliation Commission. Antjie Krog, *Country of My Skull*, Johannesburg, Random House, 1998, p. 199.
12. He had described the ANC's security apparatus as acting like 'amaBhunu' (or 'Boers') because they replicated the thuggery of the apartheid state. Trewhela, *op. cit.*

220 *Notes*

13. Gavin Evans in *Weekly Mail* (Johannesburg) 23 August, and David Beresford in *Guardian Weekly* (London) 15 September 1991.
14. Hadland and Rantao, *op. cit.*, pp. 45 and 52–3.
15. Martin Meredith, *Nelson Mandela: A Biography*, Harmondsworth, Penguin Books, 1997, pp. 411–12.
16. Trewhela, *op. cit.*
17. As cited in Seekings, *op. cit.*, p. 125. An ANC statement was distributed inside the country in 1985 which declared that there was a real possibility of a decisive national insurrection, and called on youth and other militants to take up arms. Students responded, though the ANC's underground structures were at best nebulous; in June, four students killed themselves using defective weaponry, and others died in abortive attacks. *Ibid.*, pp. 146–7.
18. Nkosazana Dlamini-Zuma, for instance, was vice-president of the South African Students Organization. 'He recruited her to the ANC and sent her back with instructions to recruit others...and to influence debates...within [BCM].' She became 'another' who 'remained loyal to [Mbeki] over the years and whose loyalty has been rewarded'. Hadland and Rantao, *op. cit.*, p. 39.
19. Patti Waldmeir, *Anatomy of a Miracle*, Harmondsworth, Viking, 1997, pp. 46–8.
20. Hadland and Rantao, *op. cit.*, p. 49. They quote Mac Maharaj as saying: 'They didn't believe it would happen.'
21. Meredith, *op. cit.*, pp. 411–12.
22. *Ibid.*, pp. 412–13.
23 Hein Marais, *South Africa: Limits to Change*, London and Cape Town, Zed Books and University of Cape Town Press, 1998, p. 52, and Michael Neocosmos, 'From People's Politics to State Politics: Aspects of National Liberation in South Africa, 1984–1994', *Politeia* (Pretoria), 15(3), 1996, p. 79.
24. Meredith, *op. cit.*, p. 412.
25. Cited in Seekings, *op. cit.*, p. 243.
26. Meredith, *op. cit.*, pp. 413 and 487.
27. Mark Gevisser, 'The Thabo Mbeki Story', Part five, 'The Deal-Maker', *Sunday Times*, 13 June 1999.
28. Waldmeir, *op. cit.*, pp. 78–9 and 99.
29. Gevisser, *op. cit.* His emphasis.
30. Seekings is non-committal here, claiming that 'it is not clear precisely how fully informed Mandela and the exiled ANC leadership kept the UDF leadership', while noting that from late 1988 'there was certainly no shortage of opportunities for the ANC to keep the internal leadership informed.' *Op. cit.*, p. 242.
31. Shubin, *op. cit.*
32. Trewhela, *op. cit.*
33. Trust and loyalty sometimes readily given. Willie Esterhuyse, for instance, after meeting Mbeki in December 1987, went back to National Intelligence in Pretoria and declared that 'I'd be prepared to entrust my life to this fellow'. Cited by Gevisser, Part five.
34. Part four, 'The Bag Carrier', *Sunday Times*, 6 June 1999.
35. At a preceding consultative conference in December, Mandela had faced 'sustained criticism' over his autocratic style and failure to consult on policy issues. Meredith, *op. cit.*, pp. 444–5.

36. *Ibid.*, p. 446. 'Over a quarter' of elected NEC members had been office-holders in the UDF, and some, in 1994, acceded to ministerial office – among them, Trevor Manuel, Vali Moosa, Sydney Mufamadi and Dullah Omar, while Popo Molefe and Patrick Lekota became provincial premiers. Seekings, *op. cit.*, p. 318. Others were conspicuously passed over, as is noted below.

37. By late 1987 most of the UDF leadership were in prison – the majority of detainees 1986–87 were members of UDF affiliates – in hiding, or dead. The UDF was banned in early 1988, but much of its remaining membership regrouped as the MDM later that year with trade unions and churches in the forefront. Marais, *op. cit.*, pp. 53 and 59. According to De Klerk, the ANC team consisted of Mandela, Walter Sisulu, Joe Slovo, Alfred Nzo, Thabo Mbeki, Ahmed Kathrada, Joe Modise, Ruth Mompati, Archie Gumede, Reverend Beyers Naude and Cheryl Carolus. Gumede, he adds, was 'included to give recognition to the UDF'. But there were 'only three main speakers' on the ANC side – Mandela, Mbeki and Slovo. For De Klerk, this was the beginning of 'structured negotiations'. F.W. De Klerk, *The Last Trek – A New Beginning*, London, Pan Books, 1999, pp. 175 and 181.

38. Cited by Hadland and Rantao, *op. cit.*, pp. 69–70.

39. *Ibid.*, p. 86.

40. 'The sense we got of Thabo', he quotes a former UDF leader saying, 'was that he was 'a corridors-of-power' person.' Part five.

41. They fail to explain the basis of this knowledge, but refer more than once to his 'powerful foresight', 'natural ability' and 'his sheer intellectual accuity'. They note too that he compensated for this fear or dislike by making 'allies', notably and enduringly of Essop and Aziz Pahad. *Op. cit.*, pp. 32–3 and 80.

42. Part four. The replacement of Mbeki and of his ally Jacob Zuma, by Ramaphosa and Slovo, on the negotiating team, was accompanied by shifts in control of the ANC's political departments from the party president's office to the secretary-general's. This occurred in early August when Mandela was absent overseas. *The Star* (Johannesburg), 22 August 1991.

43. 'ANC Conference Resolutions', in *SouthScan* (London), 6(27), 12 July 1991.

44. Reverend Frank Chikane, the committee chairman, did not even demand to see the abducted boys because, as he testified subsequently before the Truth Commission, 'this was not part of our brief'. A little later, other committee members did see wounded youths, but again did not seek their release because, in the further testimony of Sydney Mufamadi, 'we could have been charged with kidnapping'. Cited in Krog, *op. cit.*, pp. 249–50. The role of Madikizela-Mandela and the football club are discussed further in Ch. 7.

45. Meredith, *op. cit.*, pp. 378–83. The Committee's statement is as cited therein.

46. An abandoned body was found in a field or river on 7 January, but it was not identified as Stompie's until five weeks later. 'Terror United', *Sunday Times*, 19 May 1991.

47. Emma Gilbey, *The Lady: The Life and Times of Winnie Mandela*, London, Jonathan Cape, 1993, pp. 186–7. Identification of the body was eventually made on 15 February, and the forensic report said: 'Stompie Seipei's

body...was infested with maggots. The corpse had been that of a small boy.... Blood had poured out of his throat from two penetrating wounds on the right side...His lungs had collapsed. There was blood in his stomach. He was bruised all over.' Cited in Krog, *op. cit.*, p. 248.

48. Meredith, *op. cit.*, p. 385.
49. Cited in *ibid.*, pp. 385–6, and Seekings, *op. cit.*, p. 242.
50. Cited in Neocosmos, *op. cit.*, pp. 86–7.
51. *Op. cit.*, p. 257.
52. Seekings, *op. cit.*, p. 243. Calls from within the UDF and COSATU for a formal censure of Madikizela-Mandela were blocked by the ANC in Lusaka according to Neocosmos, *op. cit.*, p. 87.
53. Meredith, *op. cit.*, p. 437.
54. Albertina Sisulu worked in Dr Asvat's surgery, and could have been called to give evidence on the identity of his murderers and to disprove the validity of Madikizela-Mandela's alibi; security police personnel, with whom she closely associated, might also have offered proof of her whereabouts; and members of the Crisis Committee could have testified on the condition of some of the kidnapped youths. Gilbey, *op. cit.*, pp. 266–7.
55. *Ibid.*, p. 267.
56. As evidence subsequently emerged, in particular in the hearings of the Truth Commission in November–December 1997, and in their final Report; a number of her accomplices perjured themselves for her – to be considered further below.
57. Quoted in Gilbey, *op. cit.*, pp. 268–9.
58. Meredith, *op. cit.*, p. 442.
59. Seekings claims circumspectly that 'it is important...to acknowledge the role of the ANC in the UDF's resurgence', and that 'UDF leaders generally saw themselves as subordinate to the ANC in exile', but then adds that the ANC 'did not have the capacity to provide [the necessary] detailed direction and coordination', *op. cit.*, p. 292.
60. Marais, *op. cit.*, p. 72.
61. *Ibid.*, p. 201.
62. Hadland and Rantao, *op. cit.*, p. 75.
63. 'Tap' mobilization was a term used by Jeremy Cronin of the SACP in 1992 in describing the ANC's approach to democracy in South Africa, as what would result from agreement among elites who controlled and delivered their respective constituencies to the negotiating table. He implied that this was the dominant position on popular participation in the ANC, and was associated with Mandela himself. Noted by Neocosmos, *op. cit.*, p. 93.
64. Waldmeir, *op. cit.*, pp. 207–8.
65. Meredith, *op. cit.*, p. 479.
66. As De Klerk himself saw things, 'the government had the power and the authority and the ANC the numbers', *op. cit.*, p. 179.
67. As noted in Marais, *op. cit.*, p. 87.
68. Waldmeir, *op. cit.*, p. 241.
69. Inkatha chiefly excluded itself through the intransigence and brinkmanship of its leader, until it was brought into the electoral and governmental process by the ANC leadership at the very last minute. To be discussed below.

70. Neocosmos, *op. cit.*, p. 99.
71. Seekings, *op. cit.*, p. 241.
72. *Ibid.*, p. 294.
73. Cited in Neocosmos, 'Intellectual Debates and Popular Struggles in Transitional South Africa: Political Discourse and the Origins of Statism', mimeo, p. 37, and chapter in P. Gibbon, Neocosmos, and E. Wamba-dia-Wamba (eds), *State and Civil Society in Contemporary Africa*, Uppsala, Nordic Africa Institute, forthcoming.
74. The IEC's Investigations and Prosecutions Department 'simply fell apart'. Review by James Mitchell of *Launching Democracy in South Africa*, edited by R.W. Johnson and L. Schlemmer, *The Star*, 25 March 1996. The citations are from Johnson, p. 275.
75. The Judge frankly admitted that there was 'verneukery' (crookery), and added: 'You can't work in a brothel and remain chaste'. Cited by David Greybe, *Business Day*, 5 May 1994.
76. The ANC got 62.7 per cent of votes, comfortingly short of the two-thirds majority; the NP obtained 20.4 per cent and hence six seats in Cabinet and a Deputy Presidency; and the IFP gained 10.5 per cent of the national votes and three Cabinet seats.
77. Tom Lodge, *Consolidating Democracy*, Johannesburg, Electoral Institute of South Africa and Witwatersrand University Press, 1999, p. 11.
78. Fact and opinion in this section is based upon 'The TRC Report', Extract 3 and Extract 4, *The Star*, 4 and 5 November 1998, pp. 11 and 7–8 respectively.
79. Extract 3, pp. 11–12.
80. Extract 3, p. 11.
81. Extract 4, p. 5.
82. Just when Inkatha's terrorism was escalating, Mandela wished to 'thank Buthelezi for his long campaign to secure his release'. Waldmeir, *op. cit.*, p. 174.
83. Words of a member of the Commonwealth Eminent Persons Group who had visited Mandela in 1986, quoted in *ibid.*, p. 174. He told the same Person that 'it was the ANC's failing that blacks had resorted to violence' against each other.
84. *Ibid.*, p. 175.
85. *Ibid.*, p. 248.
86. Hadland and Rantao, *op. cit.*, p. 128.
87. The changeover was smooth and complete. As Breyten Breytenbach has framed it: 'The Afrikaner elite made a historic about-turn from one political dispensation to a completely opposing one without missing a goose-step'. Cited by Chris Louw, in 'Why we Won't Roll Over and Die', *Mail and Guardian*, 2 June 2000.
88. Interview with Kaizer Nyatsumba, in *The Star*, 6 October 2000.
89. Stephen Laufer's accurate and illuminating phraseology, 'ANC Document Could be Watershed for SA History', *Business Day*, 13 May 1997.
90. Apart from the findings of the TRC, the evidence included the Steyn Report, only made public in 1997, which described the links between Inkatha hit-squads and Pretoria until the early 1990s; the findings of the Investigative Task Unit that Marion was set up at the request of Buthelezi

and that Inkatha's paramilitary was responsible for many attacks on UDF members; and a report associated with Howard Varney that also showed that the intended task of the Caprivi 200 was to attack groups and individuals associated with the UDF. *Mail and Guardian*, 31 January, and Carmel Rickard, 'Armed With Information', in *Sunday Times*, 30 March 1997. Daluxolo Luthuli, the commander of the Caprivi squad, was explicit in interviews: 'I have absolutely no doubt that Dr Buthelezi was fully aware of every aspect of our operation'. *The Sunday Independent*, 8 June 1997.

91. Inkatha aggressively contributed to the cover-up. It responded to the findings of the TRC in Madikizela-Mandela fashion, not by reasoned argument, but by asserting that this 'villified' Buthelezi, and its 'high-ranking office-bearers' visited IFP members in prison to urge them not to apply for amnesty – hence to remain in jail – 'for fear that their applications would reveal collusion' by such senior leaders in gross human rights violations. 'The TRC Report', Extract 4, p. 5.
92. Laufer, *op. cit.*
93. Farouk Chothia, *Business Day*, 13 June 1997.
94. Reported by Chothia, *Business Day*, 17 June 1997.
95. Mark Gevisser, 'Of Politics and Hairdressing', *Mail and Guardian*, 23 August 1996.
96. Gilbey, *op. cit.*, p. 285.
97. Evans, *The Sunday Independent*, 13 April 1997.
98. Cited in *The Star*, 13 May 1997.
99. On the interrogation, torture and death of SWAPO 'dissidents', and the subsequent disappearances, see Siegfried Groth, *Namibia – The Wall of Silence*, Wuppertal, Peter Hammer Verlag, 1995.
100. Colin Leys and John S. Saul, *Namibia's Liberation Struggle: The Two-Edged Sword*, London, James Currey, 1995, p. 4.
101. Stephen Friedman, in *Business Day*, 11 November 1996.
102. Majakathata Mokoena, '"Class of '76" Leader Looks Back in Anger', *The Star*, 16 June 2000.
103. Bonner and Segal, *op. cit.*, pp. 78–93, and a review by Drew Forrest, 'Soweto's Turbulent History Examined', *Business Day*, 19 February 1999.
104. Bonner and Segal, *op. cit.*, p. 94.
105. *Ibid.*, pp. 95–100.
106. Mokoena, *op. cit.* His old political parties includes the Pan Africanist Congress along with the ANC.
107. Speaking in Cape Town, 6 December 1999, as noted in Chapter 1 above.

5 Universalizing an Incomplete Predominance

1. Richard Calland (ed.), *The First Five Years: A Review of South Africa's Democratic Parliament*, Cape Town, Idasa, 1999, pp. 104–7.
2. Report to Parliament by a Working Party, *Agenda for Change: Consolidating Parliamentary Democracy in Namibia*, Windhoek, July 1995, p. 32.
3. Calland, *op. cit.*, p. 10. He notes that these resignations 'were very destabilising', because the majority of those who left were leaders in the new parliament.

4. Cyril Madlala, 'The Grass *is* Greener', and editorial, *Sunday Times*, 12 January 1997.
5. Suttner was chair of the foreign affairs committee when he was appointed ambassador to Sweden in May 1997.
6. Spokesman Mamoepa assumed that those to be involved would be already 'members and supporters'. *The Star*, 4 March 1997.
7. Wyndham Hartley, in *Business Day*, 27 March 1997.
8. Involving specifically the ANC's Essop Pahad and the NP's Alex van Breda. *Business Day*, 18 and 21 April, and 23 May 1996.
9. The Code was initially presented publicly as an ethical instrument, 'Keep Your MP off the Gravy Train', *Mail and Guardian*, 17 March 1995.
10. Grassroots opposition to his removal was strong, and a group called the Crossroads Democratic Movement campaigned in his support under the slogan: 'Mandela made an error with Terror'. *Business Day*, 18 November 1996.
11. Editorial, *Sunday Times*, 15 December 1996.
12. Holomisa referred to Kerzner's earlier payment, either as a bribe or as extortion, of R2 million to the Mantanzima government in Transkei for a casino-rights monopoly, and to the fact that a leading member of that administration, Stella Sigcau, served then in President Mandela's Cabinet. He also pointed to Kerzner's donation to the ANC in 1994, which the party had emphatically denied receiving, and to Mbeki's and Steve Tshwete's acceptance of favours from the magnate. Mandela thereafter announced that he had personally accepted a gift of R2 million from Kerzner, two years previously, on conditions of strict confidentiality. Not even the secretary-general of the ANC knew of the matter. There was, he asserted, 'nothing unusual' in this secret transaction with such a man, and he offered no other information. *The Star*, 13 August, *Business Day*, 13 and 14 August 1996, and Carolyn Raphaely, in *The Sunday Independent*, 26 October 1997.
13. Despite ranking near the top on elections to the NEC.
14. As he told Raphaely; 'I didn't get R50,000 from Sol Kerzner, Stella Sigcau did.' *Op. cit.*
15. *The Star*, 10 December, and *Sunday Independent*, 15 December 1996.
16. John Battersby, in *The Sunday Independent*, 1 September 1996. The exiles won, according to Holomisa a year later, because people 'looked at them from afar as heroes. But it was the UDF people who were jailed and teargassed and maltreated, not the exiles. [And] it isn't really the exiles in general who have won, it's a particular set of exiles, those who were in UK and Europe … The exiles who were in Lusaka and the rest of Africa actually lost out [too]'. Interview with R.W. Johnson, in *The Star*, 1 September 1997.
17. *Business Day*, 4 and 20 October and 19 November 1996. Mbeki, for example, asked F.W. De Klerk to investigate allegations of drug trafficking against Sexwale, which was followed by a public reconciliation between Sexwale and Mbeki and a formal apology from the ANC. But 'bad blood between [the two] continue[d] to run deep.' Sexwale later attributed his fall to Mbeki's intolerance of rivals. Hadland and Rantao, *op. cit.*, pp. 115–16.
18. *The Economist*, 7 December 1996.
19. Hadland and Rantao, *op. cit.*, pp. 116–17.
20. Marion Edmunds and Enoch Mthembu, 'Strategy Behind ANC's Cabinet Offers', *Mail and Guardian*, 31 January 1997.

21. Jovial Rantao, 'Thanks but no Thanks ...', in *The Star*, 3 March 1997.
22. Hadland and Rantao, *op. cit.*, pp. 128–9.
23. Disparagement of the opposition parties, both for their smallness and their supposed opposition to democracy, was an earlier theme in Nelson Mandela's thinking. A year previously he had called for an increased ANC majority, 'to ensure that we are not interfered with by Mickey Mouse parties who have no commitment to democracy'. *The Star*, 27 November 1998.
24. All quotations above are from 'The President's Political Report', the full text of his speech to the ANC conference, special supplement, *Cape Times* (Cape Town), 23 December 1997.
25. Thabo Mbeki was unopposed as party president; Jacob Zuma as deputy-president; Kgalema Motlanthe as secretary-general; and Mendi Msimang as treasurer.
26. Steven Friedman, in *Business Day*, 12 January 1998.
27. Jacob Dlamini, in *Business Day*, 22 January 1998.
28. These are the words of an unnamed former cabinet minister. Maharaj resigned as transport minister in 1998 amid rumours of his reluctance to serve under Mbeki. Hadland and Rantao, *op. cit.*, p. 102.
29. *Ibid.*, pp. 102 and 127–8, where Steven Friedman is quoted.
30. Trewhela, *op. cit.*
31. Krog, *op. cit.*, pp. 243–6. TRC investigator, Piers Pigou, stated on 1 December that Michael Seakamela, Madikizela-Mandela's driver when the badly beaten Lolo Sono was last seen alive with her, had disappeared after he had been 'contacted' by 'Mummy'; evidence leader Hanif Vally said she had contacted at least three other former members in a bid to influence their testimony, John Morgan, Gift Ntombeni and Jabu Sithole; and TRC chairman, Archbishop Desmond Tutu, said there was 'no doubt that some people feel intimidated', Stephen Laufer, in *Business Day*, 2 December 1997.
32. Stephen Laufer, in *Business Day*, 1 December 1997.
33. Laufer and Nomavenda Mathiane, in *Business Day*, 3 December 1997.
34. Krog, *op. cit.*, pp. 246–7.
35. *Ibid.*, pp. 250–1.
36. Laufer and Mathiane, *op. cit.*
37. Evidence given to the TRC in late November indicated that the Club was 'riddled' with police informers, and at least two, Jerry Richardson and Katiza Cebekhulu, had confessed to having been informers. Charlene Smith and John Yeld, in *Saturday Star*, 29 November 1997.
38. Laufer, *Business Day*, 28 November 1997.
39. Laufer, in *Business Day*, 4 December 1997.
40. In one transcript Mobotha had fallen out of bed and Madikizela-Mandela could be heard expressing concern as to whether he had hurt himself. David Beresford, in *Mail and Guardian*, 30 January 1998.
41. *Ibid.*
42. Richardson had informed the police that Madikizela-Mandela had sent two MK guerrillas to his house, and Pretorious, off-duty at the time, was called in to make the arrest. *Ibid.*
43. The TRC evidence leader, Hanif Vally, concluded that Pretorious had entered the house alone despite the presence of 'enough policemen to fill Orlando

Stadium'. Vally said that the Commission had a statement from Pretorious' sister suggesting he had been silenced because he knew too much about the goings-on inside the Madikizela-Mandela house. Laufer, in *Business Day*, 4 December 1997.

44. De Kock's evidence. He shot Mobotha dead and blew up his corpse with explosives. *Ibid.*

45. But Seakamela had willingly repeated his earlier statement to the *Boston Globe* on 29 November. Kurt Shillinger and Peta Thornycroft, in *Mail and Guardian*, 5 December 1997.

46. When Coetsee died of a heart attack in July 2000, Nelson Mandela expressed his 'real sense of personal loss', and said: 'We shall always cherish and hold dear the memory of Kobie Coetsee as one of the main architects of transformation ...' *The Star*, 31 July 2000.

47. Cited in Shillinger and Thornycroft, *op. cit.*

48. Wall Mbhele, Peta Thornycroft, and David Beresford, 'The Cover-Up', *Mail and Guardian*, 21 November 1997.

49. Pippa Green, in *The Sunday Independent*, 30 November 1997.

50. Cyril Madlala, in *Sunday Times*, 30 November 1997. Cachalia said that, at best, Madikizela-Mandela had been aware of and encouraged the Club's criminality. 'At worst, she directed it and actively participated in the assaults.' Cited by Laufer, *Business Day*, 28 November 1997.

51. He stressed too that all previous efforts, by the church, lawyers, Oliver Tambo and Nelson Mandela, to get the Club disbanded had failed. Laufer, *op. cit.*

52. 'After Stompie's body was found', Morobe added, 'people were at the end of their tether. One thing we couldn't afford was for our people to do something on their own.' Cited in Green, *op. cit.*

53. Morobe, Cachalia and other MDM leaders spent six hours drafting their statement together. *Ibid.*, Madlala, *op. cit.*, and Green, *op. cit.*

54. Madlala, *op. cit.*, and Green, *op. cit.*

55. *The Star*, 28 November 1997.

56. Meredith, *op. cit.*, p. 413.

57. Green, *op. cit.* Like Peter Mokaba too.

58. Laufer, in *Business Day*, 5 December 1997. The term 'cabal' had originally implied, around the mid-1980s, that Indian and Coloured activists held disproportionate influence in the UDF, and that this element aimed to build the UDF into a substitute for the ANC. Seekings, *op. cit.*, p. 20. Considered further below.

59. Krog, *op. cit.*, p. 253.

60. Madlala, *op. cit.*, Green, *op. cit.*, and Laufer, *Business Day*, 1 December 1997.

61. With the TRC hearings underway, it was reported that Madikizela-Mandela, sometimes with a phalanx of bodyguards, was visiting black businessmen at night to demand money for her campaign. Charlene Smith, in *The Saturday Star*, 29 November 1997.

62. Pippa Green, in *The Sunday Independent*, 23 November 1997.

63. Stephane Bothma, in *Business Day*, 19 November 1997. In a sense he was right, in that her atrocities were committed against the youth of her own community.

64. Evidence of gang member Katiza Cebekhulu, who had participated in the assault on Stompie, cited in Madala, *op. cit.*

65. The Asvat family insisted that not a cent was taken. Krog, *op. cit.*, p. 257.
66. Anso Thom, in *The Star*, 2 December 1997.
67. He had been given a copy of the statement by the prosecutor at the trial, who said that it 'may become helpful some time in the future'. Cited by Cecilia Russell, in *The Star*, 2 December 1997.
68. *Ibid.*
69. Transcript of the interview in *The Star*, 2 December 1997. Bridgland was the author of *Katiza's Journey: Beneath the Surface of South Africa's Shame*, London, Sedgwick and Jackson, 1997.
70. Evidence leader Hanif Vally: 'I wasn't expecting this, Archbishop', as he stumbled over his response. Cited by Russell, in *The Star*, 2 December 1997.
71. *Ibid.*
72. One incomplete listing of the murders and attempted murders in which she was implicated was as follows: Stompie Seipei; Dr Asvat; Finkie Msomi, a 13-year-old girl shot dead in a Soweto house; Kuki Zwane, a young woman murdered near Orlando railway station in December 1988; Sicelo Dlomo, shot dead in January 1988 as an alleged informer; Morgan Bambisa, murdered in 1987; Susan Maripe, shot in her Soweto home in October 1987; Xola Makhaula and 'another unnamed person', killed in a shebeen brawl in 1987; Maxwell Madondo, Club member who died while kidnapping an alleged sell-out; Lolo Sono and Siboniso Tshabalala, disappeared in November 1988 and presumed murdered; Peter Makhanda, hung, suffocated with a plastic bag, and with initials carved into his body and acid smeared into the cuts; Ikaneng Lerothodi, an alleged sell-out, had his throat cut in 1989 but survived; and Sizwe Sithole, the father of a child by Zinzi Mandela-Hlongwane, detained for possession of firearms allegedly given to him by Madikizela-Mandela, hanged himself in police custody with his shoelaces. Mbhele, Thornycroft, and Beresford, in *Mail and Guardian*, 21 November 1997.
73. *Ibid.*, p. 259. Tutu's own emphasis. According to the TRC's deputy chairman, Alex Boraine, Madikizela-Mandela had challenged the integrity of the commission, and Archbishop Tutu went too far in his conciliation of her: 'His hugging of [her] during the hearing, and his declaration of love and admiration, left the commission wide open to the charge of bias.' Cited by Phylicia Oppelt, in *Sunday Times*, 1 October 2000.
74. 'The TRC Report', Extract Four, 5 November 1998, p. 8.
75. Amnesty required not only truth-telling by an applicant, but the ability to demonstrate that an act was political in nature, not merely criminal. Madikizela-Mandela would have extreme difficulty meeting either of these criteria, and Buthelezi also avoids the truth.
76. The Skweyiya Commission had reported in October 1995 into extensive corruption under Mangope's dictatorial government in Bophuthatswana. The reference is from the TRC Report.
77. Extract Five, 6 November 1998, p. 2. The ANC appears aware of the principle of unfitness for public office, and even applies it in some cases. Boksburg mayor, Eric Xayiya, resigned in October 2000 after being accused of raping a woman in his parlour. The ANC Gauteng provincial coordinator, David Makhura, explained: 'It was in the best interests of the country that no ANC member facing allegations of this magnitude can continue to hold public office.' *The Star*, 5 October 2000.

78. 'Winnie Mobutu', *Business Day*, 8 December 1997.
79. In characteristically false popular-militant style, she gave an exclusive interview in which she declared, among other things, that she was being victimized by the TRC, that the people should decide on the reintroduction of the death penalty, and that the ANC leaders had forgotten their promises. Newton Kanhema, 'Winnie's Fury: I Accuse', *The Star*, 17 November 1997. Sports Minister Steve Tshwete responded in a few days by calling her 'a charlatan who needs help', and ANC acting secretary-general, Cheryl Carolus, after more than two weeks, labelled her 'cowardly' for failing to use party structures to voice her criticisms of the ANC. But, aside from the name-calling, also announced that no disciplinary action would be taken against her. Steve Tshwete, in *The Star*, 20 November 1997, and Jacob Dlamini and Pule Molebeledi in *Business Day*, 3 December 1997. Her campaign for the ANC deputy-presidency collapsed as her popular support within provincial organizations and the Women's League withered away.
80. Cited by Farouk Chothia and Wyndham Hartley, in *Business Day*, 18 November 1996.
81. Justice Malala, 'The Power and the Party', in *Sunday Times*, 12 September 1999.
82. Carol Paton, in *Sunday Times*, 20 June 1999.
83. Editorial *Mail and Guardian*, 25 June, and editorial *Business Day*, 21 June 1999.
84. Ivor Powell, quoting Richard Calland, in *Mail and Guardian*, 25 June 1999.
85. Drew Forrest and Farouk Chothia, in *Business Day*, 20 September 1999.
86. Alan Fine and Drew Forrest, in *Business Day*, 21 October 1999.
87. Jovial Rantao, with reference to Steven Friedman, in *The Star*, 7 February 2000.
88. Sean Jacobs, 'An Imperial Presidency or an Organised One?' *Business Day*, 17 February 2000.
89. Howard Barrell, with reference to the work of James Myburgh, parliamentary researcher for the DP, in *Mail and Guardian*, 5 November 1999.
90. Hadland and Rantao, *op. cit.*, pp. 49 and 125–6.
91. Cited by Barrell, *op. cit.*
92. Citation of Tony Leon, in *Business Day*, 23 March 2000.
93. Barrell, *op. cit.*
94. Dlamini-Zuma had earlier permitted an unauthorized expenditure of R14 million on the supposed AIDS-awareness play, 'Sarafina 2'. K. Good, *Realizing Democracy in Botswana, Namibia and South Africa*, pp. 1–3.
95. *The Economist*, 20 February 1999.
96. Farouk Chothia, in *Business Day*, 30 August 1999.
97. *Business Day*, 23 March 2000.
98. Robert Kirby, 'Shoring up the President', *Mail and Guardian*, 12 May 2000. In an earlier article he had analysed what he termed 'state-of-the-art political sycophancy' on the part of the Commission's leading journalist, Snuki Zikalala. See 'Mr Toady Goes a-Courtin', *ibid.*, 11 February 2000.
99. T.J. Pempel (ed.), *Uncommon Democracies: The One-Party Dominant Regimes*, Ithaca and London, Cornell University Press, 1990.
100. The long predominance of the BDP in Botswana is related to the weakness and marginalization of civil society and opposition, and to the construction

of the notion of the growth economy by Seretse Khama and his successor Ketumile Masire, with rewards in incomes and services directed towards those who made the biggest contribution to its success. This was a hardnosed and successful programme, initiated and implemented by a disciplined and unified elite. It brought wealth to the controllers of productive resources, infrastructural development and high per capita incomes to the nation, and trickles and crumbs to voiceless communities like the San, without resources to contribute. But corruption in the early 1990s pointed to elite indiscipline and disunity, and brought the viability of the developmental state and model into question. Zibani Maundeni, 'State Culture and the Botswana Developmental State', University of Botswana, 2000, mimeo.

101. Gaetano Mosca, *The Ruling Class*, New York, McGraw-Hill, 1939.
102. *Business Day*, 30 October, and *Sunday Times*, 1 November 1998.
103. *Sunday Times*, 1 November 1998.
104. *The Sunday Independent*, 1 November 1998.
105. Janet Cherry, ' "Just War" and "Just Means": Was the TRC Wrong About the ANC?' *Transformation* (Durban), 42 (2000), pp. 14–17.
106. When prisoners from Quatro (or Quadro) were required to give a sanitized account of their imprisonment before the media in Lusaka in 1985, the event was 'hosted by Mbeki', Trewhela, *op. cit.*
107. Ivor Powell, 'Khoza Takes his Secrets to the Grave', *Mail and Guardian*, 2 June, and Tefo Mothibeli in *Business Day*, 2 June 2000
108. Hopewell Radebe, in *The Star*, 29 May 2000.
109. *Sunday Times*, 27 June 1999.
110. *Ibid.*; Kaizer Nyatsumba in *The Star*, 30 June; and Kevin O'Grady in *Business Day*, 28 June 1999.
111. Judgements quoted by O'Grady, *op. cit.*
112. *The Star*, 30 June 1999.
113. Nyatsumba, *op. cit.*
114. Tony Leon said that Mahlangu offered President Mbeki a 'golden opportunity to illustrate to the country' how he would handle corruption. 'He failed his first test.' *The Star*, 29 June 1999.
115. By 2000 all ANC premiers were selected directly by the ANC President, and the composition of their cabinets had to meet the approval of the national leadership. The Premiers' Forum, which had rotated its monthly discussion sessions among the provincial capitals, had been replaced by the President's Forum, which held monthly 'coordination' meetings with the President in Pretoria. Mondli Makhanya and Carol Paton, in *Sunday Times*, 11 June 2000.
116. World data, based on United Nations research, in *The Economist*, 22 July 2000, and UNDP/BIDPA, *op. cit.*
117. Helen Epstein, 'The Mystery of AIDS in South Africa', *The New York Review of Books*, xlvii(12), 20 July 2000, p. 50.
118. Money appeared not to be the immediate issue – in the financial year 1999–2000, the AIDS directorate in the Health Ministry failed to spend 40 per cent of its allocated funds. *Ibid.*, pp. 50–1.
119. Spokesman Parks Mankahlana took this line further, about nine months later, when he suggested, in an article in *Business Day*, that AZT was part of a corporate conspiracy against Africa. *Ibid.*

120. Cited by Adele Sulcas, in *The Sunday Independent*, 19 March 2000.
121. A group of researchers at the University of Pretoria had approached Mbeki and Dlamini-Zuma in 1997, claiming to have a cure for AIDS, and were invited to address Cabinet directly – an unusual privilege – on what they called Virodene. It consisted of dimethylformamide, an industrial chemical used, for example, in dry cleaning. It was unlikely to be beneficial, and could 'well be harmful', to AIDS patients. Clinical trials of Virodene on HIV-positive people were carried out without the authorization of the Medicines Control Council. Thabo Mbeki angrily defended his support for Virodene in an open letter to the press in March 1998, and when the Medicines Control Council tried to prevent further trials of the substance on human subjects, its chairman and some other officials were fired. Epstein, *op. cit.*, pp. 53–4.
122. *The Economist* 27 May 2000. James McIntyre, an expert on mother-to-child AIDS transmission, noted that since about half the panellists were orthodox and half dissident, it was extremely unlikely that they would achieve a consensus. Taryn Lamberti and and Pat Sidley, in *Business Day*, 4 May 2000.
123. Cited by Ranjeni Munusamy, in *Sunday Times*, 9 April 2000.
124. He emphasized that Mbeki was 'the only president in the world whose official portrait has the HIV awareness ribbon emblazoned on his breast'. *Business Day*, 20 March 2000.
125. Cited by Ranjeni Munusamy, in *Sunday Times*, 9 April 2000.
126. *The Star*, 20 April 2000.
127. 'Hogarth', in *Sunday Times*, 7 May 2000.
128. Cited by Justice Malala, 'Clause 16', *Sunday Times*, 23 July 2000.
129. Writing in *The Sunday Independent*, 2 April 2000. According to the *Mail and Guardian*, Mbeki 'appear[ed] to get his information [on AIDS] from late-night Internet trawling of what are generally considered somewhat dubious websites. But, despite this fact and … his lack of specialist medical or scientific knowledge, he apparently has no compunction in expressing forceful opinions on the subject … ' Editorial, 3 March 2000.
130. 'People whose views carry weight in Washington are puzzled and distressed and wonder what the implications might be for his handling of other pressing issues', he added. Simon Barber, in *Business Day*, 19 May 2000.
131. He toured the United States in May prepared with a little joke about filling his distinguished predecessor's shoes, which he repeated often: 'Nelson Mandela is Nelson Mandela … I did say to him when this matter was raised … that actually I would not want to step into his shoes because he normally buys such ugly shoes! So I really wouldn't want to!' Cited by Simon Barber, in *Business Day*, 31 May 2000. When he was asked specifically about his controversial AIDS policies on *The NewsHour With Jim Lehrer*, on 23 May, his replies, notes Epstein, 'were a series of evasions'. Epstein, *op. cit.*, p. 55.
132. The 'Durban Declaration', published in *Nature*, ahead of the international AIDS conference in Durban. The Health Minister, Manto Tshabalala-Msimang, added redundantly that the declaration smacked of elitism. *The Star*, 4 July 2000.
133. Reports in *The Star* and *Business Day*, 11 July 2000. Judge Cameron's address was accorded a standing ovation.

134. Smuts Ngonyama, 'A Virus Cannot Cause a Syndrome', *Business Day*, 4 October, and Charlene Smith, 'Hot Air Serves to Incubate AIDS', *ibid.*, 9 October 2000. The Minister of Health circulated a chapter of the book *Behold, a Pale Horse*, by William Cooper, which claims that AIDS was introduced into Africa by a worldwide conspiracy, to all provincial premiers and health ministers, Carol Paton, *Sunday Times*, 3 September 2000.

135. Howard Barrell, in *Mail and Guardian*, 6 October 2000. When Aziz Pahad demanded to know 'what are your objectives, Mr Barrell?', he reaffirmed the correctness of his account of the President's speech, and noted that it was well-sourced and canvassed, *Mail and Guardian*, 13 October 2000. The Treatment Action Group quickly declared that it had never received a single cent from any drug company. *Business Day*, 3 October 2000.

136. Robert Brand, in *The Star*, 4 October 2000.

137. Carol Paton and Celean Jacobson reported that Mbeki had secured the funding for the programme, 'immediately and unconditionally'. *Sunday Times*, 28 May 2000.

138. One such was the violence sweeping the country in the immediate wake of the February constitutional referendum – which delivered a sharp setback to the Mugabe government – and ahead of the June parliamentary elections. As reputable observers reported that invasions of white-owned farms and associated mayhem were being organized by the Mugabe government, and expressed grave concern for the fairness of the electoral process, Mbeki said – for example in early June – that he did not know if the elections would be free and fair, and that the issue was 'entirely speculative at this point'. Reacting to the finding of an American monitoring group in May that conditions for democratic elections did not exist, Mbeki declared: 'We do not agree ... It is not correct to be making any prejudgements', and pictured all such warnings as 'interference'. *Business Day*, 25 May, and *The Star*, 13 June 2000. The partiality of his stance was attested to in the eventual election report of the European Union: 'The evidence showed that, between February and June, Zanu-PF was engaged in a systematic campaign of intimidation aimed at crushing opposition support.' Cited by Peter Fabricius in *The Star*, 10 July 2000. *The Economist*, too, concluded on 1 July that the June elections were 'grossly unfair'. A closely related issue was the Mugabe government's displayed contempt for the rule of law, and the consequences posed by state illegality on regional economies – when Finance Minister Trevor Manuel declared in May that the crisis had not affected the rand, the markets were said to have reacted with incredulity. *Business Day*, 11 May 2000.

139. He said that 'the English can be very arrogant about [information technology]' during a tour of the Columbus IT company, on 7 June, in the company of the Danish Prime Minister, South Africa's Foreign Minister, and Columbus's South Africa director and some twenty others. When the group indicated their surprise, he said: 'There is no English person here.' Report by Justice Malala, in *Sunday Times*, 11 June 2000.

140. The premiers had met Mbeki in Skagen, Denmark, for a SA–Nordic Summit. Malala, 'Mbeki, Nordic Leaders at Odds', *Sunday Times*, 11 June 2000.

141. Speaking in a radio interview, and cited in *Business Day*, 12 October 2000.

142. Mbeki claimed that Zuma's remarks had been 'misconstrued', but Colen Garrow, an economist at ABN-Amro, stated that 'foreign investors are

looking at South Africa in a very different light – they don't want to put their money here. Zimbabwe is one of the problems.' Cited by Robert Brand, *The Star*, 13 October 2000.

143. He had then twice met the leader of the Movement for Democratic Change. *Business Day*, 30 October 2000.

144. A white farmer, Guy French, was severely assaulted and his workers beaten on 31 October 2000 when he ignored orders from squatters that he plant nothing on his farm. *Business Day*, 1 and 3 November 2000.

145. *Business Day*, 3 November 2000.

146. When Nelson Mandela spoke near the end of the Durban AIDS conference he paid somewhat exaggerated tribute to President Mbeki as 'a very intelligent man and a man of science'. He then adopted a markedly different position from Mbeki's; he called for the termination of what he described as the damaging dispute over HIV-AIDS, and stressed that ordinary South Africans and HIV-AIDS sufferers expected the government to act to limit further loss of life. Cited in *The Sunday Independent*, 16 July 2000.

147. Mike Robertson, Ray Hartley and Carol Paton, 'Face to Face With the President', *Sunday Times*, 6 February 2000.

6 Predominance and the Empowerment Goose

1. Bonner and Segal, *op. cit.*, p. 53.
2. Marais, *op. cit.*, p. 74.
3. As presented in Meredith, *op. cit.*, pp. 136–8.
4. Mbeki had appeared to distance the ANC from the latter tendency in 1984 when writing in a Canadian academic journal: 'the ANC is not a socialist party. It has never pretended to be one ... ' Cited by John Saul, 'SA's Tragic Leap to the Right', *Mail and Guardian*, 23 June 2000.
5. Marais, *op. cit.*
6. *Ibid.*
7. Seekings, *op. cit.*, p. 57.
8. Waldmeir, *op. cit.*, p. 253.
9. Both citations are from Saul, *op. cit.*
10. Waldmeir, *op. cit.*, pp. 73–4.
11. *Ibid.*, p. 255.
12. *Ibid.*, p. 256.
13. Meredith, *op. cit.*, pp. 487–8 and 3.
14. A profitable joint venture, Olivine, which produced cooking oil and also marketed Heinz products, was established too. Fintan O'Toole, 'Brand Leader', *Granta* (London), 53, Spring 1996, p. 72.
15. *Ibid.*
16. When Rhodes University gave him an honorary doctorate for services to South African journalism, in February 1998, the award met with 'more than a few raised eyebrows'. Ferial Haffajee, 'New Voice of the Establishment', *Mail and Guardian*, 13 February 1998.
17. Cited by Tom Lodge, *South African Politics Since 1994*, Cape Town and Johannesburg, David Philip, 1999, p. 66.
18. Celia Mather, in the then *Weekly Mail* (Johannesburg), 17 May 1991.

19. Mark Gevisser, quoting the estimates of 'ANC insiders', in *The Sunday Independent*, 20 April 1997.
20. *The Sunday Independent*, 16 February, *The Star*, 5 May, and *Business Day*, 25 May 1997.
21. The week after he returned from the United States, Frank Chikane, director-general in the presidency, said that the Saudi Arabian government would contribute to a land redistribution scheme in Zimbabwe which Mbeki was promoting. Justice Malala, in *Sunday Times*, 23 July 2000.
22. The full certified assessment of her expenses was presented by Susan Miller, in *The Star*, 21 March 1996.
23. *Business Day*, 7 October, and Ian Taylor, personal communication, 8 October 1999.
24. The R5 million facelift in Pretoria included R300000 on alterations to the servants quarters, and R10000 for installing a 'mobile sauna'. Henry Ludski, in *Sunday Times*, 15 and 22 August 1999.
25. Wyndham Hartley, in *Business Day*, 14 April 2000.
26. His portrait could be seen in 1998 on the windows of an exclusive courtier at the V & A Waterfront showing off the latest in Italian fashions. Jovial Rantao, 'No Flies on Mr Perfect', *The Star*, 4 December 1998.
27. Farouk Chothia, in *Business Day*, 17 March 1999.
28. Statement by government spokesperson Joel Netshitenzhe, *The Star*, 29 June 2000. Yengeni also attacked the highly critical report by the European Union, saying revealingly that the EU should 'allow Africans to be responsible. They should take their cue from us.' Iden Wetherell, in *Mail and Guardian*, 30 June 2000. When Chris Barron asked Morgan Tsvangirai, leader of Zimbabwe's Movement for Democratic Change, if the South African observer mission had been 'observing the same election as the rest of us?', Tsvangirai replied: 'They may have been on holiday.' *Sunday Times*, 9 July 2000. Yengeni's team ignored many facts: that President Mugabe had 'decided to inflame the land issue', that the land invasions had 'select[ed] farmers…known to support the [MDC]' , and the 10000 to 14000 invaders had 'prevented the opposition from campaigning in much of the countryside'. *The Economist*, 2 September 2000.
29. Chothia, *op. cit.*
30. Meredith, *op. cit.*, p. 542.
31. Lodge, *op. cit.*, p. 17.
32. *Ibid.*, p. 64.
33. Bill Krige, 'Don Quixote or Judge Dredd?' *Business Day*, 5 November 1999.
34. David Greybe, in *Business Day*, 17 September 1999.
35. Stephen Mulholland, 'Another Voice', *Sunday Times*, 25 July 1999.
36. S'thembiso Msomi, 'How Modise Got Into the Arms of Business', *Sunday Times*, 29 August 1999.
37. Ivor Powell, 'Nepotism in R32bn Arms Deal', *Mail and Guardian*, 26 May 2000.
38. *Ibid.*
39. *Ibid.*
40. Editorial, 30 June 2000.
41. Powell, 'Massive New Arms Deal Planned', *Mail and Guardian*, 23 June 2000.

42. Cited in *ibid*. South Africa was negotiating to sell the G6 to both Saudi Arabia and Kuwait in a deal that might be worth up to R8 billion. Henry Ludski, in *Sunday Times*, 16 April 2000.

43. S'thembiso Msomi, *op. cit.*

44. Editorial, 30 June 2000. Nine months earlier, Patricia de Lille of the Pan Africanist Congress alleged in parliament that ANC politicians had received bribes and kickbacks in the initial arms deals; she pointed to Jacob Zuma, and to Tony Yengeni who, as chair of parliament's defence portfolio committee, had supposedly received a Mercedes. She produced a report, but no hard evidence in substantiation, and was reviled for her efforts. See, for example, Marianne Merten and Mungo Soggot, in *Mail and Guardian*, 10 September 1999.

45. The construction, expected to cost R6 billion, would be 'hugely import intensive' with 'potential problem[s]' for the balance of payments, especially if local equity partners were involved. In addition, increasing the country's foreign debt to buy non-productive armaments, 'is bad economics'. Greta Steyn, in *Business Day*, 2 May 2000.

46. In *Mail and Guardian*, 30 June 2000.

47. Powell, *Mail and Guardian*, 30 June 2000.

48. *The Economist*, 17 May 1997.

49. Newton Kanhema, in *The Sunday Independent*, 22 June 1997.

50. See, for instance, *Mail and Guardian*, 18 November, and *Sunday Times*, 26 November, 1994.

51. Kader Asmal – portrayed as 'Mr Clean' a little earlier – declared that the public should trust 'the intuition of the 13 cabinet ministers on the [existing] National Conventional Arms Control Committee.' Marion Edmunds, in *Mail and Guardian*, 29 March 1996.

52. 'Another Voice', *Sunday Times*, 7 March 1999.

53. Thabo Kobokoane, in *Sunday Times*, 7 September 1997.

54. Cited by Sven Lunsche, in *Sunday Times*, 7 September 1997.

55. Cited by John Battersby, *Sunday Times*, 20 April 1997.

56. Carol Paton, in *Sunday Times*, 10 March 1998.

57. The number of black-controlled companies on the Johannesburg Stock Exchange had risen from five with a market capitalization of R1.8 billion five years ago to 16 with a capitalization of R36 billion in 1997. Thabo Leshilo, 'Ramaphosa Sets Cat Among Pigeons', *The Sunday Independent*, 19 October 1997.

58. *The Economist*, 15 March 1997.

59. Sophia Christoforakis, in *The Sunday Independent*, 27 October 1996.

60. Nicola Koz, in *Sunday Times*, 23 March 1997.

61. Cited by Adrian Hadland, in *Sunday Independent*, 21 December 1997.

62. Shareen Singh and Jim Jones, in *Business Day*, 27 January, and *The Economist*, 10 January 1998.

63. Haffajee, 'Are You a Member of The Network?' *Mail and Guardian*, 31 July 1998.

64. Thabo Leshilo, 'Network ... Goes Public With Party', *Sunday Times*, 26 July 1998.

65. Pule Molebeledi, 'Upwardly Mobile With Deep Roots', *Business Day*, 12 June 1998.

66. Editorial, *Business Day*, 8 March 1999.
67. *The Economist*, 17 April 1999.
68. *Business Day*, 8 July 1999. No author attributed.
69. He reappeared in the news as chairman of Mawenzi Resources when the mining and property group's operating losses reached R3.3 million. *The Star*, 3 July 2000.
70. In an interview with Thabo Leshilo, in *The Sunday Independent*, 20 April 1997.
71. He remained chairman of Johnnic and director of many other companies including Anglo American and SA Breweries. Drew Forrest, in *Business Day*, 22 February 1999.
72. Amanda Vermeulen, in *Business Day*, 21 April 1999.
73. Vermeulen, in *Business Day*, 22 April 1999.
74. Interviews by Nomavenda Mathiane, in *Business Day*, 23 April 1999.
75. Janet Parker, in *Business Day*, 6 April 1999.
76. Parker and Reuter, in *Business Day*, 7 April 1999.
77. Cited by Sipho Ngcobo, in *The Star*, 7 May 1999.
78. Mathatha Tsedu, in *The Sunday Independent*, 9 May 1999.
79. Steven Friedman, 'Govt Searches for "Patriotic Bourgeoisie"', *Business Day*, 27 October 1997.
80. Speaking at First Central Insurance, Johannesburg. Thabo Leshilo, in *The Star*, 15 July 1998.
81. Charles Phahlane, in *The Star*, 17 July 2000.
82. Edited text of his speech, in *Business Day*, 23 November 1999.
83. *The Sunday Independent* correctly recognized that Mbeki's speech was 'arguably, the most strategic intervention of his presidency', and went on to observe that his 'central point' was that 'as long as racism lives, the ANC's liberation struggle must continue'. Editorial, 28 November 1999.
84. Zakes Hlatshwayo, 'Mbeki's Speech Offers Little to Rural Poor', and 'Poor Will Reap Didiza's Ill-Considered Crop', and Drew Forrest, 'Land Reform in SA Favours Black Elite', *Business Day*, 10 February, and 4 and 11 May 2000. Hlatshwayo is director of the National Land Committee.
85. Jack had allegedly acquired state-owned farms at below their market value while in the service of Brigadier Gqozo's regime in Ciskei, and Dolny had blocked his bid to tap Land Bank funds for his private company. Mungo Soggot, 'Why Jack Doesn't Like Dolny', *Mail and Guardian*, 23 July 1999.
86. Jack also alleged that Dolny had been seeking generous salary increases for herself and the other top Bank executives, and according to *Business Day*, 'salary increases were the ultimate pretext for forcing her to resign ... at the end of a campaign of character assassination'. But Minister Thoko Didiza approved at the beginning of March 2000 the doubling of the officials' salaries, backdated to April 1999; the salary attached to Dolny's former position went up from R600 000 to R1.12 million. Dolny announced that she felt 'vindicated' by this step, and said that it 'proved that the accusations against me were personally and politically motivated'. *Business Day*, 3 March, Editorial, *ibid.*, 6 March, and *The Sunday Independent*, 5 March 2000.
87. Drew Forrest, in *Business Day*, 22 February 2000.
88. Her article, based on her then forthcoming book, in *Sunday Times*, 14 May 2000.

89. Judge Edwin Cameron, endorsing Mamphela Ramphele's views, said that public policy showed 'a lack of respect for a scientific basis for health care planning', and that government lacked a 'coherent management strategy'. *Mail and Guardian*, 31 March 2000.

90. *The Economist*, 2 October 1999.

91. *Ibid.*

92. *Sunday Times*, 14 April, and *Business Day*, 17 September 1999.

93. The richest 10 per cent of whites got 11.4 per cent, or some R7 billion.

94. Celean Jacobson, 'Richer Man, Poorer Man', *Sunday Times*, 24 October 1999. The report is also considered in *Business Day*, 1 March 2000.

95. Elvis Jack, 'Gini Out of the Bottle', *Business Day*, 27 October 2000.

96. Xolandi Xundu, in *Business Day*, 11 November 1999.

97. Sampie Terreblanche, 'The Ideological Journey of South Africa From RDP to the GEAR Macroeconomic Plan', University of Stellenbosch, mimeo, and comment on this paper by Michael Morris, in *The Cape Argus* (Cape Town), 8 March 1999.

98. *The Economist*, 2 October 1999.

99. 'Funding Development Isn't the Problem: Delivery Is', *Financial Mail* (Johannesburg), 21 July 2000.

100. Helena Dolny, in *Sunday Times*, 14 May 2000. Thabo Mbeki, as President Mandela often remarked, was running the government well before 1999.

101. Robert Greig, in *The Sunday Independent*, 11 June 2000.

102. Terreblanche, *op.cit.*, and Morris, *op. cit.*

103. Christine Qunta, 'Vantage Point', *Business Day*, 20 October 2000. Qunta is a partner in a law firm, and a regular contributor on racism and empowerment.

104. Wyndham Hartley, in *Business Day*, 4 January 2000.

105. *Ibid.*

106. 'Refocus: Black Empowerment', in *Focus* (Helen Suzman Foundation), 17, March 2000.

107. *Ibid.*

108. Quentin Wray, in *Business Day*, 1 November 2000.

109. The message had apparently fallen into the hands of the Food and Allied Workers' Union, and was then passed to Mbeki. Its significance as anything other than the personal prejudices of an individual was unclear and unexplained. Farouk Chothia, in *Business Day*, 8 February 2000.

110. As cited in *ibid.*

111. The concept apparently referred to thoughts or inclinations of which a particular person may not be aware. Howard Barrell believed that the term had first appeared in *The Sowetan* of 25 August 1997. 'Over a Barrel', *Mail and Guardian*, 3 March 2000.

112. Subliminal racism seemed a very useful notion to the new black economic elite. Reports in the *Mail and Guardian* and the *Sunday Times* about black corruption were influenced by the newspapers' own racist paradigms, not facts, according to Hale Qangule representing the Association of Black Accountants before the HRC in Johannesburg on 8 March 2000.

113. Fourteen per cent of the ANC's submission, according to Barrell, was devoted to the *Mail and Guardian*, a paper with a weekly circulation of only 36 000 copies. President Mbeki appears to be obsessed with this

journal: 'each week, word gets back to us – sometimes directly, often not ... that Thabo Mbeki ... is "enraged" or "deeply concerned" by this or that article in our columns ... the kind of article which, if published in almost any other democracy would be about as remarkable as an ANC member failing to return your telephone call'. 'Over a Barrel', *Mail and Guardian*, 14 April 2000.

114. Two pieces of evidence were adduced for these sweeping generalizations – a quote from J.B.M. Hertzog of more than 50 years ago, and a passage from J.M. Coetzee's prize-winning novel, *Disgrace*, in which the rape of a white woman by three black men is discussed. 'Over a Barrel', 14 April 2000.

115. Nomavenda Mathiane, in *Business Day*, 6 April, and the editor, *Business Day*, 7 April 2000.

116. Mathiane, *op. cit.*, and Mda in *The Star*, 7 April 2000. The style of the submission certainly suggests Mbeki's authorship in part or in whole.

117. Cited by Drew Forrest, in *Business Day*, 17 April 2000.

118. Bantu Holomisa argued much the same three years earlier: 'those of us who ... fought the struggle here are more used to working with whites and we don't have bad relations with them. We get along. It is the exiles who are far more racially bitter ... and who also don't know the issues on the ground'. Interview with R.W. Johnson, *The Star*, 1 September 1997.

119. Max du Preez, 'Maximum Headroom', *The Star*, 20 October 2000.

120. Spokesman Mankahlana's response to the criticism offered by Sipho Seepe was: 'the ANC guards its unity very jealously. We are prepared to go to war for it. If anyone wages war against us to destroy us, he can and must expect a ruthless reply'. Cited in Ibrahim Harvey, 'Left Field', *Mail and Guardian*, 21 July 2000.

121. Barrell, *Mail and Guardian*, 14 April 2000.

122. Racism's place in popular culture in South Africa is doubtful. Kwaito is a favourite dance music and a homegrown voice of township life. But race is described as 'not a big issue' for Kwaito musicians, and apartheid is 'yesterday's news'. 'One Way to Get Rich in Soweto', *The Economist*, 4 March 2000.

123. Barrell, 'Mbeki's Popularity Plummets', in *Mail and Guardian*, 20 October 2000.

124. The poll was conducted by Probe Market Research, a subsidiary of Gallup International. Mercedes Sayagues, 'Presidency on a Knife-Edge', *Mail and Guardian*, 27 October 2000.

125. Formed through an alliance between the former DP and the NNP.

126. Nomavenda Mathiane, 'Voice of the People', *Business Day*, 7 November 2000.

7 Participatory Democracy: The Reality and the Continuing Aspiration – Athens, Britain and South Africa

1. Dietrich Rueschemeyer, Evelyne Huber Stephens and John D. Stephens, *Capitalist Development and Democracy*, Cambridge, Polity Press, 1992, p. 2 and footnote 1.

2. Josiah Ober, *The Athenian Revolution*, Princeton, New Jersey, Princeton University Press, 1999, p. 19.
3. Women gained equal voting rights with men in New Zealand in 1893, in Australia in 1902 and, on random milestones, in the United States in 1920, in France in 1944, and not until 1971 in Switzerland. 'Rights', in *The Economist*, 31 December 1999. The Chartist movement in Britain, for instance, was one of the greatest popular movements of the nineteenth century. It took its name from the People's Charter of May 1838, which expressed certain fundamental demands: secret ballots; annual parliaments; salaries for MPs; the abolition of property qualifications for MPs; and, only, universal male suffrage, which was not achieved before another 80 years. A Chartist petition presented to parliament in 1842 obtained over three millions signatures and was some six miles long. Francis Wheen, *Karl Marx*, London, Fourth Estate, 2000, p. 195.
4. Ober, *op. cit.*, p. 11.
5. Robert Michels, *Political Parties*, New York, Dover Publications, 1959, pp. 21–2, and 401 and 407. First published 1911 and 1915.
6. David Beetham, *Max Weber and the Theory of Modern Politics*, Cambridge, Polity Press, 1985, pp. 102–7.
7. Ober, *op. cit.*, pp. 5 and 19.
8. *Ibid.*, pp. 11, 24 and 28.
9. *Ibid.*, pp. 28–29.
10. *Ibid.*, p. 26.
11. John Dunn, 'Conclusion', in Dunn (ed.), *Democracy: The Unfinished Journey 508BC to AD 1993*, Oxford, University Press, 1993, pp. 241–2, and Ober, *op. cit.*, pp. 23–5.
12. Dunn, *op. cit.*, p. 242. An American politician, as noted above, works hand in glove with the wealthy.
13. Ober, *op. cit.*, p. 38.
14. *Ibid.*, p. 27.
15. Ellen Meiksins Wood, *Democracy Against Capitalism: Renewing Historical Materialism*, Cambridge, University Press, 1995, p. 183.
16. *Ibid.*, pp. 185 and 188. Her emphasis of peasant-citizen.
17. The goddess Athena was patron of both the arts and crafts, she notes, but the greatest testimony to the status of free labour in Athens was seen in Plato's vehement reaction against it. *Ibid.*, pp. 190–2.
18. *Ibid.*, pp. 200–1.
19. Aylmer terms it a 'unique element' in the revolutionary preconditions. Officers and horse-troopers were volunteers, it opened a 'career to talents', and the social gulf between officers and men was probably less than in other armies before Napoleon. The mental atmosphere of the Army resembled 'a mixture of a revivalist religious congress and an extreme left-wing political debating society'. G.E. Aylmer (ed.), *The Levellers in the English Revolution*, London, Thames & Hudson, 1975, p. 13.
20. David Wootton, 'The Levellers', chapter in Dunn, *op. cit.*, p. 72. The funeral of their outstanding leader Colonel Thomas Rainsborough (sometimes Rainborough) in London in 1648 was, for example, the occasion for 'a large-scale demonstration and for the display of the sea-green Leveller colours by huge numbers of people'. Aylmer, *op. cit.*, pp. 39–40.

21. Iain Hampsher-Monk, 'Levellers', in David Miller *et al.* (eds), *The Blackwell Encyclopaedia of Political Thought*, Oxford, Basil Blackwell, 1991, p. 283, and Aylmer, *op. cit.*, p. 29 where he refers to 'the prominence of women in the Levellers cause (notably Elizabeth Lilburne and Mary Overton), but numerous others as well...'

22. Stevie Davies, *Unbridled Spirits: Women of the English Revolution, 1640–1660*, London, The Women's Press, 1998, pp. 67–8.

23. *Ibid.*, pp. 68–9.

24. The Leveller women's petitions to parliament emphasized the misery of debtors' wives and children, the horror of watching children starve, and the gross inequity of the law as it affected the poor. *Ibid.*, pp. 70–1.

25. *Ibid.*, p. 73.

26. Their spokesman, Colonel Rainsborough, during the army's Putney debates, October–November 1647: 'I think that the poorest he that is in England has a life to live as the greatest he; and ... the poorest man in England is not at all bound in a strict sense to that government that he has not had a voice to put himself under.' Quoted in Wootton, *op. cit.*, p. 74. Aylmer states that Richard Overton first enunciated the principle of parliamentary accountability to the electors in explicitly republican terms in 1646. *Op. cit.*, p. 100 and 24.

27. Hampsher-Monk, *op. cit.*, pp. 283–4.

28. *Op. cit.*, p. 79.

29. Aylmer, *op. cit.*, p. 13.

30. Quoted by Hampsher-Monk, *op. cit.*, p. 284.

31. Meiksins Wood, *op. cit.*, p. 230.

32. *Op. cit.*, pp. 87–90.

33. Aylmer, *op. cit.*, p. 9. Yet Rueschemeyer and his colleagues appear to accord them even less recognition than Athenian democracy.

34. Meiksins Wood, *op. cit.*, her emphasis again.

35. *Ibid.*, p. 231. Alexander Hamilton, for instance, affirmed that 'society naturally divides itself into the very few and the many', and James Madison believed that it was nature's design to create 'unequal faculties of acquiring property'. Quoted in Hacker, *op. cit.*, p. 48.

36. The democratic idea of freedom is one of self-determination, derivative of Rousseau's *Social Contract*. John Schwarzmantel, *The State in Contemporary Society*, London, Harvester-Wheatsheaf, 1994, p. 32.

37. Deemed to have been given when, for example, a man passed the age of 21, or when he travelled unmolested on the highway.

38. Arblaster supports Rousseau's perception that severe inequalities would prevent the development of a common interest in a society, and undermine the foundations of democracy. *Democracy*, pp. 77–8.

39. *Ibid.*, p. 81. The absence of big inequalities was a prerequisite for Rousseau's good society.

40. Roger D. Masters, 'Rousseau', in David Miller, *op. cit.*, p. 457.

41. The Diggers, their more radical off-shoot, attempted to find the solution in working common lands for themselves, until they were dispersed by organized mob violence.

42. Barrington Moore, Jr., *Social Origins of Dictatorship and Democracy*, Boston, Beacon Press, 1966, p. 418.

43. Rueschemeyer *et al.*, *op. cit.*, pp. 5–8.

44. Seekings, *op. cit.*, p. 11.
45. Cited in Bonner and Segal, *op. cit.*, p. 79.
46. Seekings, *op. cit.*, p. 11.
47. *Ibid.*
48. *Ibid.*, p. 12.
49. Ramphele, *A Life*, Cape Town and Johannesburg, David Philip, 1996, pp. 57, 65 and 72.
50. Neocosmos, 'From People's Politics to State Politics', *op. cit.*, p. 78.
51. Seekings, *op. cit.*, p. 12.
52. *Ibid.*
53. Eddie Webster and Glenn Adler, 'Introduction', in Adler and Webster (eds), *Trade Unions and Democratization in South Africa, 1985–1997*, Basingstoke, Macmillan – now Palgrave, 2000, p. 1. They write actually of the supposed 're-emergence' of the democratic movement.
54. Ian Macum, 'Growth, Structure and Power in the South African Union Movement', in Adler and Webster, *op. cit.*, p. 60.
55. Webster and Adler, *op. cit.*, p. 2.
56. Steven Friedman, *Building Tomorrow Today: African Workers in Trade Unions, 1970–1984*, Johannesburg, Ravan Press, 1987, pp. 8–9.
57. Seekings, *op. cit.*, pp. 263 and 303.
58. Tom Lodge, quoted in *ibid.*, p. 15.
59. Cited in *ibid.*, p. 17.
60. *Ibid.*, pp. 289 and 292.
61. *Ibid.*, pp. 47–8.
62. Shubin, *op. cit.*, p. 250.
63. Cited in *ibid.*, p. 171. Original emphasis.
64. *Ibid.*, pp. 172–3.
65. *Ibid.*, pp. 171 and 173.
66. *Ibid.*, p. 294.
67. *Ibid.*, p. 297.
68. The paper, 'Towards a People's Democracy', cited in *ibid.*, pp. 295–6.
69. Murphy Morobe, 'Toward's a People's Democracy: The UDF View', part of a speech made on Morobe's behalf, May 1987, *Review of African Political Economy*, 40, 1987, pp. 81–5. All emphasis was Morobe's.
70. Seekings, *op. cit.*, p. 305.
71. Marais, *op. cit.*, pp. 58–9.
72. Seekings, *op. cit.*, pp. 305–6.
73. *Ibid.*, p. 306.
74. *Ibid.*, p. 267. Sweden was a particularly generous donor. According to Howard Barrell, it gave 'more than R1.92 billion to the anti-apartheid struggle and institutions involved in it', between 1969 and 1994. Of this sum, 'more than R692 million' went directly to the ANC, and about a third of the amount was allocated for unaudited operational purposes. *Mail and Guardian*, 29 October 1999.
75. *Op. cit.*, p. 309.
76. *Ibid.*, p. 265.
77. *Ibid.*, p. 319.
78. *Ibid.*, p. 268.
79. *Ibid.*, pp. 268–9.

80. Morobe studied at Princeton from mid-1990 to June 1991, and Cachalia 'followed him the year after'. *Ibid.*, p. 270.
81. *Ibid.*, p. 267.
82. 'Hostility' is repeated at least three times, *Ibid.*, pp. 261, 278 and 284.
83. Pursued, as noted, throughout the 1990s. By contrast, as Seekings observes, other figures in the so-called cabal have done reasonably well within the ANC, including Ramaphosa and Moosa. *Ibid.*, p. 270.
84. Webster and Adler, *op. cit.*, p. 15.
85. Seekings, *op. cit.*, p. 271 and Foreword.
86. Wilmot James and Daria Caliguire, 'Renewing Civil Society', *Journal of Democracy* (Baltimore), 7(1) January 1996, p. 61.
87. *Op. cit.*, p. 276.
88. *Ibid.*, p. 264.
89. *Ibid.*, pp. 277–8.
90. *Ibid.*, p. 280. Marais emphasized widespread disgruntlement at rank-and-file level, *op. cit.*, p. 73.
91. *Ibid.*, pp. 321–2.
92. Two years after majority rule there was little or no debate on policy within the ANC parliamentary caucus according to Friedman, and Davis quoted an unnamed MP as saying: 'You don't think about sticking your neck out for fear of getting your head chopped off'. Friedman, in *Business Day*, 14 October, and Gaye Davis in *Mail and Guardian*, 4 October 1996.
93. Steven Friedman and Mark Shaw, 'Power in Partnership: Trade Unions, Forums and the Transition', chapter in Adler and Webster, *op. cit.*, p. 190.
94. Ian Macun, 'Growth, Structure and Power in the South African Union Movement', chapter in Adler and Webster, *op. cit.*, pp. 60 and 64.
95. *Ibid.*, table 3.1, p. 60.
96. Webster and Adler, *op. cit.*, pp. 2–3.
97. *Op. cit.*, p. 191.
98. Decisions specifically on things like value added tax and the broad issues of economic restructuring. *Ibid.*, pp. 194–5 and 211.
99. There was also the National Council of Trade Unions, with 7 per cent, the Federation of South African Labour, with 9 per cent, and 'other federations and unaffiliated unions' with 27 per cent. Macun, *op. cit.*, p. 60 and table 3.4, p. 66.
100. Robert Taylor, quoting data of the International Labour Organisation, in *Sunday Times*, 9 November 1997.
101. Quoted in *The Economist*, 31 October 1998.
102. Employment levels have been 'fairly stable' in the sectors 'most strongly organized by trade unions'. Tom Lodge, *South African Politics Since 1994*, Cape Town and Johannesburg, David Philip, 1999, p. 7.
103. Webster and Adler, *op. cit.*, pp. 8 and 17. Lodge affirms that unions have been 'significantly fortified by legal changes since 1994', *op. cit.*, p. 7.
104. Webster and Adler, *op. cit.*, p. 10.
105. *Ibid.*, p. 10.
106. Friedman and Shaw add that throughout the 1980s 'the unions, particularly but not exclusively those in COSATU, harboured a vision of social and economic democratization more radical than that of the rest of the anti-apartheid alliance'. *Op. cit.*, p. 192.

107. *Ibid.*, p. 8.
108. Charlene Smith, in *The Star*, 2 September, and Friedman, in *Business Day*, 24 August 1998.
109. His estimate is that the party's paid-up membership halved after 1994. *Ibid.*, p. 8.
110. *The Economist*, 27 September 1997.
111. Lodge, *op. cit.*, p. 8.
112. Shubin, *op. cit.*, p. 345.
113. Citations by Howard Barrell and Jaspreet Kindra, from documents for the conference 'Towards a Party Building Strategy and a Quality Party', in *Mail and Guardian*, 26 May 2000.
114. In 1998, five Cabinet ministers and two deputy ministers were SACP members. Essop Pahad, then deputy-minister in the Office of the Deputy President, well-known as Thabo Mbeki's 'Mr Fixit', was removed from the SACP's politbureau at the beginning of August, but replaced by Sydney Mufamadi, another minister close to Mbeki. Howard Barrell, in *Mail and Guardian*, 7 August 1998.
115. Cited by Khadija Magardie, in *Mail and Guardian*, 11 August 2000.
116. *The Sunday Independent*, 14 May 2000.
117. Interview with Jeremy Gordin, in *ibid.*
118. Jonathan Katzenellenbogen noted that Mboweni's remarks in this vein had become 'increasingly strident' recently, in *Business Day*, 11 October 2000.
119. Nirode Bramdaw and Irene Louw, in *Business Day*, 25 August 2000.
120. However, Macun emphasizes that declining employment, as during the 1990s, 'does not necessarily decrease the power of the organised workers'. Their 'ability to impose losses on employers through strike action is heightened, as is their potential solidarity'. *Op. cit.*, p. 71.
121. An anonymous official describing Treasury Secretary Robert Rubin's impressions after his visit to South Africa in July 1998, and quoted by Simon Barber, in *Business Day*, 22 October 1998.
122. Webster and Adler, *op. cit.*, pp. 14 and 15.
123. The survey was carried out by the Human Sciences Research Council, and Olivier's assessment of the normalcy of the inactivity was expressed as an undoubted good. *Business Day*, 8 February 2000.
124. Friedman, 'Worm's Eye View', *Mail and Guardian*, 22 September 2000.
125. Friedman and Shaw, *op. cit.*, p. 190.
126. A rich and colourful speech on the adoption of the Constitution Bill 1996, with the penultimate paragraph: 'Whatever the setbacks of the moment, nothing can stop us now! Whatever the difficulties, Africa shall be at peace! However improbable it may sound to the skeptics, Africa will prosper!' Text in full, in Hadland and Rantao, *op. cit.*, pp. 153–8.
127. Mbeki spent two full days at the conference which attracted politicians, academics, intellectuals and business people. Winnie Graham, 'A Sunburst of Great African Thinkers', *The Star*, 30 August 1999.
128. Pule Molebeledi, in *Business Day*, 30 September 1998.
129. Cited by Graham, *op. cit.*
130. Gwen Gill, *Sunday Times*, 26 March 2000. The book was published by Tafelberg at R149.95.

131. With Zuma and Pahad prominent among the speakers, and 1200 delegates attending. Hopewell Radebe, *The Star*, 10 April 2000.
132. *The Star*, 4 October 2000.
133. Funds came from MTN, the cellphone operator, and Nedcor, the banking group, for an initial two-year period, which could be extended if necessary. Barrell, in *Mail and Guardian, 8 September 2000*.
134. Barrell's description of the goals of the Trust, *ibid*.
135. *Op. cit.*, p. 201.
136. 'Own correspondent' in *The Star*, 16 November 1998.
137. Cited in Bramdaw and Louw, *Business Day*, 25 August 2000. Mbeki characteristically stated: 'Your discussion documents regurgitate, undigested, the most pessimistic assessments of our economy made by those whose class and national interests dictate that they propogate the understanding that our Government has failed, as all other African governments have failed'. Cited by Jovial Rantao, *The Star*, 3 July 1998.
138. Alan Fine and Renee Grawitzky, in *Business Day*, 23 November 1999. The same thing appeared to be occurring in key local government structures. The mayors of six new metropolitan cities, Cape Town, Johannesburg among them, would command budgets of up to R9 billion, amounts comparable with some provinces, and the ANC considered the appointments as almost like Cabinet positions. Competition within the ruling party through early October was described by Munusamy and Makhanya as 'one between ANC leaders who are close to Mbeki and those on the left of the [party]'. Hamnca, another observer, twice reported that Murphy Morobe was leading the race to become mayor of greater Johannesburg, and Xundu did so too. But it was also known that 'the final selection [wa]s Mbeki's prerogative'. When the six candidates were announced on 12 October, Morobe's name was not on the list. Xolani Xundu, in *Business Day*, 18 September; Ranjeni Munusamy and Mondli Makhanya, in *Sunday Times*, 8 October; and Prince Hamnca, in *The Star*, 4 and 12 October 2000. The President's choice in Johannesburg was Amos Masondo, described by Forrest as 'not known for his charisma or dynamism', and as one whose 'administrative skills have been questioned'. Drew Forrest, in *Business Day*, 13 October 2000.
139. Jaspreet Kindra, in *Mail and Guardian*, 1 September 2000.
140. Friedman, *Mail and Guardian*, 22 September 2000. He said: 'For COSATU the link between HIV and AIDS is irrefutable, and any other approach is unscientific'; Mbeki's stance 'can undermine the message that all South Africans must take precautions to avoid infection'; and that the state's concern about the costs of providing anti-retroviral drugs to pregnant women were 'often exaggerated', and they 'cannot be used to deny treatment for the millions of victims'. Cited by Nirode Bramdaw in *Business Day*, 19 September, and Eddie Javiva in *The Star*, 19 September 2000.
141. Simphiwe Xako, in *Business Day*, 13 September 2000.
142. Khathu Mamaila, and Javiva, in *The Star*, 19 September 2000.
143. Presented before parliamentary committee by Fiona Tregenna, a COSATU official. Hartley, in *Business Day*, 4 January 2000.
144. As John Matshikiza said, Mazwai has 'many well known opinions about how to make the "African renaissance" happen and is not afraid to repeat them'. 'With the Lid Off', *Mail and Guardian*, 11 February 2000.

145. Among other prize winners were Education Minister Kader Asmal and his public service counterpart, Geraldine Fraser-Moleketi. Vuyo Mvoko, in *Business Day*, 21 September 2000.
146. Cited by Eddie Javiva, in *The Star*, 12 April 2000.

The Unending Struggle

1. Lexington, 'Selling America to the Highest Bidder', *The Economist*, 11 November 2000.
2. 'As politics grow enervated', he added, 'democracy is trivialized', *op. cit.*, p. 31.
3. Zakes Mda, *The Heart of Redness*, Oxford and Cape Town, Oxford University Press, 2000, p. 197.

Index